WHAT PEOPLE ARE SAYING ABOUT MARILYN HICKEY AND *YOUR PATHWAY TO MIRACLES*...

Your Pathway to Miracles is an amazing account of all that God has done and is still doing through Marilyn Hickey's life and ministry. It will fuel your faith and give you a new passion to believe God for the miraculous in your own life.

—Joyce Meyer
Best-selling author
Founder, Joyce Meyer Ministries
Fenton, Missouri

I heartily endorse this new book by Marilyn Hickey. Her life consists of a series of miraculous events, and in this great book, Dr. Hickey expounds upon her most extraordinary, God-filled experiences, which cause this book to be one that you cannot put down.

—Reverend Dr. David Yonggi Cho
Pastor, Yoido Full Gospel Church
Chairman of the Board, Church Growth International
Seoul, South Korea

I recommend this book because it has living, real testimonies of Marilyn Hickey's personal experiences, miracles that prove that Jesus lives. *Your Pathway to Miracles* will loosen and activate the faith of many to receive a miracle. This book con̄f⸻⸻⸻ is the same yesterday, today, and forever ⸻⸻⸻⸻ ⸻s the supernatural. As a result, she is ⸻⸻⸻⸻ s, miracles, and wonders.

⸻⸻⸻ **Maldonado**
Founding Pa⸻⸻⸻⸻ ⸻⸻⸻ International Ministry
Miami, Florida

Marilyn Hickey is one of the most anointed women on earth. She not only believes in miracles...she sees them every day. Allow her new book, *Your Pathway to Miracles*, to set you on your own journey for miracles in the mighty name of Jesus.

—Richard Roberts
Chairman and CEO, Oral Roberts Evangelistic Association
Cohost, *The Place for Miracles* television program
Tulsa, Oklahoma

I believe Marilyn Hickey has regularly seen more miracles than any other minister of the gospel I know. Whether in her personal life, in the Denver church where she pastors, or in her meetings in Pakistan, Africa, Russia, or any of the other 120 countries where she has ministered, Marilyn's ministry has proven that miracles know no geographical limitations; they occur in every nation, tribe, and language—*wherever* people believe in Jesus.

—Rick Renner
Founder and Senior Pastor, Moscow Good News Church
Founder, Media Mir television network
Moscow, Russia

Your Pathway to Miracles will capture your heart and inspire you with what God has done through one woman's life. Marilyn Hickey is a treasure to the body of Christ and is truly living out what God has called us all to do. We are so blessed to have this collection of real-life miracles.

—Howie and Theresa Danzik
Danzik Enterprises
Colorado Springs, Colorado

I was captured by the real-life stories that Marilyn shared as I read *Your Pathway to Miracles*. I did not want to put it down. It will motivate every reader to believe God for miracles. This generation needs this book!

—Sharon Daugherty
Senior Pastor, Victory Christian Center
Tulsa, Oklahoma

Marilyn is a radical faith teacher. Every believer should learn from the marvelous journey of her life. Her stories will take you along with her to each one of her experiences, which will build and strengthen your faith.

—Licda. Juanita Cercone Gonzalez
Enlace International

Your
Pathway
to
Miracles

Marilyn
HICKEY

WHITAKER
HOUSE

YOUR PATHWAY TO MIRACLES

Marilyn Hickey Ministries
P.O. Box 6598
Englewood, CO 80155
www.marilynandsarah.org

ISBN: 978-1-60374-325-9
Printed in the United States of America
© 2011 by Marilyn Hickey Ministries

Whitaker House
1030 Hunt Valley Circle
New Kensington, PA 15068
www.whitakerhouse.com

Library of Congress Cataloging-in-Publication Data

Hickey, Marilyn.
  Your pathway to miracles / Marilyn Hickey.
    p. cm.
  Summary: "Marilyn Hickey describes miracles she has experienced and witnessed in her decades of ministry, provides biblical teachings on miracles, and encourages readers to trust God to work great miracles in and through them"—Provided by publisher.
  ISBN 978-1-60374-325-9 (trade pbk. : alk. paper) 1. Miracles. I. Title.
  BT97.3.H53 2011
  231.7'3—dc23

                    2011033420

3 4 5 6 7 8 9 10 11 **W** 18 17 16 15 14 13 12

ACKNOWLEDGMENTS

Certainly, I want to acknowledge my family—Wally, Reece, Sarah, and Michael—who, through the years, have encouraged me to walk a path of miracles.

I also want to thank Terri Michel for helping me put this book together. Her talents, her patience, and her love for Jesus have been a great blessing.

I want to acknowledge that God is a good God and loves us all. He wants us to live and walk in the miraculous.

CONTENTS

FOREWORD

The great nineteenth-century preacher Charles Spurgeon was known for his emphasis on divine sovereignty and soulwinning. A young minister approached him with the concern that he was not seeing conversions in his ministry, and he wondered why this was. Mr. Spurgeon asked him, "Do you expect to see conversions *every time you preach*?" "Oh no, of course not," the man replied, to which Spurgeon retorted, "And that is precisely why you aren't having them!"

As I read Marilyn Hickey's book, this story of Spurgeon and soulwinning kept coming to mind. It has been my observation that those who try the hardest to see people saved, witness the most to the lost, and seek to have people receive the gospel the soonest are the ones who see the most people converted. Those who have the highest expectancy and are unafraid to go out on a limb are those who reap the most results. So, too, it is with those who pray for God to do miracles. If some of us don't see them very often, could it be that we aren't praying for them—or expecting them?

Marilyn Hickey prays for miracles *and* expects to see them. As a result, she sees more extraordinary things happen than most people in ministry ever do! I admire her personal life, her testimony, her devotion to Christ, her prayer life, her seeking the face of God day after day, and her unashamed upholding of the gospel. Marilyn Hickey is a genuinely serious student of the Word of God. Here is a woman who has memorized vast portions of the Bible over the years. You might like to know that she has just completed memorizing 1 Corinthians—something I had not even thought of doing! And all that she is and does springs from her "prayer closet." How many people do you know who memorize the names of the nations of the world country by country in order to pray for them?

Marilyn Hickey currently has open doors for ministering in the Muslim world that most of us may never have, and she boldly and courageously faces danger all the time in countries normally closed to the majority of people. She fearlessly upholds the name of Jesus wherever she goes. Furthermore, her desire to proclaim the gospel and to see the lost saved eclipses her love of miracles, and this honors God. But, unquestionably, she sees miracles! You will be thrilled to read about her experiences in the book you hold in your hands but equally impressed with her vulnerability and honesty regarding failures. Moreover, you will have no doubt that God uses miracles to get the attention of the lost.

May this book inspire you to be unashamed of the God of the Bible. I pray it will bless you in a way that exceeds your greatest expectations!

—R. T. Kendall
Founder, R. T. Kendall Ministries
Former Senior Minister, Westminster Chapel,
London, England

Chapter 1

Everyone Needs a Miracle
What Miracle Are You Seeking?

In the United States and around the world, countless numbers of people are looking for miracles in their lives. When some people say, "I'm praying for a miracle," they are really talking about wishful thinking or a vague hope that things will get better. Others, however, mean that they are asking God to intervene in their lives based on the reality of His promises. There's a big difference! Over the years, my ministry has received numerous reports of miracles that have come through prayer and holding on to God's Word, miracles such as:

> My eight-year-old son had leukemia. I called for prayer for strength to go through the treatment. That wonderful prayer partner rebuked the disease and prayed that he be healed in Jesus' name. Now my son is healed! There is no leukemia in his body! It was such a testimony to the doctors and nurses.

> I had a nervous breakdown [and when I was feeling the worst I would] listen to you say, "This is the best day of your life!"...Little by little the joy I felt began to increase....I want you to know that my mind is healed now. I was sick for seven years. I feel the peace of God and the joy of the Lord again.

I recently requested that you agree with me to lose weight because I had reached a whopping 203 pounds. Well, praise God, the Lord has done a miracle for me. I went on a diet and have lost 53 pounds, and I'm not through yet.

You prophesied that a child who had been kidnapped by his father was going to be returned to his mother. I claimed that word as mine! I had stood in faith for 2½ years before that word; and in less than one month, my son was returned to me. I was tired and weary... ready to give up—your word from God renewed my strength to stand.

> **Miracles are available to us today because God's Word promises them.**

Everyone needs a miracle of some kind, whether it is one of healing, financial provision, a restored relationship, open doors of opportunity, favor with another person, or another intervention of God. I have experienced many miracles in my life, and I am still experiencing them. Miracles are available to us today because God's Word promises them. What miracle are you seeking?

Our heavenly Father is a God of the miraculous. From Genesis to Revelation, His Word—the Bible—is a miraculous book. It is a supernatural gift, a revelation from God, which He has given for our instruction, comfort, and guidance in life. It tells us of many miracles God has provided for His people over thousands of years. Yet the Bible doesn't talk just about past miracles; it tells us how we can experience miracles in the present and the future. God hasn't changed. He desires to do miracles for us, too!

For I am the LORD, I do not change.   (Malachi 3:6)

Jesus Christ is the same yesterday, today, and forever. (Hebrews 13:8)

A MIRACULOUS SIGN

A miracle is something that, without the intervention of God, would never have happened to the person who received it. A miracle may also be defined as something that occurs outside the natural processes of life that we would ordinarily experience in our physical world.

In October 2000, I took a group of travelers on a ministry trip to La Paz, Bolivia, and held a series of citywide meetings in the stadium there. There are many indigenous people in Bolivia whose cultural roots are steeped in idolatry, witchcraft, shamanism, and the like, and who need to hear the life-changing gospel of Jesus Christ.

One of the travelers accompanying us told me she'd had a unique dream. "I dreamed that there were three rainbows in perfect circles in the sky," she said. "I don't know what it means, but it could be the Father, the Son, and the Holy Spirit or some special visitation while we're in Bolivia." I didn't share this conversation with anyone but kept it hidden in my heart.

While we were in Bolivia, we would hold three nights of healing meetings in the stadium, as well as two days of meetings with Bolivian ministers, because we like to pour the knowledge of God's Word into the hearts of ministers. We had brought books printed in Spanish, and we had special times of instruction and fellowship with them.

The president of Bolivia invited me to join a breakfast meeting he was sponsoring, and I was asked to speak to some of the key leaders in the government. This was an unexpected and wonderful open door for ministry.

Little did I dream what God the Father would do to prepare the hearts of the people for that breakfast and our healing meetings. The first morning of our ministry training school, we were in downtown La Paz teaching the local pastors. About one thousand Bolivian leaders were there, plus the one hundred and twenty-five people from the United States who had accompanied us on the trip. One of our staff people passed a note to me while I was speaking, saying that there were crowds in the street and that traffic was stopped because there were three rainbows in perfect circles over the building we were in. I said to the people, "There is something very unusual happening outside. We must go out and look."

We walked outside, and, as had been reported, there were three rainbows in the sky above the building. All three were shaped in perfect circles. One was very distinct, and the second was more out of focus, but both appeared to be white. The third was a colored ring, more like a traditional rainbow. The three rings intersected each other, similar to the Olympics logo. We were able to capture this sight on video. No one knew what to think. I was shocked that God would perform such an unusual miracle right then and there.

We went back to the meeting and praised and worshipped God. Following the meeting, we boarded our buses to go back to our hotel. When we arrived, we saw that the three rainbows had followed us and come to a stop over the hotel. We also found that witches had gathered outside, protesting by ringing bells and banging pans. The president of the country had called a leadership conference of witches, and these witches were very upset with our being there and with the rainbows that were positioned over the hotel, and they had come to speak curses against us. But let me tell you something: You cannot curse what God has blessed. (See, for example, Numbers 22:1–24:13.)

In both the Old and New Testaments, the Bible says that Jesus took the curse of our sins upon Himself on the cross so that we could be blessed. (See, for example, Isaiah 53:4–5; Galatians 3:13–14.) Knowing this, we rebuked Satan and asked God to bring these witches to salvation in Jesus.

When I went to the breakfast, oh, what a breakfast it was, because of all the news that had been on television and in the newspapers regarding our visit and the manifestation of the rainbows. What timing the Lord has! He had given a woman on our team a dream and then brought it to pass as a sign to us and to the people of Bolivia. Because the three rainbows had appeared over the city, I knew what to say to all those attending the breakfast. I asked them, "What is God saying? He wants to bring revival to La Paz, Bolivia. God wants to move on this country, but He can do it only as we surrender our lives to Jesus Christ."

The breakfast was a wonderful opportunity to praise God. He had already sent a sign of His presence in the form of the three rainbows. The Bible says that miraculous signs will follow those who believe. (See Mark 16:17.) That was a time when signs both went before us and followed us! I built on the sign God had sent by calling the people to repentance. Then, at the stadium meetings, people were Spirit-filled, and literally thousands of people were saved and healed. There were an unusual number of people healed from growths and tumors. People also came and threw their eyeglasses onto the platform because they could see perfectly without them.

> **The Bible says that miraculous signs will follow those who believe.**

We were able to broadcast these meetings over satellite to all the Spanish-speaking countries in the world. It was an awesome time, a time when God showed up and "showed off."

WHY MIRACLES?

Why does God do miracles in the lives of His people and in relation to situations that concern them? Our experiences in Bolivia draw attention to five significant reasons God does miracles.

1. God's Miracles Reveal His Power as Creator-King

When God created the earth and everything in it, including human beings, it was a miraculous event that reveals to us His power as Creator, as well as His sovereignty over the earth. The created world continues to reveal God's nature and power.

> *The heavens declare the glory of God; and the firmament shows His handiwork. Day unto day utters*

speech, and night unto night reveals knowledge. There is no speech nor language where their voice is not heard. Their line has gone out through all the earth, and their words to the end of the world.

(Psalm 19:1–4)

The three remarkable rainbows in the sky demonstrated that this same powerful Creator God was involved in our visit to Bolivia. God spoke the world into existence at the beginning of time, and He not only continues to create wonders that glorify Him, but He also brings the things we need into existence as we speak His Word to the circumstances and problems in our lives. As He does so, He manifests His nature and His ways to us.

2. God's Miracles Reveal the Spiritual Reality Supporting Our Physical World

Miracles make known the existence of an invisible spiritual reality that is the true, ultimate reality in life. Most people live only according to what they can experience through their five senses, but there is a spiritual realm that undergirds, and is greater than, the physical reality of our world, and within which our physical world exists. The Bible tells us that Jesus, who is God the Son, the second person of the Trinity, both created and sustains our world: *"All things were created through Him and for Him. And He is before all things, and in Him all things consist ["hold together"* NIV]*"* (Colossians 1:16–17).

A miracle sign such as we saw in La Paz, and the resulting outpouring of supernatural healings and other manifestations, revealed to the Bolivian people the presence of God's spiritual realm and His desire to intervene to meet both their physical and spiritual needs.

3. God's Miracles Convey His Compassion for His People

God the Father does miracles to bless and deliver His people, because He is loving and compassionate. For example, when He sent Moses to deliver the Hebrews, who were enslaved in Egypt, He told him,

I have surely seen the oppression of My people who are in Egypt, and have heard their cry because of their taskmasters, for I know their sorrows. So I have come down to deliver them out of the hand of the Egyptians, and to bring them up from that land to a good and large land, to a land flowing with milk and honey.

(Exodus 3:7–8)

In the course of delivering the Hebrews, God performed many miracles, including the manifestations of the pillars of cloud and fire, which were signs of His constant presence with His people, and the parting of the Red Sea, through which He rescued them from their enemies. (See Exodus 13:21; 14:21–30.) And God still saves and delivers today.

God loves all the people of the world. He created them in His image and sent His Son to redeem them. *"For God so loved the world that He gave His only begotten Son, that whoever believes in Him should not perish but have everlasting life"* (John 3:16). When Jesus came to earth, His healings and other miracles were prompted by His compassion. In one instance, when two blind men called out to Him, asking for mercy, *"Jesus had compassion and touched their eyes. And immediately their eyes received sight, and they followed Him"* (Matthew 20:34).

The sign of the three rainbows in Bolivia was a symbol to the people that God knew them and loved them and wanted to move among them in compassion, healing, deliverance, and the outpouring of His Spirit.

The apostle Paul wrote that if God gave His Son to die on the cross for us, *"how shall He not with Him also freely give us all things?"* (Romans 8:32). *"All things"* includes miracles.

4. God's Miracles Promote Faith in the Truth of the Gospel

Miracles are also a way in which God the Father confirms people's faith in the legitimacy of the gospel message, helping to bring them to repentance and into a relationship with Him through Jesus Christ.

[Jesus said to His followers,] *"Go into all the world and preach the gospel to every creature....And these signs will follow those who believe: In My name they will cast out demons; they will speak with new tongues;... they will lay hands on the sick, an they will recover."...And they went out and preached everywhere, the Lord working with them and* **confirming the word through the accompanying signs**.

(Mark 16:15, 17–18, 20)

Likewise, God opened the door and validated our ministry in Bolivia by the manifestation of the rainbows, which drew the attention of the people as they saw the sign personally or heard about it through the media. Then, during our meetings in Bolivia, thousands of people were saved and healed. The healings, including those of growths and tumors, were further signs— *"accompanying signs"*—that confirmed the ministry of the gospel God had given to us for the people.

> **Jesus said we are not to seek manifestations of signs as a substitution for belief in God's Word.**

Please remember that Jesus said we are not to seek manifestations of signs as a substitution for belief in God's Word. (See Matthew 12:38–39.) And we are not to seek signs for their own sake, as a form of entertainment. However, God will use miracles to promote faith in His Word so that people will believe and be saved, be healed, and experience abundant life in Him.

5. God's Miracles Distinguish Genuine from False Spirituality

The signs accompanying our preaching of the gospel in Bolivia were a testimony of true, godly spiritual activity in contrast to counterfeit spirituality. The witches who had protested our presence there had gathered for a conference in La Paz at the request of the president, who had also invited me to speak to governmental leaders at a breakfast, so there was obviously confusion in that nation regarding what kind of spirituality should be practiced and promoted. To some people, witchcraft or shamanism may seem innocent and helpful, but these practices are false and destructive. The witches had tried to cause a commotion and disrupt our ministry, yet God showed that He is greater than counterfeit spirituality. He poured out His Spirit in a powerful way according to His love, bringing salvation, healing, and deliverance to the people.

Please be aware that false teachers and prophets can exhibit counterfeit signs and miracles. Jesus said, *"For false christs and false prophets will rise and show great signs and wonders to deceive, if possible, even the elect"* (Matthew 24:24). And the apostle Paul wrote,

> *The coming of the lawless one is according to the working of Satan, with all power, signs, and lying wonders, and with all unrighteous deception among those who perish, because they did not receive the love of the truth, that they might be saved.*
> (2 Thessalonians 2:9–10)

Genuine miracles from God, however, are recognized by those who know His ways and are enlightened by His Spirit. One of the religious leaders of Jesus' day named Nicodemus told Him, *"Rabbi, we know that You are a teacher come from God; for no one can do these signs that You do unless God is with him"* (John 3:2). And the Corinthian believers to whom Paul ministered were aware that the message and work of an apostle from God will be confirmed by signs and miracles: *"Truly the signs of an apostle were accomplished among you with all perseverance, in signs and wonders and mighty deeds"* (2 Corinthians 12:12).

Remember that true miracles bring glory to God—not to a "miracle worker." They confirm the truth of salvation through the sacrifice of Jesus Christ on the cross and His resurrection and triumph over the devil and all the forces of evil. (See, for example, Colossians 2:11–15.)

HOW DO GOD'S MIRACLES COME TO US?

God's miracles—His supernatural interventions in our lives—come to us in different ways. While there may be similarities between these ways, and they may overlap, each is important in itself. Throughout this book, we will explore various avenues through which God brings miracles into our lives. We will also discover what we need to know and act upon in order to receive our miracles. Miracles usually don't just "happen" in our lives, for, as we have seen, God does miracles for various reasons and gives them as we seek Him through faith in His Word.

We can experience miracles of various kinds throughout our lives.

Think of yourself as on a pathway to receiving the miracles you desire from God. I invite you to take a journey with me as I relate the adventures of miraculous living that I have experienced in my life, knowing that you, too, can experience the same kinds of miracles and live in the realm of the miraculous. The path to miracles is an ongoing one, and we can experience miracles of various kinds throughout our lives.

Let's be sure not to miss out on all that God has for us. There are consequences of not accepting and receiving the miracles He wants to give us through our faith in Him. The Scriptures say that Jesus *"did not do many mighty works [in His hometown] because of their unbelief"* (Matthew 13:58). We don't want to forfeit our miracle opportunities, which are part of the spiritual wonder and destiny God has planned for our lives.

If someone witnesses God's miracles but observes them only as a spectator and stays in unbelief toward Jesus and His offer of salvation, there is a high cost to him.

Then [Jesus] began to rebuke the cities in which most of His mighty works had been done, because they did not repent: "Woe to you, Chorazin! Woe to you, Bethsaida! For if the mighty works which were done in you had been done in Tyre and Sidon, they would have repented long ago in sackcloth and ashes....And you, Capernaum, who are exalted to heaven, will be brought down to Hades; for if the mighty works which were done in you had been done in Sodom, it would have remained until this day."

(Matthew 11:20–21, 23)

Not to experience a healing or deliverance God desires for you would be tragic enough, but to lack repentance and refuse to receive Christ would lead to a grim penalty. We don't want to fall short of God's purposes for our lives. Let us be able to say with Paul, *"In* [God] *we live and move and have our being"* (Acts 17:28).

Receiving Your Miracles

Through *Your Pathway to Miracles*, I want to show you how to gain a deeper relationship with your heavenly Father and how to live in the miraculous according to His plans. He has spectacular episodes for your life as you hold fast in faith. Get ready to be liberated from frustration and defeat as you set your eyes continually on His positive truths and principles, even as you contend with negative circumstances and situations. You will discover…

- how miracles begin
- the reasons and seasons for miracles
- the roles of faith, expectation, positive affirmation, and prayer
- the importance of claiming your miracle
- how to recognize the miracles in your own hands
- keys to removing mountainous problems blocking your miracles
- how to access "giant" miracles for big needs
- ways in which God gives favor and opportunity
- the nature of "miracle packages"
- how to persevere to receive God's miracle when there seems to be no solution for your problem and all seems hopeless.

My friend, whatever kind of miracle you need, read on!

Rest Stop
on Your Pathway to Miracles

1. What are God's purposes for miracles? Write down these purposes in your own words in a notebook or journal.

2. What miracle(s) have you seen in your life or in the life of someone you know? Write down what you experienced or observed.

3. Consider how you reacted to the miracle(s) you experienced or observed. In what way(s) might you see the miracle(s) in a different light after reading chapter 1?

4. What miracle are you looking for today? Record it in your notebook or journal as you begin *Your Pathway to Miracles.*

Biblical Examples and Scriptures Relating to God's Purposes for the Miraculous

- *To show God's power as Creator-King*:
  Genesis 1; Psalm 104:1–32; 19:1–4;
  Job 26:7–14; Proverbs 8:22–31; Hebrews 11:3

- *To reveal the spiritual reality supporting the physical world*:
  Genesis 28:10–17; 2 Kings 2:1–11; Matthew 4:10–11;
  17:1–5; Acts 7:54–55; Colossians 1:16–17

- *To convey God's compassion for His people*:
  Exodus 3:7–8; Deuteronomy 32:36; Psalm 86:15;
  Psalm 111:4–9; Isaiah 49:15–19; Matthew 9:36–10:1;
  14:14; 20:34; Luke 7:12–16

- *To promote faith in the truth of the gospel/God's Word*:
  Judges 6:36–40; Mark 16:15–20; John 19:34–37;
  Acts 5:1–16; 8:5–8

- *To reveal genuine versus false spirituality*:
  1 Samuel 5:1–5; 1 Kings 18:17–39; Acts 8:9–25;
  16:16–18; Acts 19:11–20

CHAPTER 2

BIRTHING MIRACLES
Where Do Miracles Start?

What is the starting point for your pathway to miracles? The journey begins by receiving a brand-new life, or having a rebirth, through Jesus Christ. Experiencing this rebirth is also called being "born again." Why is this step necessary? Because the pathway doesn't exist in your old life! Jesus said, *"Unless one is born again, he cannot see the kingdom of God"* (John 3:3). Although any person might receive a miracle from God, no one can receive eternal life or live *continually* in the miraculous without this rebirth.

The new birth moves you spiritually into an entirely new realm of life that you couldn't otherwise live in—the realm of the kingdom of God the Father, which is the realm of miracles. Physically, you still live in the realm of this world, but, spiritually, you exist in, and have access to, God's eternal grace and miraculous power.

We are able to enter into this new spiritual realm only because Jesus Christ came to earth through miraculous, supernatural means to become the Savior of the world—the Savior of all who believe in Him and receive Him. *"As many as received [Jesus], to them He gave the right to become children of God, to those who believe in His name, who were born...of God"* (John 1:12–13). Jesus lived a perfect life and died for our sins so that we could be restored to a relationship with God our Father and have eternal life.

My Entry into the Pathway of Miracles

I first entered this pathway to the miraculous when I was sixteen years old and attended a Methodist youth camp. I had been offered a scholarship to this camp, which I was very excited to accept. While I was there, a minister shared how we could invite Jesus to come into our hearts so that we could have a personal relationship with Him.

I already knew about Jesus. After all, I attended church, read the Bible, and had heard a little of the gospel—the "good news"—of Jesus Christ. However, I had not personally received Jesus into my heart. The Bible states plainly in Colossians 1:27, *"Christ in you, the hope of glory."* To receive eternal life, you cannot have Christ "outside" of you, in the sense of just reading about Him and knowing about Him; you must have *"Christ in you."* When you do, you will be connected to God and empowered to lead a miraculous life.

> **When you have "*Christ in you*," you can lead a miraculous life.**

When the minister at the youth camp invited us to pray and receive Jesus into our hearts, I prayed a very simple prayer in faith and repented of my sins. I told the Lord, "I believe in the miracle-working power of the blood of Jesus to cleanse me from sin. Jesus, I invite You to come into my heart and to be Lord of my life, and I thank You for saving me."

My new birth in Jesus Christ was the beginning of miracles for me. I can tell you openly and honestly that from that time on—from age sixteen to age eighty—I have lived a miraculous life. How did it happen? It happened because I was born again.

The Miracle-Working Power of Jesus' Blood

I just mentioned that, when I was saved, I told the Lord that I believed in the miracle-working power of the blood of Jesus to cleanse me from sin. Salvation is a miraculous process, and the role of Jesus' blood is a very important part of that process for two reasons: it was the blood of a sinless Man, and it was the blood of a sinless Sacrifice.

The Blood of a Sinless Man

Jesus' birth, life, and sacrifice on the cross for us were miracles that have special significance in regard to His blood. As you probably know, blood is the element that gives life to living beings. *"For the life of the flesh ["creature" NIV] is in the blood"* (Leviticus 17:11). However, when the first human beings, Adam and Eve, rebelled and sinned against God in the garden of Eden, they became spiritually dead, and their sinful nature has been inherited by all the human beings who have come after them, because sin had infected the very blood of humanity.

Because of this reality, when Jesus—God the Son—came to earth to be our Savior, He had to be born of a virgin. (See Matthew 1:18–24; Luke 1–2.) Why? First, in order to be a proper substitute for human beings and to take their punishment for sin, Jesus had to be a "son," or descendent, of Adam. However, He also had to be a sinless Man, so He could be an acceptable sacrifice before God. Christ could partake of a human body, which is not inherently sinful, but He could not partake of Adam's bloodline, which was completely corrupt. So, God provided a means by which Jesus could be born a sinless human being: He was conceived by the Holy Spirit, and He was also *"born of a woman"* (Galatians 4:4). God sent an angel to Mary, the mother of Jesus, with this message: *"The Holy Spirit will come upon you, and the power of the Highest will overshadow you; therefore, also, that Holy one who is to be born will be called the Son of God"* (Luke 1:35).

In the case of Jesus, a birthing miracle occurred in which a sinless Man was conceived who was both fully God and fully human. He was conceived by God the Father, through the operation of the Holy Spirit, in the womb of a woman who carried Him to term. Mary accepted her role in this remarkable state of affairs through her faith in and love for God, telling the angel, *"Behold the maidservant of the Lord! Let it be to me according to your word"* (Luke 1:38).

The Blood of a Sinless Sacrifice

Jesus' blood had to be pure from the beginning so that He could be a sinless Sacrifice for the sins of humanity. He also had to live a completely sinless life in order for His blood to remain pure. The writer of Hebrews said, *"For we do not have a High Priest [Jesus] who cannot sympathize with our weaknesses, but was in all points tempted as we are, **yet without sin**"* (Hebrews 4:15).

When the pure blood of Christ was shed on the cross, it constituted a blood covenant between God and humanity for the forgiveness of sins and for the provision of the new birth, in which we receive a new and righteous nature in Christ. *"For [God] made Him who knew no sin to be sin for us, that we might become the righteousness of God in Him"* (2 Corinthians 5:21).

Living a miraculous life wouldn't have been possible without the blood covenant through Jesus Christ.

The new birth and its resulting miraculous life could not have been possible without this blood covenant. In the Old Testament, before Jesus became the sacrifice for sin, God made temporary provision for the forgiveness of sins through the blood sacrifices of animals. The first such sacrifice indicated in the Bible was when Abel, one of the sons of Adam and Eve, sacrificed the firstborn of his flock to God as an offering. (See Genesis 4:4.) This is an example of a blood sacrifice on behalf of an individual.

Later, we see another example of a blood sacrifice offered to God by the Hebrew people. After the descendents of Abraham, Isaac, and Jacob were enslaved in Egypt, God sent Moses to deliver them. On the night of their deliverance, God instituted the first Passover observance. Lambs *"without blemish"* (Exodus 12:5) were slain and their blood applied to the doorposts of the Israelites' homes as protection. The firstborn of all the households in Egypt were to be killed that night if they did not have this protection, because Pharaoh had hardened his heart against God and refused to release God's people from their captivity. Because the Hebrews applied the blood of these lambs to their homes, they were saved from death, and then they were set free from Egyptian slavery. (See Exodus 12.) The Passover sacrifice is an example of a blood covenant that applied to entire households.

The Hebrews who were freed from Egypt became the nation of Israel, and, in Leviticus 16, we read about how the Israelites observed the annual Day of Atonement. Among the procedures on this holy day, two goats were chosen to be used for special purposes. One goat was sacrificed on the altar by the high priest as a sin offering on behalf of all the people. The other goat was brought out to an uninhabited place in the desert, far from the Israelites' camp, and released, after the sins of the people had been symbolically placed on its head by the high priest. Together, the goats represented Jesus' sacrifice for us on the cross, in which He took our sins upon Himself and removed them from us *"as far as the east is from the west"* (Psalm 103:12), so that they are never held against us again. The ritual involving the sacrifice of one goat and the sending away of another is an example of a blood sacrifice for the sins of an entire nation.

We have now noted sacrifices that were offered for an individual (Abel), for those in households (the Hebrew families in Egypt), and for a nation (Israel). But the most crucial sacrifice of all was the one that was offered for the entire world—the sacrifice of Jesus, the *"Lamb of God"* (John 1:29, 36). The previous forms of sacrifices were only forerunners to His final sacrifice.

> *For Christ also suffered once for sins, the just for the unjust, that He might bring us to God, being put to death in the flesh but made alive by the Spirit.*
> (1 Peter 3:18)

> *Such a High Priest* [Jesus]*...does not need daily, as those high priests, to offer up sacrifices, first for His own sins and then for the people's, for this He did once for all when He offered up Himself.*
> (Hebrews 7:26–27)

In Jesus' shed blood is a marvel of "divine chemistry." Revelation 7:14 says that the saints of God washed their robes white in the blood of the Lamb. Think of it—washing something in blood and having it become white! Wash one of your garments in the blood of a man and see what color it becomes. It is impossible to get a garment white by washing it in human blood, but in God's "chemical laboratory" of redemption, all the filth and stain of our sin is washed away in the pure blood of the Lamb. Jesus' sinless, supernatural blood alone can perform this miracle!

THREE MANIFESTATIONS OF THE BLOOD COVENANT IN JESUS' LIFE

I want to highlight three times during Jesus' life when He demonstrated the blood covenant. Although there are others, we will focus on these three.

At His Circumcision

First, when Jesus was eight days old, His parents, Mary and Joseph, brought Him to the temple to be circumcised, in fulfillment of the law, as a sign of God's covenant with Abraham. (See Genesis 17:10–14.) At that time, Jesus was officially named; notably, His name means "The LORD [Jehovah] is salvation," or "Jehovah is the Savior," or "Jehovah-saved."[1] (See Luke 2:21.)

You may say, "Well, many people have observed the sign of circumcision, and people continue to do so." That is true, but circumcision was an essential element of carrying out the whole law, and Jesus had to undergo it to be a proper sacrifice for us. In addition, no one but Jesus has fulfilled the other manifestations of the blood covenant.

While in the Garden of Gethsemane

A second demonstration of the blood covenant in Jesus' life was when He went to the garden of Gethsemane, which is located just across the Kidron, a valley between Jerusalem and the Mount of Olives, about two hundred yards from the city wall. *Gethsemane* means "oil press."[2] It was here that Jesus

---

1. See Merrill F. Unger and William White Jr., eds., *Vine's Complete Expository Dictionary of Old and New Testament Words* (New York: Thomas Nelson Publishers, 1985), 333, and the *New American Standard Exhaustive Concordance of the Bible* (electronic version), The Lockman Foundation, 1981. All rights reserved.
2. *Strong's Exhaustive Concordance of the Bible.*

prayed to God the Father about His imminent sacrifice on the cross. *"And being in agony, He prayed more earnestly. Then His sweat became like great drops of blood falling down to the ground"* (Luke 22:44).

On the Cross

A third demonstration of the blood covenant in Jesus' life was foreshadowed at the Last Supper, when Jesus celebrated the Passover with His disciples. There, He talked about the new covenant of His body and His blood as He blessed the bread and the wine and gave them to the disciples to eat and drink.

> *Then He took the cup, and gave thanks, and said, "Take this and divide it among yourselves; for I say to you, I will not drink of the fruit of the vine until the kingdom of God comes." And He took bread, gave thanks and broke it, and gave it to them, saying, "This is My body which is given for you; do this in remembrance of Me." Likewise He also took the cup after supper, saying, "This cup is the new covenant in My blood, which is shed for you."*
> (Luke 22:17–20)

Then, the next day, Jesus shed His blood on the cross for the sins of the world. His blood made atonement for our sins and brought us redemption. Our forgiveness and cleansing in Christ make us part of the family of God and members of the "body" of Christ, with Him as the Head. (See, for example, Colossians 1:18.)

Therefore, as essential as physical blood is to our bodies in sustaining our natural lives, the blood of the Lord Jesus Christ is to the body of Christ in sustaining us spiritually. It, too, is "fluid," reaching all of the members of His body, no matter how far those members may be from one another. And, just as physical blood supplies nourishment to the body's cells and carries away waste and poisons produced by cell metabolism, the blood of the Lord Jesus Christ is to all believers the true source of spiritual nourishment and cleansing. Jesus is our only true support and sustenance—in both the physical and spiritual worlds. He is the One who enables us to live in the realm of the miraculous.

STARTING ON THE PATHWAY TO MIRACLES

The first step in the life of the miraculous is therefore the miracle of the new birth through the sacrifice of Jesus' blood for us. It was the new birth that brought forth the wonderful, miracle-working power of God in my life. And it can be the same for you.

You may know about Jesus, you may read your Bible, and you may attend church, as I did, without having the Author of the Bible living within you. To be saved, we must all invite Jesus to come into our hearts and to be the Lord of our lives. I encourage you to begin your pathway to miracles, if you haven't already, by receiving Jesus into your heart. It will be the most important miracle of your life. At the end of chapter 14 in this book, there is a prayer you can pray to start your new life and step into the realm of the kingdom of God. Why not do so now?

If you have just prayed that prayer, you have the miracle of the new birth working in you through God's Spirit. Whether you have just invited Christ into your life or are already a believer, I urge you to receive the miracle-working power of God. Do not allow doubt or unbelief to prevent miracles from operating in your life. Instead, start living in the miraculous!

ALL OF GOD'S PROMISES ARE "YES" IN CHRIST

We wouldn't be anywhere without Jesus' miraculous birth, through which He came into the world to be our Savior, or His sacrificial life and death on the cross, through which He fulfilled His purpose of redeeming us by His blood. Again, the new birth is the foundation for receiving all other miracles. "*For no matter how many promises God has made, they are 'Yes' in Christ. And so through him the 'Amen' is spoken by us to the glory of God*" (2 Corinthians 1:20 NIV). Through our salvation in Christ, we obtain every provision we need for our lives, which we receive according to God's promises.

[God]...did not spare His own Son, but delivered Him up for us all,...shall He not with Him also freely give us all things. (Romans 8:32)

[God's] divine power has given to us all things that pertain to life and godliness, through the knowledge of Him who called us by glory and virtue. (2 Peter 1:3)

I therefore want to devote the rest of this chapter, as well as the next chapter, to discussing two other types of "birthing miracles" that Jesus has provided for us: (1) the miracle of healing that brings about physical birth where there was infertility, or barrenness, and (2) the miraculous beginnings of our God-given destinies and callings in life.

MIRACLES OF PHYSICAL BIRTH

Birthing miracles—both spiritual and physical—are those that illustrate the wonders of fertilization and new life. We can receive physical healing for barrenness, because healing was included in Christ's atonement for us on the cross, a truth revealed in Matthew 8:16–17:

When evening had come, they brought to Him [Jesus] many who were demon-possessed. And He cast out the spirits with a word, and healed all who were sick, that it might be fulfilled which was spoken by Isaiah the prophet, saying: "He Himself took our infirmities and bore our sicknesses."

In fact, the first healings recorded in the Bible were birthing miracles. They involved the healing of women who were unable to conceive and bear children. In Genesis 20, the women of childbearing age who lived in the royal household of King Abimelech of Gerar suddenly could not have children because of a circumstance in which Abimelech had taken Abraham's wife, Sarah, into his harem. He thought that she was Abraham's sister and desired to make her his wife. Because he had taken Sarah, God caused the other women's wombs to be closed. However, God warned the king in a dream that Sarah was married, and he immediately gave her back to Abraham. God protected her, because the child and heir that God had promised to Abraham, through whom all the nations on earth would be blessed, would come through Sarah. Then, according to God's instructions, Abraham prayed, and God healed Abimelech, his wife, and the other women of Gerar, so that they were able to have children again. (See Genesis 20:17.) In this case, both the barrenness and the renewed ability to bear children were miraculous situations that revealed God's nature and purposes.

The birth of Isaac, the child God had promised to Abraham and Sarah, was an extraordinary miracle. Sarah had been barren during her childbearing years, and now both she and Abraham were old and well past the age of having children. Yet God fulfilled His promise, despite the physical realities and despite what the outward circumstances looked like. Abraham was one hundred and Sarah was ninety when Isaac was born.

> *And the* LORD *visited Sarah as He had said, and the* LORD *did for Sarah as He had spoken. For Sarah conceived and bore Abraham a son in his old age, at the set time of which God had spoken to him.*
> (Genesis 21:1–2)

> *Sarah herself also received strength to conceive seed, and she bore a child when she was past the age, because she judged Him faithful who had promised. Therefore from one man [Abraham], and him as good as dead, were born as many as the stars of the sky in multitude; innumerable as the sand which is by the seashore.* (Hebrews 11:11–12)

Forty years later, Isaac married Rebekah, and the couple soon discovered that she, too, was barren. But Isaac prayed for Rebekah, and they received a double miracle of physical birth: twins named Jacob and Esau. (See Genesis 25:21–26.) In a repeating pattern, Jacob grew up to marry Rachel, who was also unable to bear children. Yet the Bible says that *"God remembered Rachel, and God listened to her and opened her womb. And she conceived and bore a son"* (Genesis 30:22–23). That son was Joseph, whom

God later used to save the lives of his exended family during a time of severe famine. In so doing, He preserved the families whose descendents would become the nation of Israel.

Do you desire a miracle of physical birth? God still does the same type of miracles today. I know this reality personally. The birth of my daughter, Sarah, was a definite miracle. There is no question that God gave her to my husband, Wally, and me in a supernatural way.

I had married at twenty-three, and I'd wanted to be pregnant by twenty-six. However, after a few years of being unable to have a child, I went to a doctor, who sent me to a specialist. This doctor, in turn, sent me to another specialist. All of them told me the same thing: "You have an inherited condition that prevents you from conceiving a child."

Yet, Jesus said, *"All things are possible to him who believes"* (Mark 9:23). Believers can stand on the Word of God and establish miracles in their lives, and so Wally and I believed that God would miraculously give us a baby.

> **Believers can stand on the Word of God and establish miracles in their lives.**

When I was still twenty-six, we went to a big Voice of Healing tent meeting in Dallas, Texas, during an unforgettably hot summer. An evangelist named William Branham was there, and he called me out of a crowd of five thousand people to come up to the platform. Then, he told me through a word of knowledge[3], "You are not from here. You are from a wooded area. You are from Denver, Colorado. You would like to have a baby. Go home and receive your baby."

Before he said this to me, I had a frightening experience as I stood facing him on that platform because I saw an unusual manifestation of the presence of God. In sharing this story with you, I must stress that I am relating my personal experience.

---

3. Specific or special knowledge given by God to a believer, often for the purpose of ministry to others. The word of knowledge is one of the gifts of the Holy Spirit listed in 1 Corinthians 12:7–10.

Between the evangelist and me was what I can describe only as a "wheel within a wheel," which turned. I could literally hear the wheels turning; they made a swooshing sound. I related what I saw to the description of a wheel within a wheel that is found in the book of Ezekiel. But in the biblical account, those were huge wheels that had to do with angelic beings. (See Ezekiel 1:15–21.) These were small and low to the ground.

Yet, in my heart, I felt that this was a manifestation of the presence of God. When William Branham told me to go home and receive my miracle, a very curious thing happened. The wheel within a wheel seemed to go into my feet and up into my body. Of course, I thought, *I know we will have a baby very quickly*, because the evangelist had said, "Go home and receive your baby."

However, we did not have a baby quickly. In fact, *ten years went by*, and there was no baby. To be very honest, I wondered if there ever would be, but my husband always believed during those ten years that God would give us a natural child. In the meantime, we adopted our son, Michael, and we were thrilled with this sweet little boy. But we had no biological babies.

Then, when I was thirty-six, something happened to me physically. I went to the doctor, and he asked me, "Why are you here? What do you think is wrong?"

I said, "I believe I am pregnant."

He proceeded to examine me and said, "No, you are not pregnant. You are most likely going through an early change. It is impossible for you to be pregnant, as you have a condition that is inherited, and you cannot have a child."

I went home, and I did have some changes! My stomach began to extend, so I decided to see another doctor. He examined me, and, this time, I was told, "This is a five-and-a-half-month pregnancy." Such a miracle!

My miracle daughter is now in her early forties, and you can see her on the television program that we cohost, *Today with Marilyn and Sarah*.

I had to make an appointment to go back to the first doctor, due to insurance purposes, and at my follow-up appointment, he said to me, "Why are you here?"

I told him I had just given birth.

He said, "Oh, you adopted a child?"

I said, "No, I didn't adopt a child. I had a baby."

He said, "Well, that's impossible."

I said, "Well, I had a baby anyway."

Sarah is certainly a real miracle and a blessing in my life, as are her husband and children. Sometimes, we are told by other people that certain things are impossible, but if we will stay in faith, we can birth miracles through the Word of God.

If you desire to have a child, or if you have loved one who would like to have a child, I encourage you to believe that God can bring about a miraculous birth. In my travels all over the world, I have prayed for people to have children, and I've seen wonderful birthing miracles.

Several years ago, I prayed in Singapore at a large church that had received repeated reports about couples in the congregation who could not have babies. Since then, I have learned that the *opposite* is now the case. Many babies are being born, and, in fact, some couples are even having twins. I felt like God had given me a greater anointing to believe for miracle births, even to the level of twins and triplets.

BIRTHING MIRACLES AWAIT YOU

Jesus' birth was the most significant "birthing miracle" of all, and His supernatural life was evident throughout His ministry on earth. He brought miracles to many people's lives, and I believe there are miracles awaiting you, too. If you need a miracle of spiritual birth, physical birth, or any other kind, it is available for you through Christ. What matters is not your age, your skin color, or your gender. God is looking for your faith. Receive all the miracles He has prepared with your name written on them.

> **Receive all the miracles God has prepared with your name written on them.**

REST STOP
ON YOUR PATHWAY TO MIRACLES

1. Do you have *"Christ in you, the hope of glory"* (Colossians 1:27)? If so, remind yourself of how He brought you into the new birth, give Him thanks, and remain open to the miracles He has made available to you. If you have not yet received Christ, remember that you can do so right now, using the prayer at the end of chapter 14. After you have prayed this prayer, record your decision in a notebook or journal.

2. Write down two miracles you want to see birthed in your life. Then, write a promise from God's Word that corresponds to each one of these desired miracles.

3. Pray regularly according to God's promises for the miracles you want to see birthed.

4. Write down the name of someone you can tell about the two miracles for which you are believing. Then, ask that person to join with you in prayer for these miracles to come to pass.

BIBLICAL EXAMPLES AND SCRIPTURES RELATING TO BIRTHING MIRACLES

- *Miracle of the "Word made flesh" (the Logos)/miracle of the virgin birth*:
  Isaiah 7:14; John 1:1–18; Matthew 1:18–25;
  Luke 1–2

- *Miracle of John the Baptist's birth*:
  Luke 1

- *Miracle of the new birth*:
  John 3:1–16; Romans 6:4; 1 Peter 1:23;
  Hebrews 10:16–22; James 1:18

- *Miracle of closed and opened wombs*:
  Genesis 20

- *Miracle of Isaac's birth*:
  Genesis 17:15–19; 18:10–14; 21:1–8

- *Miracle of Samson's birth*:
  Judges 13:1–24

- *Miracle of Samuel's birth*:
  1 Samuel 1

- *Miracle birth of a son to the woman at Shunem (through the ministry of Elisha)*:
  2 Kings 4:8–17

CHAPTER 3

THE SEEDS OF MIRACLES
What Has God Sown in Your Life?

We are often unaware that God has sown the seeds of a miracle and that they are taking root. Yet miracle seeds will be sown in our lives in good soil as we are obedient to God, have faith, pray, and grow in our relationship with Him. In fact, His seeds of destiny were sown even before we are aware of Him and His plans for us.

The Scriptures indicate that God made plans for us before we were even born:

> *You know my sitting down and my rising up; you understand my thought afar off....Your eyes saw my substance, being yet unformed. And in Your book they all were written, the days fashioned for me, when as yet there were none of them.* (Psalm 139:2, 16)

> *Then the word of the LORD came to* [the prophet Jeremiah], *saying: "Before I formed you in the womb I knew you; before you were born I sanctified you; I ordained you a prophet to the nations."* (Jeremiah 1:4–5)

SEEDS OF A MINISTRY

When I reflect on the path of ministry on which God has taken me over the years, I can see that the miracles connected to it did not suddenly start when I hit my fifties and sixties. Their seeds were planted early in my life, when I started reading the Bible and having an interest in God's Word.

When I was ten, my family lived on an apple farm in Sewickley, Pennsylvania. I had a room upstairs in the farmhouse, and I would go there and look out the window at the pine trees. I felt very drawn to God and wanted to be connected to Him, and I began to pray and read my Bible, though no one pushed me to do so or encouraged it. I remember even memorizing some Scriptures at that time. So, from the age of ten to sixteen, even though I was not yet a born-again Christian, I was reading the Bible, loving what God had to say to me, and believing that the Bible was truly His Word. I also remember visiting different churches and thinking to myself, *What do they have, and how can I connect to God better?*

Those were important times in my life, although I did not assess them as such until much later in life. I see now that everything I experienced at that time was pointing me to God's calling on my life, one I never would have dreamed of, which is "to cover the earth with the Word," based on Isaiah 11:9: "*The earth shall be full of the knowledge of the* LORD *as the waters cover the sea.*"

We all have spiritual beginnings in our lives. I encourage you to look back and consider how God began to draw you to Himself, how you first started to have a hunger for Him, and how you responded to Him. Those were important steps toward your salvation and the life to which God has called you. These "miracle beginnings" are the initial and early stages in the process through which God works to draw us to Him so that He might communicate His will and we might fulfill His divine plan for us.

> **Every human being has a divine destiny from God.**

I'm certainly not the only one God has called. I believe every human being has a divine destiny from Him. When you have an understanding of God's purpose for you, and when you know His promises and what Christ has given you access to through His death and resurrection, God can work miracles in your life through His mighty power.

A TRANSFORMED PURPOSE

Another way the seeds for later ministry and miracles were planted in my life was through my early love for foreign languages. I started learning Latin when I was only about twelve years old, and I fell in love with it. Then, I took Spanish and French. I enjoyed learning about other cultures and international relations, and I thought, *Someday, I want to be a foreign ambassador.* So, in the beginning, my plan was to get my degree, teach in a foreign country at some point, and then come back to the United States and get into the political arena of education.

However, when I was twenty-three and teaching my first year of school, I met my future husband. Wally attended the same church as my mother. He had recently recommitted his life to the Lord and received a wonderful outpouring of the Holy Spirit in his life. I liked him, but I didn't like the church, because it was what people called "Spirit-filled."

My mother had always wanted me to go to church with her, but, frankly, I was uncomfortable there. When I became interested in Wally, though, I went for purely social reasons. Wally would take me to church, and then we would usually go out to dinner. After nine months of dating, our relationship became serious, and we got engaged.

One night, Wally was to come over to our home to have dinner with us. Yet, strangely, even though he loved my mother's cooking, he called and said, "I will not be over for dinner, but I will be over later to see you." This left me puzzled.

When he arrived, I asked him, "Why didn't you come to dinner?"

His response was, "Because I'm fasting."

Shocked, I asked him, "What are you fasting for?" I knew about fasting, because my mother was dedicated to fasting and praying for my father, who had a very serious mental condition.

He said, "I am fasting for you."

I was highly insulted by this statement. *I'm a born-again Christian,* I thought. *I don't need his fasting and prayer.* So, I reacted by asking him, "Do you want your engagement ring back?"

This was his answer: "I want you to be a committed Christian. Marilyn, before I was born again, I served the devil with all my heart. Now, I'm going to serve God with all my heart, and I'm not marrying a woman who is halfhearted. So, I am on a three-day fast."

My heart dropped. I loved Wally and wanted to marry him, but I didn't want to be as "wild and radical" for Jesus as he was. But there I was, being told he was fasting for three days because of me, and he did not know if our marriage would come to pass.

I went to bed that night troubled. God began to deal with me about a greater surrender to His will and to the power of the Holy Spirit, which I had pushed away. I did not sleep well all night. The next morning, I got up to go to work, but teaching twelve- and thirteen-year-olds takes a lot of energy and activity, and I was already exhausted.

The second night, I did not sleep well again. God kept dealing with me about a full surrender, and I kept refusing. The next morning, I was even more exhausted. I'd now gone two nights without a restful sleep, and I still had to go to work and teach young teenagers.

The third night, God dealt with my heart once more. I'll never forget what He finally said to me: "I have dealt with you about the baptism and power of the Holy Spirit for four years now, and you have refused. I will not deal with you again after this night. I will show you what you will do if you do not surrender to My will: You will not marry Wallace Hickey. You will go to California. You will get your master's degree. You will marry, and you will have a good life and a good career. You will be happy, and you will go to heaven because you'll have Jesus in your heart. But," He added, "if you surrender, I have something so wonderful for you that you could not imagine."

That broke my heart. I began to weep, and I cried out to Him, saying, "God, whether I never marry Wallace Hickey, I want all You have for me. I want to be filled with the Holy Spirit. Do what You want with me, because I want to be what You want me to be."

Well, of course, I did marry Wallace Hickey. I never imagined that, three years later, God would call my husband into full-time ministry. It completely shocked Wally, and, by then, it only partially shocked me. It was never on my agenda to be a pastor's wife or to become active in ministry. But, truly, I wanted to follow God. And He had sowed the seeds of ministry in me as I surrendered to His will.

Little did I dream of the opportunities God would open to me. He fulfilled the desires of my early life, according to His own purposes, for He has provided many occasions for me to travel to other countries as an ambassador for Him. Yes, I did become an ambassador! Not in the manner I had originally thought, but in the way of God's call, which has led me into a miraculous way of life.

When I submitted to His will, did I ever think that I would someday speak to 120,000 people in Pakistan? Did I imagine that I would minister to 65,000 people in Khartoum, the capital of the nation of Sudan? Did I ever envision that I would go to Bolivia, see the sign of the rainbows, and have wonderful healing meetings in a stadium? Did I ever dream that I would minister in Hungary to 100,000 people in a church and witness unusual miracles? I did not dream any of those things. God has such wonderful plans for us, and we need to let Him birth these miracles by yielding to Him.

Yes, I believe that, before the foundation of the world, God planned miraculous beginnings and endings for His people and that He will lead you into His purposes for your life.

> **God imprints His miraculous design on each of us.**

He imprints His miraculous design on each of us. Why would my seventh-grade

Latin teacher inspire me to devote myself to studying foreign languages? Because God had a purpose for them in my life.

What is God's design for you? Think about your abilities and what you like to do. What are you talented in? What *aren't* you talented in? If you have children, observe their talents and abilities and encourage them to develop them. My daughter, Sarah, was a German education major. She can also speak Chinese well, has taken several years of Hebrew and Greek, and can speak some Spanish. She always says, "I love languages." God gave her that design in her DNA for a purpose. Now, I'm observing the interests and gifts of my grandchildren. My granddaughter loves languages, the same as her mother and I do. My grandsons love math and science, as does their father, Reece.

SMALL BEGINNINGS

I have been observing how God's divine design unfolds and noticing that it starts with small beginnings. If those beginnings are encouraged and developed, they will increase abundantly. For example, my budding interest in foreign languages in the seventh grade eventually led to my going to minister in 125 countries of the world. The seeds of ministry that were sown with my surrender to God's will grew gradually. Another way of describing the development of my calling is that I was in the "birth canal" of ministry; the process of being "birthed" in ministry allowed me to become more mature in my faith and gave me experience in teaching the Word and praying for people. I did not speak to thousands of people right away. I began by teaching home Bible studies. Both men and women came to these gatherings, and over a cup of coffee and a cookie, they received Jesus and learned the Bible. Then, as the number of Bible studies I was involved with grew, people started speaking to me about producing a five-minute radio program once a week. I thought, *How would we meet that budget?* But the people in those Bible studies—I had twenty-two Bible studies by that time—paid for that radio budget. It cost sixty dollars a month—a sizeable amount for us at the time.

The radio program gained in popularity and went from five minutes once a week to fifteen minutes every day. Eventually, it led to a television program, which is now called *Today with Marilyn and Sarah* and has a potential viewing audience of more than two billion every weekday. All this was part of God's plan because media has a massive impact in reaching the world with the gospel of Jesus Christ, His healing power, and the outpouring of the Holy Spirit. Truly, the birthing of miracles is a process. It involves not only an initial surrender to God but also a continual surrender.

I said earlier that each miracle has a beginning, and the television ministry had its own birthing process. When I recognize how many opportunities we have today and how many countries we reach through television, I think back to the early 1970s to a group of nine men at the television studios of Channel 9 in Denver, Colorado, with whom I met to see if I could have a program on Sunday mornings called *Life for Laymen*. They looked at me and said, "You will never make it. Stick with the radio. You are radio material but not television material."

Yet, in my heart, I felt God had called me to television. Although I had no Bible school training and had not been raised in a Spirit-filled home, I had the passion and the fire inside.

I'll never forget one Catholic man in that group of nine who spoke up and said, "Well, let's try her. I think she'll pay her bill." The others agreed. I was on Channel 9 for eight years, and I always paid my bills. Forty years later, I am still in television. Why? Not because of great ability or academic degrees but because of the call of God on my life and the vision and passion He has put in my heart. Birthing a miracle is a process of not giving up and not allowing other people, or Satan, to undermine it.

Do not give up on receiving your miracle; otherwise, you can have a "stillbirth." I believe God wants all the ideas He puts in our hearts to be birthed. But there is much to the progression of God's purposes: it requires faith on our part, the details often take time to unfold, and the plans may be attacked as we seek to carry them out.

Today, wherever I travel throughout the world, almost invariably, someone will approach me and say, "I watch you and Sarah on television." That is a miracle, and it was birthed from God's call on my life, which, again, is "to cover the earth with the Word." And, take note: I didn't even receive the definition of my call until the age of forty-two.

> **We need to daily pray, "God, I believe You for the miraculous today."**

Every day is a miracle day for the believer. We need to daily pray, "God, I believe You for the miraculous today." We should not give up, even when circumstances look bad, because God loves to do the supernatural in and through the lives of His people.

REST STOP
ON YOUR PATHWAY TO MIRACLES

1. What early "seeds" do you feel led you to where God has you today? How might they have prepared you for a miracle in your life?

2. Memorize Psalm 139:2, 16 and Jeremiah 1:4–5.

3. Write down your thoughts on your calling in life. As you do, think about your abilities, preferences, gifts, and special direction/guidance from God.

4. If you have a clear idea of your call, try to describe it in one sentence, and then write down a Scripture verse that corresponds to it (this might be general or specific). If you do not yet have a clear idea of your call, are you willing to wait for God to define it for you as you continue to obey Him according to what you do know?

5. What have you been told you cannot do but feel you should be doing? How are you asking God to move you into what you should be doing?

6. What miracle are you praying for in order to progress in your God-given destiny?

BIBLICAL EXAMPLES AND SCRIPTURES RELATING TO THE SEEDS OF MIRACLES/GOD'S CALL

- *God the Son's/Jesus' calling*:
  Psalm 2:7–12; Matthew 1:18–23; Hebrews 1:1–9

- *Abraham's calling*:
  Genesis 12:1–7

- *Jeremiah's calling*:
  Jeremiah 1:4–10

- *Moses' calling*:
  Exodus 3:1–4:17

- *Joshua's calling*:
  Joshua 1:9

- *Paul's calling*:
  Acts 9:1–22; 26:2–20; 2 Timothy 1:11

- *Timothy's calling*:
  2 Timothy 1:5–8

- *Believers' callings*:
  Genesis 1:26–27; Psalm 139:16; Romans 8:28–30;
  1 Corinthians 1:2–9; Philippians 3:20–21;
  2 Timothy 1:9–10; Revelation 1:5–6; 5:9–10

CHAPTER 4

REASONS, SEASONS, AND LIFETIME INFLUENCES

Whom Are You Meeting Along the Pathway?

Joyce Meyer has said, "People come into your life for reasons, for seasons, and for a lifetime." God has certainly brought people into my life for those purposes. He has used people, as well as situations and circumstances, at various points in my life—or for an entire lifetime of influence—to help me along the pathway to fulfilling His vision for me. There are reasons, seasons, and lifetime influences along God's miracle pathways for you, too.

ENCOUNTERS FOR A REASON

Paul and Ananias

One biblical example of a person being used in another's life at a specific point in God's miracle timeline is when God called Ananias to minister to Paul at his conversion. Paul was originally called Saul, and he was born in Tarsus, which today is in south-central Turkey. He was an Israelite from the tribe of Benjamin. He was also a member of the Pharisees, a religious group dedicated to strict obedience to the law of Moses (but whose rules and interpretations went beyond that law and burdened people). He had been educated in Jerusalem by the notable and respected teacher Gamaliel. And, he was a Roman citizen, which meant he held privileged status in society.

This young Pharisee had consented to the stoning death of Stephen (see Acts 8:1), a leader in the early church, and he joined in persecuting the followers of Christ, seeking their imprisonment and death. Persecution of Christians had scattered many of the believers who'd been living in Jerusalem. Some had apparently sought refuge in Damascus, and the Bible says that Saul, *"breathing threats and murder against the disciples of the Lord"* (Acts 9:1), determinedly went to the high priest, Caiaphas, to obtain letters on his behalf addressed to the synagogues of Damascus, so that he could travel to that city and forcibly bring Christians back to Jerusalem for trial. (See verses 1–2.)

But the one who tried to arrest the believers was "arrested" himself as he traveled on the road to Damascus. "High noon" for Saul was the time of his decisive encounter with the One whom he would later refer to as *"the Lord from heaven"* (1 Corinthians 15:47). As Saul made his way, a great light suddenly shone from heaven. He *"fell to the ground, and heard a voice saying to him, 'Saul, Saul, why are you persecuting Me?'"* (Acts 9:4).

One can hardly imagine the sight of a grown man on his knees, shielding his eyes with his hands, hoping to see through the brightness, and wondering who was speaking to him. He answered, *"Who are You, Lord?"* (verse 5), and he heard this startling reply: *"I am Jesus whom thou persecutest: it is hard for thee to kick against the pricks* ["goads" NKJV]*"* (Acts 9:5 KJV).

What were the painful "pricks" that Saul had kicked against? Perhaps, after Stephen died, his words stayed in Saul's memory and haunted him: *"Lord, do not charge them with this sin"* (Acts 7:60), as well as the fact that even while Stephen was being accused, his face had been *"as the face of an angel"* (Acts 6:15). In addition, Saul may have continually thought about the love, zeal, and courage of the Christians whose death sentences he had helped bring about. Again and again, God had tried to reach Saul through the followers of Jesus, but Saul had continued to ignore Him.

Yet, from this time on, Jesus would be Lord in Saul's spirit, mind, and will. That day, the old Saul died, and the new Saul stood forth in Christ. He exalted Jesus as perhaps no other man has ever done.

Saul had been blinded physically by the bright light, but he now saw clearly with his spirit. The men accompanying him could see with the human eye, but they saw nothing of spiritual value in what had happened because they had failed to see Jesus. (See Acts 9:7–8.) Saul's obedience to the Lord gave him the miracle of new birth and the beginning of another miracle—his God-given calling.

> **Saul's obedience to the Lord gave him the miracle of new birth and the beginning of his God-given calling.**

Have you ever been to a harbor and watched the tiny tugboats as they guide the huge ocean liners in and out of port? In the story of Saul, Ananias was God's "tugboat" who was given the purpose of launching this giant-of-the-faith-to-be into his ministry.

Ananias was a believer living in the city of Damascus. The Lord appeared to him in a vision and told him to go to Saul, who was staying in a house on a street called Straight, saying that Saul had seen a vision of Ananias coming and laying his hand on him so that he would regain his sight. (I love the fact that Saul was staying on a street called Straight. God changed his crooked path!)

Ananias had heard about this destroyer of disciples who now sought additional Christians to persecute. So, he questioned the Lord, who immediately put his fears to rest. Ananias went and laid his hands on Saul, who'd been fasting for three days. Saul received his sight and was baptized a Christian. (See verses 9–18.) Perhaps, in this way, Saul came into Ananias's life for the reason of showing him that God can reach anyone with His love and salvation, even this great persecutor of believers.

What Saul did with his life from that point on serves as a keystone in the Christian religion. He called himself a *"bond-servant of God"* (Titus 1:1), and his conversion revolutionized the world. His name was changed to Paul, reflecting His new life in Christ, and he became a preacher of the gospel, as well as an apostle. *"Paul, an apostle (not from men nor through man, but through Jesus Christ and God the Father who raised Him from the dead)"* (Galatians 1:1). He also wrote thirteen epistles—half the books of the New Testament.

Paul gained eternal life not only for himself but also for those whom he touched with the saving gospel of Jesus Christ. Aren't you glad that Ananias was obedient to the command of the Lord at that point in time—and for that special reason—so that Paul could experience the miraculous beginning of a life of miraculous ministry?

Ministry Opportunities

Miracle encounters in God's purposes are waiting for you, too. He will direct people to come into your life for specific reasons, and some of them may help you to reach unsaved people. Remember the man who was on the board of Channel 9 when I wanted to start my television ministry? The rest of the board told me I was not television material, but that one man said, "I think she'll pay her bill." I didn't have a lifetime relationship with him, but one of the reasons he was appointed to that board was to help me in the process of the miracle God was unfolding in my life as He opened the door to television ministry. And that ministry has led to my being the "reason" for the miracle of spiritual birth in many others' lives.

Some years ago, a woman who had watched our telecasts and become a Christian called to ask if I would be willing to speak at a Mormon women's retreat in Illinois. I said, "Of course, I would be delighted to speak." I would consider speaking at a Mormon retreat, a Jehovah's Witnesses meeting, or wherever opportunities open their doors to me.

She said, "I have to ask seventy-two elders and get their permission, but if I get it, would you come?"

"I will come," I assured her.

She got the permission of the elders. However, when I arrived, I didn't have a warm reception. I was concerned about what I should teach, and so I prayed, and the Holy Spirit said, *Teach them like they are born-again Christians.* At the Friday night session, I taught on Joshua 1:8 and how to meditate on the Word of God. The women were very interested and asked questions. I encouraged them to sign up to read through the Bible with me.

By the third session, every woman had signed up to read through the Bible. They were open to hear more about what the Scriptures had to say.

I asked the leader if I could invite people to receive Jesus as their Savior, but she said, "Absolutely not. You cannot do that."

I continued to teach the Bible. During my last service on Sunday morning, I was preparing to close the service when the Lord said to me, *Have an altar call for them to receive Jesus as their Savior.*

I argued, *Lord, they told me I can't do that.*

He said, *Do it, because you're leaving anyway. They won't throw you out.*

I invited those two hundred women to receive Jesus as we stood in a great circle. All but one—the woman who had already become a Christian—raised their hands and prayed to receive Christ into their hearts.

I never received another invitation to their retreat, but that experience was powerful. The opportunity came because of a divine connection with a woman who watched our television program and was open to the Holy Spirit and to the Word of God.

Job 8:7 says, *"Though your beginning was small, yet your latter end would increase abundantly."* We look at many situations in our lives and say, "What good can come out of this?" Yet I would have to say that the above Scripture describes my life. I believe so strongly in destiny and the sovereignty of God that I know He designed me, before the foundation of the world, for the destiny and plan He had for my life. I believe the same is true for you and that He

> **God uses people in our lives for specific reasons in the process of unfolding His purposes.**

uses people in our lives for specific reasons in the process of unfolding His purposes.

RELATIONSHIPS FOR A SEASON

God also brings people into our lives for "seasons" of time to help us along the pathway. They are with us for longer than a specific moment but not for a lifetime.

Jesus and John the Baptist

John the Baptist was a relative of Jesus and a prophet. God used him in Jesus' life during an important season—the initiation of Jesus' public ministry. John's birth had been miraculous, and God had ordained him before he was born to be a herald for Jesus. While John was still in the womb of his mother, Elizabeth, he was filled with the Spirit when Elizabeth heard Mary's greeting. (See Luke 1:5–57.) The Bible tells us that John was sent to *"bear witness of the Light* [Jesus]*"* (John 1:7); he was also known as the *"voice...crying in the wilderness: 'Prepare the way of the LORD.'"* (See, for example, Isaiah 40:3; Luke 3:2–6.)

Since the religious system of the Jews was full of ritual but spiritually empty, John was sent to the people of Israel from outside the religious system. He lived in the wilderness, and when he was thirty years old, he began to preach, pointing out the spiritual barrenness of Israel and calling the people to repentance in order to prepare their hearts for receiving the Messiah.

John was the *"voice"* and Jesus was *"the Word"* (John 1:1). The Word existed before the voice spoke or even was born. (See verses 2–3.) John knew exactly what his role was and what the Messiah was called to do. John's role was to announce Jesus' coming, prepare people's hearts for Him, baptize Him, and confirm His messiahship to the people. Although John was uncomfortable with baptizing the Messiah, Jesus told him, *"Permit it to be so now, for thus it is fitting for us to fulfill all righteousness"* (Matthew 3:15). Jesus had to fulfill all righteousness, including baptism, to be our perfect Substitute and Sacrifice. The fact that Jesus was the promised Messiah was validated to John when he saw the Spirit descend upon Jesus at His baptism, a sign God had revealed to him ahead of time. (See John 1:32–33.) Then, he declared, *"Behold! The Lamb of God who takes away the sin of the world!"* (verse 29). John fulfilled his special role at a significant period of time in the unfolding of God's plan of redemption through Jesus.

Significant Relationships Through Church and Ministry

God has brought people into my life for seasons in order to further the ministry He has called me to. Early on, He did so to move me into teaching home Bible studies. A couple brought their children to our church's vacation Bible school. Although they did not attend our church, they came because the church was located close to their home. The wife then asked me if I would ever consider having a Bible study, and she offered their home. I was inspired and thought, *How exciting to go into a home and teach a Bible study.* I had never had that kind of invitation before, but I agreed. Seven women attended the first Bible study as we began a study on the Holy Spirit. I held Bible studies in that home for seven years, and out of it grew twenty-two home Bible study groups.

Yes, God brings people into our lives in unexpected but wonderful ways. During that time, a woman named Mary Smith, who had been Oral Roberts' secretary, came to work with Wally and me at our church as an administrator. She was very familiar with Oral Roberts' ministry, and she felt that God had a special call on my life. Mary was with me until she retired at age seventy. What a blessing she was, and how she believed in me. God used her as a great encouragement to increase my faith for what God had planned for me.

About the same time, I became involved in the radio ministry. The home Bible studies were growing to the point where I was holding them not only in Denver, but also in various other cities in Colorado, such as Boulder, Fort Collins, and Greeley. I even had a study in Cheyenne, Wyoming. God began to build financial support for the ministry because the people in the Bible studies partnered with me to pay the radio bills and later the television bills. This was indeed a time of new beginnings.

We decided to have a partner event one night and invite people from each of the Bible studies to a dessert time at the Hilton Hotel in downtown Denver. It was a big step of faith for me. About thirty-five or forty people attended, and I presented our ministry's vision for our radio program, which would encourage people to read their Bibles and get them turned on to Jesus. I also presented information about our new project, our television ministry. We gave them an opportunity to sign pledge cards stating that they wanted to be partners and commit themselves to give a certain amount of money toward the ministry. I have to be honest—I had a lot of fear about taking this step, and I began to question if it was truly in God's will. Was I really following the Holy Spirit's leading?

After the partner event, I walked out of the Hilton Hotel on that warm summer evening in July and looked up at a tall building that was being constructed opposite the hotel. It was slated to be a bank and was advertised as the tallest building in the city. The Lord spoke to my heart, saying, *You will have the tallest outreach in Colorado.* I was floored. I had twenty-two small Bible studies at that time. Yes, I had a fifteen-minute daily radio program, but it was broadcast just in Denver, and I was only in the beginning phases of our television program, which was being shown for thirty minutes on Sunday mornings, also in Denver alone. Yet God had told me of something greater He wanted to do. Why? Because, before the foundation of the world, He had prepared a lifestyle of miracles for me, but the fulfillment of the miracles took a process of faith.

I have never forgotten the experience of standing in front of that new structure, and, even now, when I'm driving on the freeway and see that tall building, I am reminded of the words God spoke to me so many years ago. It is amazing to me what He has done. It is His vision, and it has truly been a miraculous one.

He has also prepared miracles for you, as well as for your spouse, your children, your grandchildren, and other family members. At times, your faith walk will be a battle, and you will become concerned about whether you are hearing from God and whether the miracles will come to pass. You will even "blow it" on occasion and not make the right decision. But if you will hang on to God, He will come through for you. You can experience the unfolding of God's purposes if you will put your confidence in Him, read and meditate on the Word, speak the Word in faith, and obey the Word.

> **You can experience the unfolding of God's purposes if you will read and meditate on the Word, speak the Word in faith, and obey the Word.**

I learned a lesson in faith and obedience the year we started our church in Denver. We had only twenty-two people at the first Sunday service, but we really believed that God had called us to that city, and, during that first year, the church grew to seventy people.

At that time, world-renowned evangelists T. L. and Daisy Osborn came to Denver for the purpose of raising money for their building project in Tulsa. In my opinion, the Osborns have probably done more to bring the gospel to the whole world than anyone else in my generation. That night, my husband spontaneously gave them the thousand dollars that we had carefully saved for a car. Our current vehicle was in bad shape, and I was very upset with him for doing that because I thought, *How are we going to get to church if our car breaks down?* And now, we didn't even have a down payment to purchase another car.

I awoke in the middle of the night and said to him, "Why don't you wake up and worry?" He did wake up, but he didn't worry. He said, "Marilyn, I'm not going to worry. God told me to give the money, so He will provide the money for the car. Now, go to sleep and put your trust in God."

Then, someone borrowed our old car and wrecked it. So, now, we had no car to drive to church. We were the pastors, and we had no money for another car because my husband had given it all away! We had to ask someone to pick us up and take us to church. Little did I know that God had a miracle with our names on it.

Soon afterward, John Osteen, the founding pastor of Lakewood Church in Houston, Texas, and the father of current pastor Joel Osteen, came to minister at our church. We did not know him personally, but when he stood up to speak, he said, "Pastor, I see the letters C-A-R over your head. Do you need a car?"

Do we need a car? Wally answered, "Kind of."

That morning, John Osteen raised the money for the car we needed, but that was not the end of the miracle. About five years later, I began to travel a little. I received invitations to various speaking engagements due to the radio program, and I was asked to speak in Tulsa. I took the opportunity and very boldly called the Osborns' ministry and asked if I could take T. L. and Daisy to lunch. I was shocked and pleased when they said yes. When I walked into the private dining room at the restaurant, Daisy stood up and greeted me. This was the first time we had met, and she said to me, "Marilyn, God is going to use you to be a world evangelist. You will affect leaders of nations, and you will have many audiences." I was overwhelmed and thought, *How can this be? That's Daisy's call.* I noted that "Daisy" and "crazy" rhymed, but I tucked the word in my heart. Certainly, after all these years and 125 countries later, it is clear that was a prophetic word. However, I really believe it all started with my husband's obedience in sowing that seed for a spiritual harvest through the Osborns' ministry. Daisy died some years ago, but, to this day, T. L. Osborn blesses my ministry with special gifts.

Elijah and Elisha

Another biblical example of a season of spiritual influence is the mentorship of Elisha by Elijah. The miracles connected with both of these prophets are powerful, and I will return to them several times in this book.

Elijah was a tremendous prophet who moved in the miraculous. He was called by God to minister during a very dark period in the history of the Israelites. Their nation had been divided into the northern kingdom, which was called "Israel," and the southern kingdom, which was called "Judah." Ahab and Jezebel were the king and queen of the northern kingdom, and they were evil leaders who rejected God and His ways and turned the nation to the worship of Baal, the false god of a religion that even included child sacrifice. (See, for example, Jeremiah 19:5.) Elijah preached against them, and the nation made a turnaround during the time of his ministry.

Then, God called Elisha to be Elijah's successor, and he became a *"servant"* or *"attendant"* to Elijah for a time. (See 1 Kings 19:16–21 NKJV, NIV.) Elisha apparently learned from observing Elijah; he saw how God had anointed his life with power to fulfill what he had been called to do. Therefore, when it came time for Elijah to be taken to heaven, Elisha was very bold, telling the older prophet, in effect, "I want a double portion of the anointing you have from God." (See 2 Kings 2:9.) Elijah replied, *"You have asked a hard thing"* (verse 10).

If you want a double portion of God's anointing, don't think of it as a little thing. It is a hard thing. But Elijah told Elisha that if he saw him when he left, he could have what he had asked for. Here is how that transpired:

> *Then it happened, as they continued on and talked, that suddenly a chariot of fire appeared with horses of fire, and separated the two of them; and Elijah went up by a whirlwind into heaven. And Elisha saw it, and he cried out, "My father, my father, the chariot of Israel and its horsemen!" So he saw him no more. And he took hold of his own clothes and tore them into two pieces. He also took up the mantle ["cloak" NIV] of Elijah that had fallen from him, and went back and stood by the bank of the Jordan.* (verses 11–13)

After receiving Elijah's mantle, Elisha repeated what Elijah had done a little while earlier (see verse 8), to enable them both to cross the Jordan River: *"Then [Elisha] took the mantle of Elijah that had fallen from him, and struck the water, and said, 'Where is the LORD God of Elijah?' And when he also had struck the water, it was divided this way and that; and Elisha crossed over"* (2 Kings 2:14).

If you count the miracles of Elijah in the Bible, you will see that there are eight. If you count the miracles of Elisha, you will find sixteen. Elisha did receive a double portion of the anointing!

Let me tell you about one of Elisha's first miracles. He went to the city of Jericho, which was infamous among the Israelites. Let me give you some background to this city. You probably know that shortly after they entered the Promised Land, under God's instructions, the Israelites marched completely around Jericho once a day, for six days. Then, on the seventh day, they marched around the city seven times and shouted. Jericho's walls fell down, and the Israelites defeated the people who lived there. (See Joshua 6:1–20.) That was the first city the Israelites took after entering the Promised Land.

There are other situations in the Bible that involve Jericho, in both the New and Old Testaments, but I want to mention for our purposes that God had spoken a curse on that city. Its people had been so evil and vile that God had said, in essence, "If anyone tries to rebuild this city, his oldest and youngest sons will die." (See verse 26.) Later, a king named Hiel decided to rebuild the city, and his oldest and youngest sons did die. (See 1 Kings 16:34.) So, the city and the area surrounding it had a negative reputation and were under a curse. But, while Elisha was prophet, the people who lived in the area of Jericho came to him and said, in effect, "This is a hard place in which to live. There's something bad in the water here. We water the trees and the gardens, but we still don't harvest the crops that we should. We don't know what to do about it." They knew that the ground was unfruitful because the water was somehow cursed. (See 2 Kings 2:19.) These people were desperate. Wouldn't you be desperate if your crops were failing, if your trees were not giving the fruit they should, and if your garden wasn't producing?

I love what comes next. Notice that the people didn't accept their situation but went to Elisha for help, believing that a miracle could occur. Likewise, you need to know that God can give you a miracle. If you are just sitting there, thinking, *Well, a miracle couldn't happen to me*, stop thinking like that! That's not biblical. You have moved out of faith and into unbelief.

What kind of miracle do you need? A restored relationship? An open door of opportunity? A job?

The people of Jericho went to Elisha, the man with the double portion, expecting something good. When you ask for prayer for a miracle, don't go to just anyone, who may not believe at all. Go to a person of faith.

> **When you ask for prayer for a miracle, go to a person of faith.**

Jericho was under a curse, but the people believed that the curse could be broken by the anointing of God. I believe that, too. The anointing of God can break any curse, whether it is physical, mental, emotional, or spiritual. Many times, we think we and our families have to remain under a curse. The curse may be physical affliction, poverty, alcoholism, or something else. People will say things like, "Oh, my family's always lived in poverty." You don't have to remain in a cursed situation, because Jesus has already redeemed you from the curse. "*Christ has redeemed us from the curse of the law, having become a curse for us..., that the blessing of Abraham might come upon the Gentiles*" (Galatians 3:13–14).

What was Elisha's response to the people of Jericho? "*Bring me a new bowl, and put salt in it*" (2 Kings 2:20). That action could seem insignificant, but it was the means through which the miracle came. The people could have refused to do what Elisha said, saying that it wouldn't accomplish anything. They could have tried a different method, or they could have gone halfway, such as bringing an old bowl rather than a new one. But they did exactly as the prophet said.

Then, Elisha went out to the spring of the waters. Significantly, he didn't go to where there was a trickle or a little stream of water, or to an irrigation ditch, but to the *source* of the waters. He took the bowl of salt and threw it into the water. As he threw it, he proclaimed, "*Thus says the* LORD: *'I have healed this water; from it there shall be no more death or barrenness'*"

(2 Kings 2:21). Although he had received from God the revelation of using the bowl and the salt, Elisha also had to *speak* to the source of the problem for change to occur. And, from the time of Elisha, the water of Jericho has been fine, and that area of Jericho has been very prosperous.

Miracles are a part of the anointing that God wants His people to receive, and I encourage you to believe for your miracle today. There was a time in my life when I was sick and, instead of getting better, I seemed to get worse. But I had a faith friend, Frances Hunter, whom I would call almost every night for encouragement.

She would always ask, "How was your day?"

I always tried to be positive, but one day I answered, "It was a hard day."

She replied emphatically, "This is your last bad day."

I wrote it down—*This is my last bad day*—and I repeated it out loud.

The spoken word is powerful and wonderful. My strength and energy came back—Frances had declared it, and I had declared it.

> **The Bible says we can all speak in faith and see results.**

You may say, "But Elisha was a prophet, and Frances Hunter had a healing ministry." However, the Bible says we can all speak in faith and see results. Jesus said, "*For assuredly, I say to you, whoever says to this mountain, 'Be removed and be cast into the sea,' and does not doubt in his heart, but believes that those things he says will be done, he will have whatever he says*" (Mark 11:23). Notice that it says "*whoever.*"

Sometimes, it is not only people but circumstances that come into your life for a reason, so that you can pray about them and speak to them in order to receive the blessing God has for you. What is your Jericho? What are your "bad waters"? What do you need to speak to that has been blocking God's blessings from your life?

A LIFETIME OF INFLUENCE

A biblical illustration of a long-term relationship of influence is the association of Paul and Timothy. The seeds of their connection started during Paul's first missionary journey (see Acts 16:1–5) and likely continued right up until Paul's death in Rome. Paul considered Timothy his *"true son in the faith"* (1 Timothy 1:2). He wrote to the Philippians,

> *For I have no one like-minded, who will sincerely care for your state. For all seek their own, not the things which are of Christ Jesus. But you know his proven character, that as a son with his father he served with me in the gospel.*   (Philippians 2:20–22)

Timothy was constantly loyal and helpful to Paul, and he learned to follow Christ through the apostle's lifestyle and teaching. Theirs was a mutually supportive, enduring relationship of mentorship, friendship, and dedicated service to God.[4]

In this regard, I want to share a personal example of someone who has had a great influence on me for many years ·because of his lifestyle. Let me give you some background. A great charismatic renewal had begun in the denominational churches, for example, among Catholics, Presbyterians, Lutherans, Baptists, and Nazarenes. Anglicans were also coming to Jesus and becoming Spirit-filled. In conjunction with this renewal, I began to cohost a charismatic conference in Niagara Falls with a pastor from Buffalo, New York, by the name of Tommy Reid. Hundreds of people attended, especially Catholics. They became born again, Spirit-filled, healed, and transformed. Approximately 5,000 people would attend the meetings at night, with 1,500 or more at the daytime meetings.

We would each choose a guest to speak at the conference. One time, I asked Fred Price to come, and he was a great blessing because he was a person of strong faith. Tommy Reid invited Dr. David Yonggi Cho. Dr. Cho's church in Seoul, South Korea, is the

---

4. Merrill C. Tenney, gen. ed., "Timothy," *The Zondervan Pictorial Bible Dictionary* (Grand Rapids: Zondervan Publishing House, 1967), 855–856.

largest church in the world. He's retired now, but his church is still growing. He came to the conference because Tommy had met him as a young man and had ministered with him at his church.

I was in awe of Dr. Cho. He considered his church small since it had "only" about 200,000 members. Can you imagine a 200,000-member church being small? I really wanted to be around him and learn from him, so, during the speakers' luncheon, I sat with him and listened as he talked a little about the things in his heart, such as passion, vision, and how to walk and live in the vision. I thought, *Oh, God, this man has such an anointing of faith. He oozes faith, and I would really like to get around him more, but how could I do that? He's in South Korea, and I'm in the United States. I'm just a pastor's wife, and I have children. Yes, I have home Bible studies and a radio program, and I do a little television, but how could I connect with his vision?*

I found out that Dr. Cho had an American board of directors for his Church Growth International ministry and that there were twenty-two pastors on that board. So, I asked one of these pastors if there were any women on Dr. Cho's American board, and he said no. I told him that I thought it would be good if there was a woman on the board, and he asked, "Whom do you have in mind, yourself?" I said, "Absolutely."

> **"Don't give up" is an extremely important principle in receiving your miracle.**

He asked the other twenty-one pastors, and they said, "No, we don't want her on the board." However, I did not give up, and that is an extremely important principle in receiving your miracle. Don't give up, because people will say no, circumstances will say no, you may feel inadequate, and there might be a thousand things that the devil will throw at you to keep you from moving forward on the miraculous walk that God has for you. Don't give up!

What did I do? I prayed, "Lord, if Dr. Cho were to invite me to be on his board, then no one could say no." And I continued to pray. About six months later, I received a personal letter from

Dr. Cho inviting me to be on the board. I was faithful to attend those board meetings when he came to the United States. I didn't go there to say anything; what did I have to say? I went to receive. I believe that when you get around radical faith people, their faith is contagious, and Dr. Cho's was contagious in my life. Then, I began to have a desire to speak at his church. *I would love to speak at his big church*, I thought to myself, *but he can get any speaker in the world, so why would he invite me?* But when you exercise faith in God, He can do anything. So, I began to pray that God would put it on Dr. Cho's heart to invite me to come and speak at his church.

Four months later, I went to a board meeting in Orlando, Florida, that I will never forget. My flight was late in arriving, and when I walked into the meeting, Dr. Cho stood up and said, "Oh Marilyn, I'm so glad you're here, because I want to invite you to come and speak at my cell leaders' conference. I have twenty thousand cell leaders."

Of course, I went, and that was the first time I spoke at his church. After that, Dr. Cho invited me to serve on his international board, which I've been on for many years. And I have had the pleasure of speaking at his church numerous times. Why do I tell you all this? To show you that you need to get around radical faith people, because radical faith will come upon you, too.

There is no question that the people you listen to and fellowship with have a great deal of influence on your life. There are people whom God will bring into your life for longer than just a season to help you progress in your faith and service for Him. Being on both Dr. Cho's American and international boards has been a big thing for me and a great blessing. It's brought about the blessing of radical faith.

I want to encourage your faith because I believe God has big things waiting for you.

BE FAITHFUL TO GOD'S DIRECTION IN YOUR LIFE

We don't always know when God will bring people into our lives for a specific reason, a season of mentoring or ministry, or a long-term influence for His purposes. However, I encourage you to be faithful in learning and growing in the ways He is teaching you, knowing that He is in the process of leading you along the miraculous path He has planned for you.

REST STOP
ON YOUR PATHWAY TO MIRACLES

1. How did God first draw you to Him?

2. After reading this chapter, what additional thoughts do you have about what God has called you to? Write them down and pray about them.

3. Consider how God has brought various people into your life for a reason, a season, or a long-term/lifelong influence. Then, take some time to thank Him for these "divine connections."

4. What seemingly small beginnings have turned out to be part of God's big plan for your life?

5. Write down the names of two people in whose lives God has placed you so that you may be an encouragement to them. Pray His promises for them. Then, think about how you can bless them in a specific way.

6. Ask God to move in your life in relation to one of your heart's desires. For example, you might long for someone to be prompted to do something on your behalf.

7. Who are the "radical" faith people in your life? Pray that God would enable you to learn more from them.

BIBLICAL EXAMPLES AND SCRIPTURES RELATING TO REASONS, SEASONS, AND LIFETIME INFLUENCES

- *Miracle healing of waters by Elijah for people of Jericho*:
  2 Kings 2:16–18

- *Miracle healing of centurion's servant*:
  Matthew 8:5–13; Luke 7:1–10

- *Miracle healing of man with withered hand*:
  Matthew 12:9–13; Mark 3:1–5; Luke 6:6–10

- *Miracle of Jesus' word of knowledge regarding colt*:
  Mark 11:1–10

- *Ananias's spiritual encouragement/miracle of
  healing for Saul (Paul)*:
  Acts 9:9–18

- *Seasonal mentorship of Moses and Joshua*:
  Exodus 17:8–16; 24:12–18; 32:17–18; 33:7–11;
  Numbers 11:24–30; 13:1–14:38; 27:12–23; 32:25–28;
  34:16–17; Deuteronomy 3:21–28; 31:1–8, 14–23;
  32:44; 34:9; Joshua 1:1–9

- *Seasonal mentorship of Elijah and Elisha*:
  1 Kings 19:16–21; 2 Kings 2:14–15

- *Seasonal relationship of Jesus and John the Baptist*:
  Matthew 3; John 1:1–36

- *Miracle encounters with Jesus (leading to lifetime
  influence)*:
  John 1:40–51; 4:28–29, 39

- *Lifetime influence of Paul and Timothy*:
  Acts 16:1–5; Philippians 2:19–22; 1 and 2 Timothy

CHAPTER 5

EXPECTING YOUR MIRACLE
Prepare to Receive God's Blessings

There is a saying that goes, "Don't expect anything, because then you won't be disappointed when it doesn't happen." I say, "Don't expect anything *and* you won't be disappointed!" In other words, there is a direct connection between expecting and receiving, and vice versa. Expectation is a vital attitude to have if you are to progress on your pathway to miracles.

Can you imagine the level of expectation the prophet Elijah had when he was used by God to do miracles? Again, you may say, "Yes, but he was a prophet." Yet the Bible says, *"Elijah was a man just like us..."* (James 5:17 NIV).

Jesus calls all of us believers to do the works that He did, including miracles. In fact, He said, *"Most assuredly, I say to you, he who believes in Me, the works that I do he will do also; even greater works than these he will do, because I go to My Father"* (John 14:12). Picture that: greater works than He did. That should raise your level of expectation!

YOUR FOUNDATION FOR MIRACLES

Did you know that when the Bible refers to hope, it means "confident expectation"? So, I define *expectation* as "confident belief or strong hope that a particular event will happen." *"This hope we have as an anchor of the soul, both sure and steadfast"* (Hebrews 6:19). We receive miracles through expectation, as the Bible tells us in Mark 11:23.

71

Since hope, or confident expectation, is so important to receiving miracles, you have to purposely place yourself around influences that will build hope and faith within you—that will help you build an expectation that God does indeed want you to live in the miraculous. He has a divine destiny for you; you're not an accident. Remember that He *"knit you together"* as He said in Psalm 139:13 (NIV). He even gave you the Bible, which tells you what He would have you to do.

OVERCOMING NEGATIVE THINKING

> **We have to change our thinking to "positive expectation."**

One of the problems many of us have in exercising faith for miracles is that we were taught "negative expectation" as children; we learned to expect negative results instead of positive ones. We therefore have to change our thinking to "positive expectation."

When I was growing up, my mother told me that I would probably never be good in athletic events. She unknowingly planted a negative idea in me. I listened, my expectation was negative, and, as a result, I was always the last one chosen for sports teams at school. However, when I got older and began to work out, I thought, *Athletic success is primarily practice.* As I exercised, I realized that I had a body that could perform well in athletic events.

On the other hand, when I was in grade school, I was apprehensive about spelling tests and thought that I would not do well on them. In this area, my mother reinforced positive expectation, telling me, "You will do well because you are a smart girl." The result was that I did do well in spelling during my grade-school years, and I also did well academically in high school and college, because she had told me, "You are a smart girl."

This positive outlook carried over to my walk with God as I read the Word, and I began to build expectation for what He wanted to do in my life. If we do not live in expectation, we live without hope, and it is depressing to be hopeless.

KEYS TO BUILDING A FOUNDATION OF EXPECTATION

1. Develop Faith in God's Promises

As I began to build a foundation of biblical expectation, both Kenneth Hagin and Bill Gothard were instrumental in my life. The first year Wally and I were married, we went to a Foursquare church and heard Kenneth Hagin speak. He was not a well-known preacher at that time. I remember hearing him teach on how the Word of God can work in your life. The truths he taught became so real and wonderful to me that I remember clearly, more than fifty-five years later, exactly what I thought when I got home: *If the Word of God can work like that for him, it can also work that way for me.*

My newfound belief that the promises of God *do* work brought an expectation in my life that formed the solid groundwork on which I could base my anticipations. It may take time, and it may take God dealing in our lives, putting us through various situations that enable us to learn how to trust Him. Yet having expectation in regard to God's promises is a must for all of us if we are to fulfill His purposes for us and experience His miracles.

Kenneth Hagin has been a mentor to me throughout my life (one of the "lifetime influences" we talked about in the previous chapter) because, once I heard how the Word could work and about the power of the Holy Spirit, and how they connected, I was "hooked." Over the years, I would go to his meetings, listen to his tapes, and read his books, because his teachings were such an inspiration to me and built my faith. Faith teaching totally modeled my life. People would ask me, "Are you a faith teacher?" and I would respond, "I am a radical faith teacher."

I would have to say that the salvations and healings I've seen, the life transformations I've witnessed, the negative circumstances I've seen turn around, and the nations I've observed change for the better have all been results of people exercising faith in God's Word and in His power. Exercising faith is a process—and it's a challenging one at times.

I have explained how God puts various circumstances in our lives to teach and direct us. But, as we have seen, He also puts people in our lives to mentor us—people who are spiritually stronger than we are and who bring us revelation from God's Word to help us. To this day, I thank God for Kenneth Hagin and the influence his teachings have had on my life. He was a wonderful encouragement.

2. Meditate On and Memorize God's Word

Meditating on the truths and principles of God's Word and memorizing Scripture is the next key for developing an attitude of expectation because you need to get the Word within you to nourish your faith.

Some years ago, I went to a four-day seminar called Institute in Basic Youth Conflicts (now called Institute in Basic Life Principles). It was taught by Bill Gothard, who, along with Kenneth Hagin, has been another great encouragement to me through his teaching. Basic Youth Conflicts was a wonderful seminar for learning how to deal with various life issues in a biblical and practical way, such as how to address problems that arise with your children and other difficult circumstances.

> **Meditating on and memorizing God's Word is where the *real* miracle of expectation comes from.**

However, the last meeting of the seminar turned out to be the most important for me, because Bill Gothard taught about meditating on and memorizing God's Word. In my experience, participating in these practices is where the *real* miracle of expectation comes from, and meditating on and memorizing Scripture has continued to nurture me on a daily basis.

Another reason I began to meditate on God's Word was that I took Joshua 1:8 to heart. This Scripture says, in effect, that if you meditate on the Word of God day and night, if you speak the Word day and night, if you do the Word of God day and night, you will make your way prosperous and successful.

To *meditate on* really means "to chew." This is one situation in which you will want to chew with your mouth open! In other words, say the Scriptures out loud; repeat them over and over, because meditating on them will make you successful.

What did Joshua meditate on? In his day, the Scriptures available to him were the Pentateuch, or the first five books of the Bible: Genesis, Exodus, Leviticus, Numbers, and Deuteronomy. (In certain Jewish circles today, men are required to memorize the whole Pentateuch.) What was the result of Joshua's meditating? What God had promised him came true. He was successful in everything he did. He was vigorously healthy, and he was victorious in conquering the Promised Land, which took five or six years. Undoubtedly, he meditated on and spoke the Word often. Joshua ended up living in a town called Timnath Serah in the hill country of Ephraim, which was his tribe. (See Joshua 19:49–50.) When he was in his eighties or nineties, he didn't retire to a little cottage. Instead, he was just beginning his conquest of Canaan. People say they're too old or too busy to pursue God's purposes, but they have a promised land to take—the fulfillment of His promises.

In addition to meditation on the Scriptures, memorization will allow you to get the Word inside you so that you can build expectation based upon it. At the Basic Youth Conflicts seminar, Bill Gothard shared his testimony of how he had almost been held back in school but had a Sunday school teacher who got her class of boys to memorize Scripture. They began to memorize small books of the Bible, and, as Gothard continued to memorize the Word, his grades went up. He continued a life of mediating on the Word of God. The Word is life-giving!

Bill Gothard's account of what Bible memorization did for him was so inspirational to me that I went home and thought to myself, *I am going to memorize the book of Proverbs.* This was quite a book to take on, as it has thirty-one chapters. At that time, my son, Michael, would have been fourteen years old, and my daughter, Sarah, would have been six, and I would recite what I'd memorized to my children. I didn't worry about how long it took to memorize but just worked at it faithfully.

I thought that Bible memorization would be great for Michael and Sarah, as well, so I pushed and pulled them to memorize, and, in those early years, they memorized the first part of Proverbs.

Saying Scriptures out loud to other people is an important part of the process. I asked another woman to be my Bible memorization partner, and we would call each other every day, early in the morning. Sometimes, I would talk with her while I was packing school lunches for my children. We tried to do one verse a day. Our system was to say our verses to each other and then share what they meant to us. We would also review verses we'd memorized in the past. Unfortunately, my partner backed out of the arrangement, but, within nine months, I finished memorizing all thirty-one chapters of Proverbs, and the experience was absolutely transformational for me. God's Word was like a burning fire within me.

The following is the method I used. I took Proverbs 6:22 as my guide, which talks about taking the teachings of one's parents to heart: *"When you walk, they will guide you; when you sleep, they will watch over you; when you awake, they will speak to you"* (NIV).

I decided to begin in the morning, corresponding to the phrase, *"When you awake, they will speak to you."* So, when I got up each day, I would say my memory verse ten times.

In the afternoon, I would say the verse one time, in conjunction with the phrase, *"When you walk, they will guide you."*

Then, at night, I would recite my verse once before going to bed, and I would say the verse for the next day one time, in relation to the phrase, *"When you sleep, they will watch over you."* It's been said that the last thing you hear at night goes through your mind seven times.

The point of memorization is not just to be able to say that you can quote the first three chapters of this or that book of the Bible. The significance is what God says to you through the Scripture passages—the insights, truths, and wisdom you receive. Therefore, when you begin to memorize the Bible, use a notebook or journal to record what God is saying to you in those verses. Sometimes, memorization can seem like a very dry process, but as you say the verses and say them and say them, suddenly, they will open up, like the shell of a nut when it cracks, and you will get to the "meat" inside. You'll discover truths you never could have if you'd only read the Bible. In this way, memorization and meditation come together, as they should.

For some reason, the hardest book of the Bible for me to memorize was the gospel of John. I don't know why; it could have been the enemy trying to keep me from its wonderful truths. It took me at least three years to memorize the gospel of John. It also took me almost three years to memorize the book of Revelation. Both of these books were challenging to me, but they were well worth the time!

In John 8:12, Jesus said, *"I am the light of the world. He who follows Me shall not walk in darkness, but have the light of life."* When I came to that verse in the process of memorizing the book, I was so excited about it because of the preceding story about the woman taken in adultery. As I meditated on this Scripture and what had come before it, I saw that no sin was too dark that the light of God could not penetrate it. The Lord said to my heart, *You're very excited about this verse because of this woman, but I'm not very happy because I wanted her accusers as much as I wanted her. I lost them.* Getting that kind of revelation has made all of my memorizing worth the effort.

Even after I lost my early-morning memorization partner, I continued practicing memorization with my children, repeating my Scriptures to them so they could hear them, too. When Sarah got older, she would sometimes scratch my back as I spoke the passages I had learned. On occasion, she would tell me, "Just one chapter, Mom." If I tried to go further, she would say, "Now, Mom, I know what you're doing."

Currently, I'm memorizing with my grandchildren. Recently, I babysat for them, and as the youngest was going to bed, I asked him, "Do you mind if I recite First Corinthians, chapter fifteen?" I warned him that it was long, but he agreed and calmly heard me practice. He sat through all fifty-six verses.

Another time, I did 1 Corinthians, chapters 13 and 14, with my middle grandchild. It is a blessing to me and, I hope, to them.

So, for more than thirty years now, I have started each day by memorizing Scripture. Scripture you have memorized will stay with you. If someone were to ask me to repeat chapter 5 of a specific book, I probably could not do it. But, as I review the passage, it comes back to me.

> **Speaking the Word, thinking the Word, and doing the Word gives you intimacy with God as He speaks revelation from His Word into your life.**

Meditating on the Word helped me to be a better wife, a better mother, and a better partner in ministry with my husband. It helped me to teach the Bible better because I was not just reading the Bible; the Bible also began to "read" me. In other words, speaking the Word, thinking the Word, and doing the Word gives you a kind of intimacy with God as He speaks revelation from His Word into your life daily—sometimes from hour to hour and from moment to moment.

Yes, there have been times when I've become discouraged and thought, *What's the use?* and have given it up for a while. However, I have always come back to it because when I wasn't memorizing, I felt as if a big part of my life was missing.

"Your word I have hidden in my heart, that I might not sin against You" (Psalm 119:11). Hiding God's Word in our hearts and allowing it to work within us, building our expectation for the fulfillment of His promises, are essential components of a healthy spiritual life. Daily, there are interruptions, obligations, urgent situations, and the like that pull on us, and, if we aren't careful, they will keep us from what the Lord wants us to receive through meditating on and memorizing the Word. Speaking the Word, thinking the Word, and doing the Word will keep our focus on the fact that God has planned miracles and a miraculous lifestyle for His people, if they will live in an attitude of continual expectation.

FEAR IS THE ENEMY OF FAITH AND EXPECTATION

When you wholeheartedly believe God to do special things in your life, He will do them, but you need to maintain your faith, no matter what the circumstances look like or how long it takes.

The devil tries to "move into" your brain and put fear in you. Fear attacked even the prophet Elijah, right after he had won a mighty victory over four hundred fifty false prophets of Baal, and God had to reassure him that He was still in control. (See 1 Kings 19:15–18.) The good news is that you don't have to rent out space in your brain to fear. Instead, you can put up a "No Vacancy" sign. Fear is a terrible burden; it always brings you down. But the opposite of fear is faith, and it is a wonderful blessing. We can say to God, "Okay, I want faith to move into my brain permanently." You can make that choice, and then you can make it a reality in your life through a purposeful process that will also build your expectation for miracles.

Have you ever noticed that fear usually comes into our lives as a process? We start out with a little, anxious thought, and then we feed it and feed it, to the point where it can become an overwhelming, negative force that influences our perspectives and decisions. Yet both faith and fear have the power to grow within us. You can start out with a little faith, but then, you can feed it and feed it with God's Word. As you read the Word and practice what it says, your faith will grow significantly and crowd out the fear.

> **As you read the Word and practice what it says, your faith will grow significantly and crowd out fear.**

Of course, not all types of fear are negative. There is something the Bible calls *"the fear of the LORD."* (See, for example, Psalm 34:11.) This does not mean we are to be afraid of God; to have a fear of the Lord means to reverence Him or to be in awe of His majesty. It means that we respect Him and take what He says seriously. We read in Proverbs that *"the fear of the LORD is the beginning of wisdom"* (Proverbs 9:10). God's wisdom will bring us success, and we can hang our expectation on that. When we train our brains to dwell on faith and not the negative kind of fear, we will change our attitudes and expectations from negative to positive, too.

FAITH GROWS MIRACLES

When discussing the topic of fear and faith, I can't help thinking about Dr. David Yonggi Cho. As I mentioned earlier, the church he founded, Yoido Full Gospel Church, is the largest in the world. It had close to 800,000 members at the beginning of 2010, before the church decided to form twenty independent "satellite" churches (involving approximately 360,000 members) out of the main congregation. Both the parent church and these offspring churches have grown since then.[5]

It seems as if, all over the world, you can meet Koreans who are there to share their faith. When I go to Sudan or Pakistan, I meet Koreans. Almost anywhere I travel, I could shake a tree, and ten Koreans would fall out! It is because Dr. Cho is such a man of faith, and he believed that God could reach his countrymen.

Let me tell you how he started the process of building his church. As I do, I want you to truly take hold of the fact that although fear often comes through a process, so does faith. Again, you can make the choice to tell fear that your mind is not for rent and then invite faith to take up permanent residence there.

I personally heard Dr. Cho tell the following account. After the Korean War in the 1950s, South Korea was terribly poor. There was widespread starvation, and it was a very depressing time. Dr. Cho was about twenty years old then, and he decided to start a church, so he went into an old army camp, raised a tent, and held services for about thirty people.

5. Adrienne S. Gaines, "Pruning the World's Largest Church," *Charisma,* November 15, 2010, http://www.charismamag.com/index.php/news/29486-pruning-the-worlds-largest-church.

The Buddhists came to him and said, "This is Buddhist territory. You can't put a Christian church here."

Dr. Cho answered, "We can put a Christian church any-place."

They said, "Well, you can't put it here. If you leave that tent up, we'll burn it down."

Then, a crippled woman came along, barely walking across the street because her body was twisted and limp. Everybody in this area of Seoul knew about her and her physical problems.

So, Dr. Cho said, "If God heals that woman, will you believe we need to be here?"

They said, "Yes, but you have thirty days."

Dr. Cho and the members of his church went to the woman's house. They prayed and prayed over her. They cleaned her house. They prayed even more. Nothing happened. Then, on the twenty-ninth night, Dr. Cho had a dream in which he saw an image of a being that was half-woman and half-animal, with long nails and long teeth, hanging at the bottom of his bed. The woman said in a seducing tone, "Why can't we live together in peace?"

In his dream, he jumped out of bed and said, "Devil, there'll never be peace with you," and he pulled the being down and stomped on it.

The next day, the thirtieth day, he was walking toward his tent church when the Buddhists came with fire torches in their hands.

A woman from across the street yelled, "Oh, Dr. Cho, isn't it wonderful what God did?"

It was the crippled woman, only she was walking perfectly! He thought, *This must be her sister*, and so he said to her, "Where is your sister?"

She replied, "Dr. Cho, you came and prayed for me, and God healed me."

His church was allowed to continue, and he stated, "What an opportunity that was for faith in my life, but that was the beginning."

God's Promises Will Come to Rest

When you carry out the key principles we've been discussing in this chapter, you'll find that God's promises come to rest in your house. I remember an unusual miracle that happened with our ministry's finances. As I said previously, my early budget for radio was sixty dollars a month. Of course, as the radio program began to grow and finally became syndicated, it required a much larger budget. And, in the meantime, I had also started my television program on Sunday mornings.

That was forty years ago. At that time, there were very few ministers on television. I remember that Charles Blair, a pastor from our city of Denver; Oral Roberts; and, on occasion, Billy Graham were on television during the week or for special broadcasts of evangelistic crusades. So, for me to go on television was a big thing, and it cost a lot of money. My husband told me clearly that I could not depend upon the church's finances to fund the television program. He said, "It's going to have to be your faith."

> **I believed in God's provision and had faith that He would bring in the money, and our bills were paid.**

I believed in God's provision and had faith that He would bring in the money, and our bills were paid. A man who owned an automobile dealership began to watch our television program and came to our church with his five children. He was Italian, and his family lived in San Jose. His mother had been in a car accident, and she was experiencing bleeding that the doctors couldn't stop. I went to see him and his mother and prayed for them. The mother was healed, and they both received the Lord. This man began to give a sizeable amount of money to support my weekly television program.

However, at one point, we still got behind by $5,000. I went to my husband and asked if our church would be willing to help, and he said, "No, but I'm willing to pray with you that God will give you a miracle."

At the time, I was disappointed by his response. I would much rather have had him say, "Yes, we will give you the money." I accepted his prayer but wondered inwardly, *How is God going to do this?* Even when you meditate on the Scriptures, doubt may enter your mind, but when you are filled with the Word, it becomes greater than the doubt.

That day, I was teaching a Bible study at an Episcopal church in Fort Collins, Colorado. At lunchtime, a couple asked me to eat with them. I thought they wanted me to settle a fight between them, and I was trying to think of Scriptures to help them navigate their war zone. Yet that was not their agenda at all. The woman said to me, "Marilyn, how much does it cost you to be on the radio?"

She acted as though she was going to go on the radio herself. I said, "In Denver, it costs fifteen dollars and fifty cents a day."

She said, "No, that is not what I mean. What does it cost you to be on for a year?"

I said, "Well, you multiply it out. Fifteen fifty times five, times fifty-two." She replied, "No, you figure it out." So I did, and I told her the amount.

She turned to her husband and said, "Honey, write Marilyn a check for six thousand dollars."

I thought, *Honey, do it!*

Our radio bill was already paid, but she was fine with my using the amount toward the television program.

The automobile dealer supported us in both the second and third years of our television show. He also supplied a car for us for several years from his dealership. God answers prayer, and provision always goes with the vision.

EXPECTING THE "IMPOSSIBLE"

Through the years, there have been many "honeys" who have helped me to finance radio shows, television programs, overseas crusades, books, and all kinds of open doors for ministry. I can't even begin to enumerate the partners in ministry who have been such a blessing, blessing, *blessing* in the past forty years. It is just beyond my comprehension. But, again, expectancy is the key—living in a place of faith and meditating on the Word, saying the Word, thinking the Word, and acting on the Word. This is often an ongoing challenge as new difficulties arise, even in the midst of blessings. Let me give you an example.

> **The inner tug of the Holy Spirit kept me looking for a "small cloud" that would indicate the coming of rain after a long drought.**

As my radio ministry expanded at a fast rate and multiplied in popularity, I really did not feel I had the money to continue in television because it was such a financial drain. Yet, I still felt that God had called me to minister through television. The inner tug of the Holy Spirit kept me looking for a "small cloud" that would indicate the coming of rain after a long drought, as Elijah the prophet did.

Elijah said to King Ahab, "*Go up, eat and drink; for there is the sound of abundance of rain*" (1 Kings 18:41).

An "*abundance of rain*"? How could that be? It hadn't rained in over three years, according to Elijah's word, because Ahab had encouraged the people to reject God and to engage in the worship of Baal, a false god. Well, the people had repented, turning back to the one true God. They had seized the prophets of Baal, and Elijah had killed them at the Brook Kishon. (See verse 40.) And God had said that if His people obeyed Him, He would open the heavens and bring them rain. (See, for example, Deuteronomy 16:13–17; 28:12.)

Elijah had not even seen one cloud yet, but he knew God's Word does not return void. (See Isaiah 55:10–11.) He withdrew to pray privately, climbing to the top of Mount Carmel, bending toward the ground, and placing his face between his knees. Then, Elijah said something to his servant that showed he was operating in faith and expectation: "'*Go up now, look toward the sea.' So he went up and looked, and said, 'There is nothing.' And seven times he said, 'Go again'*" (1 Kings 18:43).

I want you to notice what occurred. The servant had not seen anything the first *six* times, but each time, Elijah sent him back.

I heard from a man who attends our church that he sent out fifty-eight applications for jobs but had only sixteen interviews. He did finally get a job, and he said, "I never gave up, and, Marilyn, this is the best job I've ever had in my life." Part of waiting in expectation is not giving up.

> *Then it came to pass the seventh time, that he said, "There is a cloud, as small as a man's hand, rising out of the sea!"* (verse 44)

If I saw a cloud that was only the size of a man's hand, I don't know that I'd think it was going to rain, yet Elijah knew the people had done what God had said and that He was faithful.

"*So [Elijah] said, 'Go up, say to Ahab, "Prepare your chariot, and go down before the rain stops you"'*" (verse 44). In other words, he said, "That's it! Let's go."

The last part of this passage says,

> *Now it happened in the meantime that the sky became black with clouds and wind, and there was a heavy rain. So Ahab rode away and went to Jezreel. Then the hand of the LORD came upon Elijah; and he girded up his loins and ran ahead of Ahab to the entrance of Jezreel.* (verses 45–46)

The hand of the Lord touched Elijah, and he ran faster than the horses of Ahab's chariot! God's miracle power—the power of His Spirit—came upon the prophet. We need to wait in expectation and then move forward when God says it's time.

Well, the "cloud on the horizon" for my television ministry—the beginnings of a new miracle—came in the form of a woman named Louise who was the director of educational television in Denver. She came to one of my home Bible studies and was born again, Spirit-filled, and delivered from cigarettes. One day, she said to me, "Have you ever thought of teaching the Bible on educational television?"

Of course, I had thought of it, but I wondered how that could ever happen.

> **The miracle of expectancy says that God can do *all* things.**

The miracle of expectancy, though, says that God can do *all* things. It says that nothing is impossible to him who believes. (See Mark 9:23.) So, Louise stimulated my faith, and we began to look at the possibility of my teaching the Bible on educational television.

At that time, such a thing was unheard of, but we went to the president of the Denver station and talked to him. He said, "Marilyn, I'm willing to try two pilot programs, and we would like for you to do the programs on Bible characters. Let's do two sample programs, and then I'll see if we can use them." He asked Louise to direct them.

I taped the two programs. The first one was about Rahab, the prostitute in Jericho who helped the Israelite spies who had come to do reconnaissance so they could conquer the city. Rahab and her family were spared from death, and Rahab married an Israelite and was the grandmother of King David. I titled the program "Hope for Broads." The second one was about Gideon, the timid Israelite whom God called to deliver the people from the attacks of their enemies, the Midianites. That program focused on dealing with an inferiority complex.

Several weeks passed before the president called me about the programs, saying, "No, I don't think we'll do this. I don't think it will work."

I answered, "I think it will work," and I stayed in a place of expectancy. Three weeks later, he called and said, "Well, let's try it for six weeks during the summer. "So, we taped six programs, each thirty minutes in length. I chose special Bible characters and told the story of their lives and explained how they were involved with God, and then I taught on the process of how God is involved in our lives.

At the end of the six weeks, the president of the station called me and said, "We've had the best response to these programs of any we've ever produced." After that, I had a regular Monday evening slot for my program for the next two years.

I want to encourage you to stay in faith and in an attitude of expectancy. Let the Word give you expectancy when circumstances look bad.

I find it interesting that, for two years, I taught the Bible on educational television every week and was actually paid to do it. That is a miracle of miracles. During that time, a group of people went to the Denver Public School administrator asking that our program be taken off the air because it was teaching the Bible. However, when push came to shove, the Denver Public School Administration stood with us, and the educational channel stood with us. So, the program continued. During those two years, wonderful things came to pass. The program opened many doors. People who watched it began to come to our church and attend our Bible studies. They received Jesus as their Savior and became Spirit-filled and healed. All these things were the result of the "law of expectancy."

LIVING BY FAITH

Miracles are what come out of a life of meditating on the Word, because you get into a spirit of faith. What I believe basically happens is described in 2 Corinthians 4:13: *"And since we have the same spirit of faith, according to what is written, 'I believed and therefore I spoke,' we also believe and therefore speak."* Expectation brings you to a place of continually believing and speaking the Word of God.

I want to relate some additional examples to show you how you can build expectation in your life by relying on what

> **Expectation brings you to a place of continually believing and speaking the Word of God.**

God tells you to do. As my Bible studies continued to grow, God began to bring partners into our ministry from other cities around the United States. I mentioned earlier that, at this time, I did a little traveling and even hosted special Partner Breakfasts where I was able to meet and thank people personally.

At our initial Partner Breakfast, I received an inner impression from the Lord that there were three people in attendance who had growths on the roofs of their mouths. He said He would heal them and asked me to have them stand.

But I argued with Him, saying, *Three people out of the thirty? I will look like an idiot if this is not true. Are You really talking to me?*

I continued to protest, but He impressed it upon me once again and said, *You are always asking Me to give you words of knowledge. I give them to you, and you turn them down. I'm going to stop giving them to you.*

So, I said, *Oh, Lord, I'll do it.*

I spoke out and said, "I believe there are three people here with growths on the roofs of your mouths. If that's you, stand up, and you will be healed."

To my shock and delight, three people stood up who had growths on the roofs of their mouths, and they were healed. It was a wonderful learning time for me, and, again, it put me into a place of expectancy.

Also, during this time in my life, I began to accept speaking invitations and do some traveling, but I was not used to speaking in churches because, back then, women didn't speak much in churches. Therefore, when God started to deal with me about teaching the Bible in churches, I said to Him, "Lord, I am a woman. What about that?"

He said to me very clearly, *Your being a woman will never be a problem to you. That will be My problem. The biggest problem you will have will be your faith.*

That has proven to be true. I've gone all over the world, even to Muslim countries; I've gone to places where women are not customarily allowed to speak or teach, including men's sections of federal prisons where I've held Bible seminars; and it has remained true that being a woman has never been a problem in preventing me from ministering. But it has been a problem for me to live by faith. That's been a daily challenge, and sometimes it has been a greater and more serious challenge than at other times. This is why it's important for us to follow the law of expectancy, keeping our faith in God's Word strong.

Job said, *"I have not departed from the commandment of His lips; I have treasured the words of His mouth more than my necessary food"* (Job 23:12). He said God's Word was more important to him than food. Again, I encourage you to meditate on the Word, to soak yourself with the Word.

Do you wonder what God can do to address an issue in your family, your workplace, or any other situation? He can do anything. I have seen expectation based on the Word work miracles in my own family. Our son was in the drug scene for nine years, but I claimed Proverbs 11:21: *"Though hand join in hand, the wicked shall not be unpunished: but the seed of the righteous shall be delivered"* (KJV).

I'd wake up in the night thinking, *My son is sleeping in a park. Will someone kill him?* But, then, I would speak the above Scripture. I must have spoken that Scripture thousands of times. Eventually, my son was completely delivered from drugs and alcohol. I believe that God's Word works in more ways than you and I can imagine or understand.

We need to step out in faith in this law of expectancy. Sometimes, we may make mistakes, but we have to realize that learning to discern God's leading is a process. We can't let our failures prevent us from trusting Him for miracles in the future. I went out on a limb one time and accepted an invitation

> **We can't let our failures prevent us from trusting God for miracles in the future.**

to minister at an Assemblies of God church in New Jersey. I asked the pastor how long he wanted me to speak, and he said, "As long as you're anointed, and when you're not anointed, I want you to sit down. If you don't sit down, I'll tell you to sit down."

His answer scared me. I thought, *Oh, God, I don't know if I can speak here at all. I am so frightened already.*

I got up to speak, and I wanted to be anointed, so I tried to be very loud. To this day, I ask myself why I did this, but in the middle of speaking, I saw a man way in the back of the auditorium who was sitting in a wheelchair. I could see the man from only the waist up, and I told him, "In Jesus' name, get up and walk." Well, he didn't get up and walk. So, I got very loud and "anointed," and I said, "In, Jesus' name, get up and walk." But he still did not get up and walk. One of the assistant pastors was standing beside him, and I said, "David, get him up. He's going to walk."

David shook his head no.

I said, "David, where is your faith? Get him up; he's going to walk."

David shook his head again and replied, "Marilyn, he doesn't have any legs."

I was crushed and shattered. But the Lord spoke to my heart, *Marilyn, if you will stay in faith, there will come a day when people will get out of wheelchairs in your meetings.*

It took a process of faith and expectancy for me, but, today, I can tell you about people whom I've seen get up out of their wheelchairs, walking in wholeness. I especially remember a time in Grand Rapids, Michigan, where a woman had been in a wheelchair for thirteen years. During a Sunday night service, she walked out of her wheelchair and is walking to this day. That's right here in United States, not overseas. So, stay in faith; stay in expectancy.

Yes, I've had disappointments. Yes, some people for whom I've prayed for healing have died. But I've seen more live than die.

One time, I was very disappointed about the death of a young girl with leukemia for whom we had been praying for two years. We'd even had all-night prayer meetings for her. We prayed and fasted for her, yet she died. At that time, I was just beginning to teach Sunday school and home Bible studies and to do the radio program. I said to the Lord, "I'm never going to pray for the sick again. I'm not going to do it. I thought it was Your Word, but it didn't work."

However, I was studying the book of Daniel one night, reading about how Shadrach, Meshach, and Abed-Nego refused to bow to King Nebuchadnezzar's golden image but honored and trusted the Lord. God revealed to me wonderful truths, saying, *Look at the example of the three Hebrew young men. They said,* "He will deliver us out of thine hand, O king." *That is faith. But then, the young men said,* "But if not, be it known unto thee, O king, that we will not serve thy gods, nor worship the golden image which thou hast set up." *That's faithfulness. Marilyn, will you be faithful when it seems like your faith has failed?* (See Daniel 3:17–18 KJV.)

I have found that God wants to develop these two things in all of us: faith and faithfulness. Both will keep us in expectancy.

As we cultivate the right influences in our lives, meditate on and memorize God's Word, replace fear with faith, and believe God for the impossible, our expectancy will increase. Our hope, or confident expectation, will grow, leading to the miraculous. Stay with it, my friends. Stay in expectation, and miracles will come!

REST STOP
ON YOUR PATHWAY TO MIRACLES

1. Do you believe the Word of God works in your life? In what ways?

2. What can you speak with expectation daily over your life and the lives of others?

3. How can Proverbs 6:22 help you to memorize the Scriptures? What Bible memorization method will you put into place in your life?

4. Write down the names of two people who need you to encourage them to believe with expectation concerning something in their lives. Then, write down two promises you are going to pray for them during the next seven days.

5. Call someone today and encourage him or her to keep believing that God will intervene in a difficult circumstance.

6. Write down an example of how a disappointment became a "divine appointment" in your life as God taught you a truth or principle from His Word.

7. Write down a time when you stood in faith, even though it didn't seem as if any good would come out of a situation. What was the result?

8. Whom do you know whose life is evidence that the Word of God works? How can his or her life inspire you to believe that the Word of God will work for you in a similar way?

BIBLICAL EXAMPLES AND SCRIPTURES RELATING TO MIRACLES OF EXPECTATION

- *Miracle of the conquering of Jericho*:
  Joshua 2; 6

- *Miracle of Elijah ending the drought*:
  1 Kings 18:41–46

- *Miracle of Hezekiah's healing*:
  2 Kings 20:1–11; 2 Chronicles 32:24; Isaiah 38

- *Miracle of water turning into wine at wedding in Cana*:
  John 2:1–11

- *Miracle cleansing of leper*:
  Matthew 8:1–4; Mark 1:39–45; Luke 5:12–15

- *Miracle healing of paralytic*:
  Matthew 9:2–7; Mark 2:1–12; Luke 5:17–26

- *Miracle healing of woman with flow of blood*:
  Matthew 9:20–22; Mark 5:25–34; Luke 8:43–48

- *Miracle healing of two blind men*:
  Matthew 9:27–31

- *Miracle of Jesus walking on water*:
  Matthew 14:22–33; Mark 6:45–53; John 6:16–21

- *Miracle deliverance of Syro-Phoenician woman's daughter*:
  Matthew 15:21–28; Mark 7:24–30

- *Miracle healing of blind Bartimaeus*:
  Matthew 20:29–34; Mark 10:46–52; Luke 18:35–43

- *Miracle cleansing of ten lepers*:
  Luke 17:11–19

- *Miracle healing of nobleman's son*:
  John 4:46–54

- *Miracle of receiving the Holy Spirit at Pentecost*:
  Acts 2

CHAPTER 6

THE "I CAN" ATTITUDE
Develop a Miracle Magnet

Along with raising your level of expectation, an attitude of "I can"—*"I can do all things through Christ who strengthens me"* (Philippians 4:13)—will make all the difference in receiving your miracles. It's what will put us "over the top" when we face adversity, obstacles, enemies, and discouragement. An "I can" attitude is the magnet that will attract miracles to our lives. I have seen this to be true as I've ministered throughout the world.

"I Can" Do All Things Through Christ

After the Iron Curtain fell in Eastern Europe in the late 1980s and early 1990s, I felt directed by the Holy Spirit to go to the former Soviet Union because, for the first time in seventy years, the doors were open to freely preach the gospel there.

We had a creative idea that would enable Russian Christians to help us to preach. On one visit to Russia, we leased a boat on the Volga River that would hold 150 people, and we invited fifty Russian pastors and their wives to go with us for six days. Twice a day, the ship would stop at ports, and we would get out and have street meetings. The Russian pastors would preach, and we would pass out Russian Bibles and Christian literature. The hunger for God among Russian people of all ages was fabulous. Most had not seen a Bible for seventy years, and they would kiss your hand when you gave them a Bible.

> **I felt that if they witnessed miracles, it would settle the issue for them of whether God was real.**

For each trip to the former Soviet Union, we would select one city in which to hold a two-night healing crusade. The people who came knew nothing about the Bible. In my heart, I felt that if they witnessed miracles, it would settle the issue for them of whether God was real, which, as we saw from chapter 1, is one of the reasons God uses miracles. When someone who is an atheist is healed, it tends to stop him from arguing about the truth of the Bible. So, it's important that people see miracles. My prayer for our trips was that God would again "show up and show off."

On one such trip, we were in a sports arena in Zaporozhye, Ukraine. With us was a team of 100 Americans and forty to fifty Russian pastors and their wives. Of course, I had to preach through an interpreter, and our prayer was that we would have truly anointed interpreters.

I feared that if great miracles did not occur, we would leave a bad impression of the gospel. But I had to remember that "*I can do all things through Christ who strengthens me.*" At the meeting, I felt that the Spirit of God gave me a word of knowledge to pray for people who had growths and tumors. So, I asked the people who had these maladies to stand, and perhaps 100 in an audience of 2000 stood. After I prayed, I asked them to examine themselves for a miracle. Then, I asked them to come forward and share their miracles.

A number of people came forward, and my daughter, Sarah, was helping with the testimony line. One woman in line, who was perhaps in her mid-thirties, had a right arm that was black and greatly swollen. Through an interpreter, Sarah asked if she had received a miracle. The woman was crying and said, "Yes, I had a huge growth in my armpit, and it is no longer there."

Sarah examined her and found no growth. There were eight or nine people in front of this woman at the time Sarah spoke with her. But, by the time she reached the front and testified, her arm was natural in color and size!

Many people received Jesus as their Savior at this meeting. They had seen and experienced God's power. Often, when I face audiences such as this one in Ukraine, I have to repeat to myself, *"I can do all things through Christ who strengthens me."* I know that it is not my power or my name that can accomplish these miracles, but the power and name of Jesus.

I encourage you to be a strong "I can" person. You can do everything God has called you to do through the strength of the Lord Jesus Christ.

Planting an "I Can" Attitude Within You

As we talked about in earlier chapters, miracles have beginnings, but they don't begin by themselves. God plants miracle seeds in us, and He is working in our lives in many ways through His Spirit to fulfill His purposes. We need to cooperate with the ways in which He is leading us.

> **God is working in our lives in many ways through His Spirit to fulfill His purposes.**

When Sarah was in third grade, I went into her room one evening to pray with her before she went to sleep. To my surprise, I found her in tears, and I asked, "Sarah, what is wrong with you?"

She said, "Mom, every year on field day, I get the lowest number of ribbons out of all my classmates. I'm just not good at athletic events."

I said to her, "Sarah, you're so good in academics, you're a wonderful Christian, you have a beautiful personality, and you are very attractive. You can't be good at everything."

Remember, I had heard that attitude from my mother, and now I was passing it along to my daughter. But the Lord spoke to my heart, *You are teaching your child unbelief. Why can't she be good at everything?*

I thought, *God, You're right. I am so sorry. I repent of this.*

So, I said to Sarah, "Forgive me. You can be good at everything. You can be good at athletic events, so let's begin to say positive Scriptures about what you're going to do on field day."

I asked her how many first-place ribbons she would like to receive, and she said, "Mom, I've never gotten a second-place ribbon, much less a first-place one."

I said, "Well, we are going to believe big."

"I want two first-place ribbons."

"Okay, every night, for the next three weeks, we're going to speak Scriptures before you go to sleep."

And, every night, I spoke positive Scriptures to Sarah, such as Philippians 4:13, which I mentioned above. We spoke affirmations such as: "I'm more than a conqueror" from Romans 8:37, "Thanks be to God, who always leads us as captives in Christ's triumphal procession" from 2 Corinthians 2:14, "All the promises of God in Christ are Yes and Amen, to the glory of God" from 2 Corinthians 1:20, and *"Be of good cheer, I have overcome the world"* from John 16:33. We spoke about ten Scriptures every night.

Then, field day arrived. Chairs had been set up on the field for the athletes in the competition, and Sarah was sitting in one of them, so I went over to her and whispered, "How are you?"

She whispered back, "I can do all things through Christ who strengthens me. I'm more than a conqueror. I always triumph in Christ. I have His Spirit of faith in me."

She spoke her Scriptures—and then won two first-place ribbons! Her athletic life was completely turned around. From that time on, she has proven to be an excellent athlete. In high school, Sarah got involved with basketball and played on the varsity team. She amazes me with her athletic ability, but it started with "I can do all things through Christ who strengthens me."

Miracles start with "I can," not "I can't."

AN "I CAN" ATTITUDE OF BLESSING YOUR ENEMIES WILL SET YOU FREE

In 2 Kings 6, there is an account of a certain king who had a very ugly attitude. His name was Ben-Hadad, king of Syria, and the captain of his army was Naaman. Ben-Hadad knew that Naaman had been miraculously healed from leprosy through the prophet Elisha. In fact, it was Ben-Hadad who had given Naaman permission to go to Elisha for healing in the first place. (See 2 Kings 5:1–6.) However, this miraculous event wasn't enough to convince Ben-Hadad to turn his life over to the God of Israel. He continued to rebel against Him and His people.

The problem was that Ben-Hadad wanted to capture Israel. Yet, no matter how well he planned his surprise attacks, he couldn't succeed with his plans. It seemed that, for some strange reason, Israel knew his every move before he made it. He got so upset that he accused his own men of tipping off the enemy. One of them stood and said, "It's not us—it's Elisha. His God tells him everything." (See 2 Kings 6:11–12.)

Ben-Hadad was a troublemaker, and he must have been extremely frustrated. If you were a warrior, you'd hope to be good one, right? But old Ben-Hadad couldn't even find the army he was supposed to raid! God kept warning the Israelites of what he was up to. So, with failure after failure on his record, he decided to come up with "plan B" and capture Elisha. He figured the only way to stop God from talking to Elisha the prophet was to capture him and put him in jail.

Similarly, Satan thinks that if he can get you into a bad situation, then God will "forget" where you are and what you are doing—or, that you will feel sorry for yourself and shut yourself off from God. For example, the devil may try to get you into strife with a neighbor to the point where your neighbor becomes a full-fledged enemy, and you are distracted

> **We need to keep our focus on God, no matter what the circumstances.**

from God's purposes. We need to keep our focus on God, no matter what the circumstances.

> *So* [Ben-Hadad] *said, "Go and see where* [Elijah] *is, that I may send and get him." And it was told him, saying, "Surely he is in Dothan." Therefore he sent horses and chariots and a great army there, and they came by night and surrounded the city.*
>
> (2 Kings 6:13–14)

Elisha's servant got up the next morning and was horrified to see the city totally surrounded by the Syrian army. There are many Christians who are like this servant. When they see bad circumstances, they yell, "What shall we do? Help! We need help." They run to God, but if He doesn't answer fast enough, then their winning attitudes turn into sinning attitudes. With their faith turning to fear, they can't see beyond the enemy's lines. But God intervened with a tremendous miracle.

> *So* [Elijah] *answered* [his servant], *"Do not fear, for those who are with us are more than those who are with them." And Elisha prayed, and said, "Lord, I pray, open his eyes that he may see." Then the Lord opened the eyes of the young man, and he saw. And behold, the mountain was full of horses and chariots of fire all around Elisha.* (verses 16–17)

When you get in line with God and focus your "I can" attitude on His miracles, then you, too, will see the armies of God surrounding your situation to deliver you.

What happened to the army of Syria? Elisha prayed that they would be blinded. He didn't pray that God would kill the enemy, although he could have. But what would that have done to his "I can" attitude? Instead of slaying the soldiers with the sword, he led them to Samaria, which was the capital of the northern kingdom of Israel.

When they arrived, he prayed that the Lord would open their eyes so they could see. *"And the Lord opened their eyes, and they saw; and there they were, inside Samaria!"* (2 Kings 16:20).

Then, Jehoram, the king of Israel, asked Elijah if he wanted him to kill the Syrians.

> *But he answered, "You shall not kill them. Would you kill those whom you have taken captive with your sword and your bow? Set food and water before them, that they may eat and drink and go to their master." Then he prepared a great feast for them; and after they ate and drank, he sent them away and they went to their master. So the bands of Syrian raiders came no more into the land of Israel.* (2 Kings 16:22–23)

As I said earlier, the devil wants to give us an attitude problem. He wants us to seek vicious vengeance on our enemies in order to keep us from becoming all that God wants us to be. Yet God wants us to free our enemies by forgiving them and praying that God would show them love and mercy. (See, for example, Proverbs 25:21; Matthew 5:43–45.)

I have had some attitude problems in my life. "So-and-so didn't treat me right," I would complain. But, one day, the Lord told me that I would never change people with that kind of attitude. I was acting from the attitude of the old, sinful nature and griping about persecutions instead of rejoicing. I was walking in an "I can't" frame of mind. The Bible tells us,

> **We will never change people if we complain and say, "So-and-so didn't treat me right."**

> *Put off, concerning your former conduct, the old man which grows corrupt according to the deceitful lusts, and be renewed in the spirit of your mind, and that you put on the new man which was created according to God, in true righteousness and holiness.* (Ephesians 4:22–24)

Setting our enemies free by extending forgiveness, kindness, and mercy will set us free, as well, and give us the ability to continue on our "I can" pathway to miracles. (See, for example, Matthew 6:9–15.)

An "I Can" Attitude
Opens Doors of Opportunity

One of Sarah's friends from high school had already graduated and was attending Oral Roberts University (ORU) in Tulsa, Oklahoma, where Sarah would later earn her degree. She asked if I could come and speak at their Sunday evening chapel service, and I was honored to be invited. I spoke at chapel and was very touched by the warm reception of the student body. After that, I received an invitation to speak at a regular weekday chapel service attended by all of the students.

God had been good to me, and, of course, I spoke His promises before this service, such as "He surrounds me with favor like a shield" (see Psalm 5:12) and *"I can do all things through Christ who strengthens me"* (Philippians 4:13). I believed I could speak like the oracles of God into the students' hearts and help bring about a positive change in their lives.

After that, I was invited to speak at ORU's chapel two or three times a year. Eventually, I had the opportunity to meet Oral Roberts. Dr. Roberts had held a tent meeting in our city when Wally and I were just starting our church. To meet him was a great honor. Of course, who didn't want to meet him? I had watched his television program with my mother in my early years, and my mother had even received healing from a tumor after placing her hand on the television set as he prayed during one of his broadcasts.

Shortly after meeting Oral Roberts, I received a letter from ORU saying that they would like to give me an honorary doctorate of divinity. I could hardly imagine that I would receive an honorary doctorate from ORU. Yes, I had a bachelor's degree in foreign languages, with a minor in English, but I had never gone on to get my master's degree, and I certainly had not progressed to a doctoral program. Again, I was greatly honored, and even more so when I found out that I was only the second woman to receive a doctorate from ORU.

I do not have an earned doctorate; I have an honorary doctorate. But Oral Roberts said the honorary doctorate had come through much harder learning than an earned doctorate. Regardless of what he said, I thank him and I thank God for giving me that degree. To this day, particularly when I go to other nations, people call me Dr. Hickey, and having that title helps to open doors for ministry.

At that time, Oral Roberts prophesied over me and spoke what I considered to be unusual but encouraging words. Although I was just beginning in the ministry, he told me that God would use me in international ways.

Out of the experience of receiving the degree, I was invited to be a member of ORU's board of regents. At that point, Sarah was attending school there. It was a wonderful opportunity. Not only was I honored to be on the board, but it was also a blessing for me because I was able to see Sarah an additional two times a year when I traveled to Tulsa for board meetings.

I learned many things from that appointment. A number of people from well-known ministries were also on the board at that time, and I had the opportunity to meet them and learn from them. Then, something else unexpected happened. After I'd been on the board for only one year, Dr. Roberts spoke to me one night after a dinner and told me that the chairman of the board was resigning. He asked if I would be willing to accept the position.

What? How would I call a meeting to order with such people as John Hagee and Kenneth Copeland in attendance? I was very uncomfortable with that idea, and I said, "No, I don't think I could even consider it." But Dr. Roberts said, "Well, if you were unanimously voted in, would you be willing to be chairman of the board? Would you think it was God's will?"

I replied, "First of all, I need to ask my husband. Second, I need to ask Sarah how she would feel about my being chairman of the board. Then, yes, if I would receive unanimous approval, I would take that as the will of God."

That's exactly what happened. My husband said yes, Sarah said yes, and the board unanimously said yes. I had the privilege of being chairman of the board of regents at ORU for nineteen years, the longest term anyone had ever served. And all of it happened through the miracle of "I can."

Many times in my life, I could have said "I can't": "I can't teach a Bible study." "I can't have a radio ministry." "I can't go on television." "I can't serve on Dr. Cho's board of directors." "I can't be chairman of the board of ORU." "I can't go to other countries and preach." "I can't hold a healing meeting." "I can't, I can't, I can't...." If I had taken that attitude, I never would have ended up doing any of those things or experiencing the miracles connected with them.

What things could be opportunities that you have been saying "I can't" to?

An attitude of "I can, I can, I can..." will take you places you never would have dreamed of. What are some things that could be opportunities for you that you have been saying "I can't" to? As you've been reading this chapter, has God been encouraging you to say "I can"? He is such a wonderful, loving heavenly Father. He doesn't want you to say "I can't" but "I can"!

An "I Can" Attitude Enables God to Work Through You

An "I can" attitude will keep you receptive to the opportunities God brings your way. When you say "I can, through God's strength," He can use you to reach others with the gospel.

For example, I like to speak to people about Jesus when I'm traveling by plane. Now, I'm not obnoxious. I try the "door" to a person's life first, and if he or she indicates that the door is closed, I am not rude or uncouth. I leave it at that, knowing that at least I have made an attempt.

Here is what I usually do: I say to the person next to me, "Where are you going?" or "What do you do?" After answering my question, people will often ask me what I do.

I say to them, "I'm a pastor's wife, and I teach the Bible on television. I go all around the world because of the opportunities of teaching the Bible on television."

They say, "How did you get into this?"

That question opens the door, and I tell them, "When I was sixteen, I prayed one prayer that totally changed my life. I asked Jesus Christ into my heart, and He has never left me." From there, I can share the whole gospel with them.

Do I always feel like talking to people when I'm traveling? No, but sharing Jesus with others is something God has shown me I can do, even when I feel that I can't or don't want to.

"I can't" stops the miraculous in your life, but "I can" brings miracles!

One of the most dramatic miracles I have witnessed in this regard was when I changed my confession from "I can't" to "I can" after an exhausting ministry trip. I had been speaking at a large church in the country of Hungary. This is a wonderful church, and I have been there twice since 1989. It has more than 100,000 members. Can you imagine?

After a very intense time of ministry, I got on a plane in Budapest to travel to London, where I would board another flight going directly to Denver. I planned to sleep from Budapest to London. I wasn't feeling "spiritual," and I felt I couldn't witness to anyone at that time.

Then, a tall Asian man boarded the plane and sat next to me. I prayed, *Lord, I don't think this man speaks English, so it probably would not be worth trying to see if I could witness to him.* Then, I thought, *He is probably not very open to Christ, as Asian people usually are not, so I don't know that I can be an effective witness.* I made all of these "I can't" excuses. But then, I thought, *Okay, I will try the door.* So, I said to the man, "What were you doing here in Budapest?"

He said, "I'm an executive with Toyota. I fly all over the world and look at the Toyota businesses. I was here for four days in Budapest." It turned out he was from Japan and spoke perfect English. Then, he asked me what I was doing in Budapest.

I said, "I was here speaking at Faith Church. It is a wonderful church." I told him that I teach the Bible on television and travel around the world.

He said, "Do you know any stories about Jesus?"

I almost fell out of my chair. I thought, *Well, forget napping on this plane! I can do it. I am not too tired. I can be a witness.* I answered, "Yes, I do know stories about Jesus. How do you know about Jesus?"

He told me, "When I was small, there was a Sunday school in our neighborhood, and I would go to it. They would always tell the story about Jesus, and they would always give us some candy. I loved the stories about Jesus. Do you know any stories about Jesus?"

I answered, "Oh yes, I've read through the four Gospels, which are the part of the Bible that really tells about Jesus. But, more than just telling you stories, I want to tell you about how I have Jesus in my heart."

"What? You have Jesus inside you?"

"Yes, I do, and the Bible says it is '*Christ in you, the hope of glory.*'"

He said to me, "How did you get Jesus in your heart?"

So, I told him that when I was sixteen, I prayed and invited Jesus to come into my heart, and that He had come into my heart and become the Lord of my life.

The man was astonished and asked, "Do you think He would come into my heart?"

It was absolutely the most open opportunity I have ever had to lead someone to Christ.

I said, "I don't think it; I know it." I told him exactly how to pray, and he opened his heart to God. I have cards with the "sinner's prayer" printed on them that I like to give people. I tell them that this prayer changed my life forever and I would like to share it with them. I use those cards a lot, and I gave one of the cards to him. We talked all the way to London about Jesus and how wonderful He is. We discussed how he could read the four Gospels and how God would make Himself real to him as he did.

When we got off the plane, I wanted to dance. The opportunity God had given me with that man was very exciting, but it started with my getting out of the "I can't" frame of mind and into the "I can" attitude. This is so important for all of us to do.

One time, we took a team of people to Eritrea, a small country in Africa next to Ethiopia, for healing meetings. We already had a committee of local Eritreans in place, and we had a tent that would seat about 5,000 people.

I met with the committee, but the head of the committee said to me, "We don't want you to pray for the sick, because when you pray for the sick in Muslim countries, it is offensive. It would be offensive here. You can preach the gospel, and you can pray to have them receive Jesus, but don't pray for the sick."

I responded, "I go to Muslim countries all over the world, and I've never found that healing was offensive to Muslims. I have found just the opposite to be true. It draws Muslims to Christ when they experience His healing power. They want Him in their hearts."

> **Muslims are drawn to Christ when they experience His healing power.**

They said, "But we don't want you to do it here."

I was furious with them. I thought, *I'm paying for this meeting. If I want to pray for the sick, I'll pray for the sick. I'll do whatever I want.*

The Lord intervened by speaking to my heart, saying, *Calm down, calm down. You can do all things if you keep your faith in Me.*

So, I said to them, "Would you let me pray for the sick the first night? If, after I pray for the sick, you are unhappy with me, then, on the other five nights, I will not pray for the sick."

They agreed. That night, before I went out to preach, I prayed, "Lord, You better show up and show off. This is Your name on the line, not my name."

"*I can* do all things through Christ who strengthens me" ran through my spirit.

And, while I was preaching, I heard this word from the Holy Spirit: *Have people stand who have a problem with their wrists or hands.*

Now, that sounded like such a small thing to me, but I was obedient to the Holy Spirit. I asked, and the people who had problems with their wrists or hands stood. I prayed for them and "sent" the Word into their hands, so that it would deliver them from destruction. (See Psalm 107:20.)

All at once, a tall man from the audience came running up onto the platform, holding his hand and flashing it open and closed. The audience went wild. In Africa, when people go wild, they ululate, which means they make a long, wavering, high-pitched sound; it has a trilling quality and sounds like "la, la, la, la." The sound grew louder, and I didn't know what was happening, so I said to the head of the committee, "What is going on?"

He told me, "That man is our number one war hero. He was shot in the wrist and could not open and close his hand. He has had a miracle, and Jesus has healed him." Then, he said, "You need to pray for the sick every night."

We can take offense when we face resistance and say things like, "I can't do it. It won't work. People won't let me." We can let fear take over when God opens doors of opportunity to us and say things like, "I'm not strong enough. I don't know the Bible well enough." Or, we can say, *"I can do all things through Christ who strengthens me"* (Philippians 4:13).

I'm telling you, if you want a lot of miracles working in your life, then get into the miracle attitude of "I can." You can do all things through Christ who strengthens you.

An "I Can" Attitude
Overcomes Discouragement

A winning, "I can" attitude is essential to gaining and sustaining success. It illustrates the difference between a person who has lost everything but starts over, and a person who has lost everything but gives up.

The force of discouragement in our lives can be devastating, robbing us of hope and strength. Did you know that discouragement is the opposite of courage? I will show you why with a brief English lesson.

The prefix *dis* indicates "not" or "the opposite of." Therefore, the *dis* in front of a word tells us that it is the opposite of the root word it precedes. For example, *disobey* means "to not obey." Likewise, *discontent* means to "to not be content." Therefore, when you are discouraged, you are without courage.

In 2 Kings 4, we read about another discouraging situation in Israel. There was again a famine in the land, and food was scarce. The people were hungry, tired, and generally in despair.

The prophet Elisha made a trip to Gilgal to meet with the sons of other prophets. After visiting together for a while, the men began to get hungry, and the Bible says,

> *So one went out into the field to gather herbs, and found a wild vine, and gathered from it a lapful of wild gourds, and came and sliced them into the pot of stew, though they did not know what they were. Then they served it to the men to eat. Now it happened, as they were eating the stew, that they cried out and said, "Man of God, there is death in the pot!" And they could not eat it.* (2 Kings 4:39–40)

The men ate the stew with the gourds and almost immediately began to feel sick. They cried out with pain and said, in effect, "Hey, Elisha, this stuff is poisonous! You're a man of God. Help us." Since idolatry was so pronounced in the land, you might think that someone would have cried, "Baal, Baal. Come quickly." But the men sought after the God of Elisha.

Elisha knew the men were reaching out to God. They were, in essence, hungering and thirsting after righteousness. When you are down-and-out, sometimes you cry out to God because there is no one else to turn to and you know His ways work. What Elisha did was interesting. Just as he had poured salt into bitter waters to heal them, he poured meal into the stew to heal it so that it was no longer poisonous. What a miracle of grace and hope for those sons of the prophets in a time of deep discouragement and distress!

Please realize that Elisha didn't use "healing meal" or anything like that to effect the miracle. The meal was simply the means God instructed the prophet to use to heal the food. It was a symbol, just as the salt in the water had been a symbol. The salt symbolized God's purification and preservation of the people[6], and the meal symbolized Jesus, the Bread of Life.

> **When you hunger and thirst after God, your attitude will change to faith and courage, and you will receive His blessings.**

When you hunger and thirst after God, your attitude will change from discouragement to faith and courage, and you will receive His blessings. *"Blessed are those who hunger and thirst for righteousness, for they shall be filled"* (Matthew 5:6). Discouragement won't keep you in doubt and unbelief. You'll be free to say, "I can."

I hope that in reading the above testimonies and biblical accounts, you have received into your spirit the revelation of how important it is to have the attitude of "I can," so that God will be released to bless your enemies, open doors of opportunity for you, use you to reach people for Him, encourage you in times of discouragement, and take you places in your life that are truly miraculous!

6. Charles Pfeiffer and Everett F. Harrison, eds., *The Wycliffe Bible Commentary* (Chicago: Moody Press, 1962), 342.

Rest Stop
on Your Pathway to Miracles

1. List several things you've always thought you couldn't do. How might you do those things through an "I can" attitude?

2. Memorize Matthew 19:26, Philippians 4:13, and Psalm 5:12.

3. Write yourself reminders about how you can be victorious in Christ and put them where you will see them often (for example, you could use the password on your computer as a reminder).

4. Listen to the dialogue you carry on with yourself. See if you can catch the times when you tell yourself "I can't." Write down what you have been saying and change it immediately by applying your memory verses to your situations, confessing them in faith.

5. Speak the renewing of your inward man, according to 2 Corinthians 4:16.

6. Do you think you can lead others to Christ? If not, how can you change your attitude toward being a witness, based on what you have read in this chapter?

7. What enemy or enemies do you need to set free today through forgiveness, kindness, and mercy, so that you can live in the miraculous?

BIBLICAL EXAMPLES AND SCRIPTURES RELATING TO THE "I CAN" ATTITUDE

- *Miracle of the burning bush, through which God called Moses to deliver the Hebrews from slavery in Egypt*:
  Exodus 3:1–14; Acts 7:30–36

- *Miracle of Elisha's deliverance*:
  2 Kings 6:11–23

- *Miracle of David defeating Goliath*:
  1 Samuel 17:20–54

- *Miraculous abilities*:
  Exodus 31:1–11; Psalm 18:29; Matthew 14:22–32

- *Miracle of the rebuilding of the walls of Jerusalem*:
  Nehemiah 1–6

- *Miracle of Peter's trance, through which God revealed to him that the gospel could be preached to the Gentiles*:
  Acts 10

- *Miracle vision of encouragement for Paul*:
  Acts 18:5–11

CHAPTER 7

MIRACLES FROM THE PRAYER CLOSET

Pray the Promises of God

Unless we believe and stand on God's Word, it will remain dormant in regard to us and our circumstances. Obviously, in that state, it cannot be effective for producing miracles! But we can bring about miracles by incorporating the Word into our prayers and praying in the way Jesus taught us to.

WHAT KIND OF PRAYER DOES GOD REWARD?

Some of the Pharisees, or religious leaders, in Jesus' day liked to be seen praying because they wanted people to believe they were very pious. Jesus taught that such prayers may make you look good in the eyes of others but are totally ineffective for getting God's attention. God loves "closet" prayer because it's private—directed to Him only—and because it helps to keep us from praying out of a motivation of pride or to gain attention for ourselves. Jesus often went and prayed alone to God the Father (see Mark 1:35; 6:45–46; Luke 4:42; 5:16; 6:12), and He taught us,

> *But you, when you pray, go into your room ["closet"* KJV], *and when you have shut your door, pray to your Father who is in the secret place; and your Father who sees in secret will reward you openly.* (Matthew 6:6)

PRAYER IS A PLATFORM FOR MIRACLES

Prayer is a platform for miracles, a major element of the miraculous life. As you worship and praise your heavenly Father and offer your concerns to Him, you will receive His guidance, encouragement, and strength, and He will act on your behalf.

The practice of consistent, biblically based prayer is a very important part of your pathway to miracles.

Your "prayer closet," as it is often called, is simply a designated place where you set aside everything else to talk to God daily. It doesn't have to be a separate room or a small, enclosed space. It can be anywhere you choose that is quiet and private. And, of course, you can pray anywhere and at any time. I often pray in my car. However, the practice of consistent, biblically based prayer is a very important part of your pathway to miracles.

SPIRIT-LED PRAYER

Prayer that results in miracles is Spirit-led prayer. When my mother was forty years old, she reached out to God to receive the baptism of the Holy Spirit out of desperation concerning my father's mental illness. Because he was mentally broken, he'd become verbally and physically abusive. My mother had heard the radio program of a Spirit-filled pastor in our city, so she attended his church and was filled with the Spirit. It totally changed her life.

Shortly after this, my father was admitted to a mental hospital, and the doctors said he would never come out again. Yet my mother began to pray and fast, and, within one year, my father was healed. This was the beginning of my mother's prayer ministry. She lived to be ninety years of age and prayed intensely for everything.

In my early twenties, I began dating a man whom my mother was very uneasy about. He was not a Christian, and, in reality, he had a hidden agenda: I found out after several months that he was married. Interestingly, the first time she met him, my mother said to me, "There's something wrong with him," and she began to pray about the situation.

At that time, I was teaching at Centennial High School in Pueblo, Colorado. Whereas, previously, I would hear from this boyfriend all the time, he suddenly stopped contacting me. Mom said she prayed him out of my life. I told her to be sure to pray someone *else* in! Within three weeks, I met Wally Hickey, and we were married for more than fifty-five years before he went to be with the Lord. These miracles happened as a result of my mother's time in her prayer closet.

DAILY INTERCESSION

I'm a strong believer in miracles being birthed through prayer. Praying is good, but praying daily is better.

Christ For The Nations has a vision of "bringing the life-changing message of the Gospel of Jesus Christ to all nations"[7] as they provide spiritual and material support to people around the globe. The organization has produced many Christian leaders in most of the countries of the world. I heard Freda Lindsay, who started Christ For The Nations with her husband, Gordon, tell how she prayed over every nation in the world, every day, and I thought, *How can this woman do that?* It seemed impossible to me.

Later, we were both invited to speak at a convention. I saw her eating breakfast one morning, and I asked if I could join her. As we ate our meals, I said, "Freda, how can you pray over every nation every day?"

She shared with me that she'd taken a map and begun to memorize the nations. It really helped me when she said, "Marilyn, it doesn't take so long to memorize the nations by heart if you do it by continent." I thought, *I can do that.*

So, I memorized the nations of the world by continent. The most challenging continent for me was Africa because it had more nations than any other continent, and, on top of that, it seemed that the names of many of the African nations kept changing. However, the rest didn't appear very hard to memorize. Europe and then Asia were the most challenging after Africa, but North America and South America were not difficult.

7. http://www.cfn.org/.

I took to heart my task of learning the countries, and I memorized the map. My practice was to take about an hour each day to pray over every nation. This experience was very interesting to me because, as I prayed over those countries, there were certain nations that stood out to me and warmed my heart. I thought, *What is God is doing? Why do some nations just burn within my heart?*

> **The miracle of open doors to 125 countries started with consistent intercession in my prayer closet.**

Little did I dream years ago that when God called me to memorize and pray for the nations of the world, I would eventually go and minister in 125 of them. At the time, I didn't imagine that God was preparing me to go to those nations. I just wanted to be faithful to Him by praying for them. Yet the miracle of the open doors to those countries started with consistent intercession in my prayer closet.

I began to realize what God was doing when a man who was visiting our church approached me and said, "I help a certain ministry go to the nations of the world. I'm now living in Denver, and if there are any nations you would ever like to go to, and I'm available at the time to be of service, I would be happy to help you." I thought, *Wow, this is really something.*

I told him there was a nation that I had such a warm feeling toward when I prayed, and that it was Pakistan. He replied, "How interesting that is. A leading pastor I've worked with in helping set up meetings in Pakistan is in Denver right now. He is visiting with some of his family." He asked me if I would like to meet and speak with him, and I said I would. We met, and the Pakistani pastor told me that he would love for me to come to Pakistan and hold a meeting. However, he did not have a good track record with Americans. "We do all the work, we set it all up, and the Americans back out on us," he said. "So, if you tell me you're going to come, then don't back out; please come." I gave him my word that I would come.

DIRECTION AND WISDOM
FROM THE PRAYER CLOSET

A year later, we went to Lahore, one of the largest cities in Pakistan, and held a healing meeting. I had never hosted a healing meeting before, much less in a Muslim country, so this was really unusual. Most Muslims at that time didn't like Christians. They weren't wild over women, either, let alone a Christian woman.

Needless to say, I had sought a lot of counsel on the situation, and most of the feedback I received was that it would be a bad thing to go and that it would never work out. "Don't go; someone could kill you," people said. Even a Pakistani man from our church whom I talked to said, "I don't think it's wise for you to go. When you stand up to speak, half of the audience will walk out when they see you're a woman." He added, "Marilyn, it is true; you could be killed. There are a lot of radical Islamic groups, and they could make plans to kill you."

However, I still had the passion for Pakistan that had been birthed in my heart in the prayer closet. I made the decision to go, but, before I went, I repeated over and over again, "I just love Muslims, and Muslims love me." You see, I had a passion to say what I believed God could do.

Approximately 4,000 people attended the first meeting we organized. You can imagine the wild thoughts I had ahead of time about them leaving, but, to my surprise, when I stood up to speak, I didn't see anybody walk out. Not one. It was a powerful time of ministry. God did a wonderful miracle of healing a Muslim woman who had not walked in twelve years. She came up on the platform and gave her testimony that Jesus had healed her. This really touched the crowd. The next night, more than 8,000 people attended—double our previous number. We had advertised in the largest newspapers with a notice that simply said, "Come and be healed." It also showed a picture of me dressed in their native dress with my head covered. People from all over the city came and were healed.

> **Word of the miracle spread, and people from all over the city brought the sick and demon-possessed for healing and deliverance.**

I'll never forget one night when a beautiful young Muslim woman, who was about twenty-five years old, was delivered from a demonic power. She had attended the meeting with her sister, and, after her deliverance, she stood up and told how important and wonderful her deliverance was. The woman's sister even testified that she had been demon-possessed as a little girl. Word of the miracle spread, and people from all over the city came and brought the sick and demon-possessed for healing and deliverance. On the fourth night, more than 20,000 people attended, and numerous people were healed.

Each night, I would teach one miracle of Jesus from the Bible, and then I would tell the people how they could receive Jesus into their lives. I explained that He would not only heal their bodies but also come into their hearts and heal their souls. I would ask them, "Would you like to receive Jesus into your heart as your Savior?" And, every night, many people stood to receive Jesus. That put even more passion and fire within me for the people of Pakistan. Because of the success of these meetings, I really wanted to go back there to minister.

What was happening? God was placing Pakistan in my heart. I wasn't just going to Pakistan; Pakistan was coming in to me. And it all started with my taking a world map, memorizing it, and praying over the nations.

About a year and a half later, we held another series of meetings in a Pakistani city called Rawalpindi, and my daughter, Sarah, accompanied me. The last night we were there, we had a crowd of more than 70,000 people. In Pakistan, as in India, the people sit on the ground, and they crowd in together like packed sardines. We put down mats, and the people squeezed in. They sat, they listened, they responded, and I witnessed some of the most unusual miracles I have ever seen.

For example, one woman dressed in black had a tumor on the side of her face, and the tumor disappeared. She came forward and gave her testimony. An imam (a leader of a mosque) came forward and testified that he had been blind in his left eye for over five years, but Jesus had healed his eye. These miracles were just superb.

That same week, another wonderful opportunity presented itself. I was asked if I would be willing to be interviewed on a popular, hour-long television talk show during which people called in and discussed a designated topic. They wanted to know if I would be okay with callers asking questions about healing. Well, this could have been a very dangerous thing. The program was national, similar to our *Good Morning America* program, except it was *Good Morning Pakistan*. If I were to say something wrong or offensive, I could be thrown out of the country.

I asked myself, *Is this a trap of the devil, or is God speaking to me to do something very special?* This opportunity would give me the potential to advertise the meetings in a bigger way than I ever could have done on my own—or, it could close us down. So, what did I do? I went to my prayer closet, because that's where miracles come from. After praying, I felt a peace and sensed that the Lord wanted me to do it, so I went to the television station.

A handsome young man was the host, and he reaffirmed that people would call in and ask questions about healing. Then, he said, "Perhaps you can talk about some of the healings that are going on in the services," so I did.

I specifically remember one woman who called in halfway through the program and said, "You say you pray in the name of Jesus and that He heals people, but couldn't you pray in the name of Buddha or the name of Muhammad and have the same results?"

I was so grateful to the Holy Spirit for giving me the answer. As I heard myself saying it, I thought, *I'm not that smart,* so I knew it was the wisdom of the Spirit of God. This is what I replied: "Well, I have no experience praying in the name of

Buddha, and I have no experience praying in the name of Muhammad, so I really can't tell you whether those names work or not. I do, however, have lots of experience praying in the name of Jesus, and I've seen many people healed all over the world praying in His name."

God's greatness is revealed as we are faithful to His Word and prayer.

Do you know they were happy—happy—happy with that answer? Later, we found out that people were healed while hearing and believing what I said during the broadcast. Of course, as a result of the program and the miracles that occurred in connection with it, larger and larger crowds came to the healing meetings. Miracles happen when you pray in your prayer closet. God's greatness is revealed as we are faithful to His Word and to prayer.

I want to share something else that happened on that trip to Pakistan. All week, the meetings had been held in an open field, and we had experienced various distractions. For example, people had played ball at the back of the field, and motorcyclists and bicyclists had ridden through the property. In addition, at the Islamic call to prayer, people had gotten up, gone to pray, and then come back and sat down when they'd finished. We'd had to stop the meetings and wait until the call to prayer was over before continuing. So, there had been a continual atmosphere of restlessness and confusion.

However, on the last night, Sarah and I arrived early, and we immediately noticed there was an atmosphere of peace on the property. Children were not throwing balls, no one was riding motorcycles or bicycles, and people were not getting up and walking around. There was no other activity at all. We ended up with the largest crowd we'd had to that point. The quiet, peaceful presence of God rested upon the audience, people stood to receive Jesus as their personal Savior, and God began to move in the most unusual healings and miracles.

As these signs were going on, I was "caught up" in the Spirit. (See 2 Corinthians 12:2.) I was looking down at the crowd and at myself as I was preaching and praying. It was a most glorious experience. I thought, *Lord, I don't want to go back. Just take me on home with You, because this is so wonderful.* Later, Sarah said to me, "Mom, you know how restless the crowds have been every night. I prayed Genesis 1:2, that the Spirit of God would brood over the crowds as He had brooded over the waters before the creation of the world and brought chaos into orderly cosmos. I prayed there would be unity—that the presence of God would bring peace in the crowd tonight and that when you got up to preach, there would be great peace and the people would be very receptive to receive Jesus and His healing power." It was a wonderful, superb time in Rawalpindi.

PRAYING THE WORD

Miracles absolutely are birthed in prayer closets. If you need a miracle, bring your request before God in prayer. About two years ago, I received a phone call from a couple in the United States whose son and daughter-in-law were getting a divorce. The son had gotten into an immoral relationship with another woman, and the daughter-in-law was in the process of a mental breakdown. It was a heartbreaking situation.

Divorce is a terrible thing. It appears that everyone involved loses. So, we began to pray according to Colossians 1:20: *"And through him to reconcile to himself all things, whether things on earth or things in heaven, by making peace through his blood, shed on the cross"* (NIV). The blood of Jesus is so powerful that it can reconcile us to the Father, and it can reconcile us in regard to earthly relationships, too. We stood on this Scripture. We believed, we prayed, and we spoke words of faith. Yet nothing happened, nothing happened, nothing happened. On the day the divorce was to be official, the son awakened and said, "God spoke to me that He does not want this divorce, and He has given me a new love for my wife." He explained this to his wife in the attorney's office, and they were reconciled right there. Today, they give their testimony of how Jesus has given them a miracle marriage. They are helping many other couples who are having serious marital problems.

> **If you want the miraculous, you must pray the promises of God that correspond with the problems you are dealing with.**

How did this miracle happen? It happened as we prayed the promises of God in the prayer closet. If you want the miraculous, you must pray the promises of God that correspond with the problems you are dealing with. So many times, we pray problems, problems, problems, and we don't see answers. We must pray promises, promises, promises, and see God intervene. There are more than seven thousand promises in the Bible. These promises are God's supernatural provision for the problems we face.

In chapter 4, we talked briefly about Ahab and Jezebel, who were the wicked king and queen of the northern kingdom of Israel during the time of Elijah the prophet. These two were really "the pits." Remember that they led the people away from worshipping the one true God, Jehovah, and into worshipping the false god Baal.

In Deuteronomy, we find one of the warnings God had given Israel about the worship of false gods.

> *Take heed to yourselves, lest your heart be deceived, and you turn aside and serve other gods and worship them, lest the LORD's anger be aroused against you, and He shut up the heavens so that there be no rain, and the land yield no produce, and you perish quickly from the good land which the LORD is giving you.*
> (Deuteronomy 11:16–17)

In great faith and boldness, Elijah went to King Ahab and told him, in effect, "I'm coming from the presence of God, and it is not going to rain, according to my word, for three-and-a-half years." (See 1 Kings 17:1; Luke 4:25.)

Considering Ahab's wicked nature, you may be thinking, *How could Elijah say that to the king? He could have been killed immediately.* I believe the answer to that question comes from a careful reading of 1 Kings 17, where *"word"* occurs seven times.

When Elijah spoke to Ahab, what was he speaking? He was speaking God's Word. If we have faith, God will use us in bold and wonderful ways. Remember, the Bible says that Elijah was just as human as we are. (See James 5:17.) Yet he was also a man of the Word and of prayer.

All of us can be people of the Word, and all of us can pray. Tell yourself out loud, "I am a person of the Word and of prayer." If you will pray God's Word, His Word won't return to Him void but will accomplish His purposes. (See Isaiah 55:10–11.)

Therefore, when you face a circumstance that's really bad, what do you need to do? Speak the Word and obey the Word, as Elijah did.

> *Then the word of the* LORD *came to* [Elijah], *saying, "Get away from here and turn eastward, and hide by the Brook Cherith, which flows into the Jordan. And it will be that you shall drink from the brook, and I have commanded the ravens to feed you there."*
>
> (1 Kings 17:2–4)

Elijah went and did according to...what? *"The word of the* LORD.*"*

God took care of Elijah during the time of drought. The prophet went and stayed by the Brook Cherith, and ravens brought him bread and meat. That's not shabby, is it, when you have both those things to eat? He was probably one of the best-fed prophets at the time. And he also was able to drink from the brook.

Cherith means "a cut" or "cutting place." I think of this definition in terms of Elijah being totally cut off from family, friends, and everybody else. He had to do a disappearing act because he was well-known, and he might be killed for being God's prophet and for being instrumental in bringing God's judgment in the form of the drought.

You, too, may feel as if you're in a "cutting place." But if you give up and go somewhere else, allowing the devil to invade your mind with fears, you may miss out on the miracles God has for you. We need to stay in the place of God's provision.

We need to stay in the place of God's provision.

When Wally and I had been in the ministry for about three years, there weren't many people in the congregation, and we certainly didn't have a lot of money, but we were getting by. We didn't take secular jobs because we felt we could trust God, even though our resources were slim. At that time, a woman from Texas sent me some vitamins, telling me, "These are very good." So, I took them, and they were a great help to me physically. Then, this woman traveled to Denver, and she met with me and said, "I sell these vitamins, and I think they could be a good income source for you, too."

God spoke to me about it and said, *I'm going to lead you in, and when I tell you to come out, I want you to come out. I'm going to prosper you during that time.*

The company's headquarters were in California, but its representatives would periodically travel to Denver. I signed up but told them, very boldly, "If you have a meeting on a Sunday, I won't be there. If you have one on a Wednesday night, I won't be there. I'm going to do what God wants me to do first. God is first, and then the vitamin business will come after that."

I really prospered. In one month, I made $36,000. You may think that's not much, but this was in the 1960s. With that $36,000, we purchased the house we lived in for thirty-one years. Doesn't that excite you? I thought, *Wow, I'm really doing well, prospering, and I've gotten to lead a lot of the people in the business to Christ.* It was a good opportunity.

After about six years, the Lord said to me, *Come out.*

Come out? I thought. *I could be rich, and You want me to come out?* But God wanted me to learn to rely on *His* provision, whether it came from the vitamin business or something else. So, my "brook" began to dry up, and the "ravens" came less frequently, because God doesn't have only one way of blessing us. Faith is a process of trusting God day by day. Please don't forget this truth. Again, He is not always going to use the same methods of providing for us and leading us, because we go *"from faith to faith"* (Romans 1:17).

That is exactly what happened to Elijah. The Brook Cherith dried up because of the drought, so his former source of sustenance was no longer available. Then, God told him to go to the town of Zarephath for his provision. (See 1 Kings 17:8–9.) *Zarephath* means "refinement," or "the place of refining," or "smelting place." God had told him there was a widow in that city who would feed him.

So, Elijah went from the "cutting place" to the "refining place." He went from faith to faith, just as we do, as he obeyed the word of the Lord. After he had traveled seventy-five miles to reach Zarephath, he found the widow. Now, this wasn't a rich widow. Wouldn't you hope to find a rich widow, if she was meant to provide for you? But she wasn't rich. Instead, she was out gathering sticks so that (in her mind) she could make a fire to cook the last meal she and her son would eat before dying of starvation.

Elijah said to her, *"Please bring me a little water in a cup, that I may drink"* (verse 10). When she went to get it, he called to her and said, *"Please bring me a morsel of bread in your hand"* (verse 11).

> So she said, *"As the LORD your God lives, I do not have bread, only a handful of flour in a bin, and a little oil in a jar; and see, I am gathering a couple of sticks that I may go in and prepare it for myself and my son, that we may eat it, and die."* (verse 12)

Let me ask you: to whom do you think she was "renting" her brain? There seems to be a *"spirit of fear"* (2 Timothy 1:7) in her words. Yet, in contrast to the spirit of fear, there is a *"spirit of faith"*: *"And since we have the same spirit of faith, according to what is written, 'I believed and therefore I spoke,' we also believe and therefore speak"* (2 Corinthians 4:13). You can resist the spirit of fear, and you can invite a spirit of faith into your heart. Remember how we discussed replacing thoughts of fear with

> **You can resist the spirit of fear and invite a spirit of faith into your heart.**

thoughts of God's Word? That is a major way to resist a spirit of fear.

When Elijah heard the widow's reply, he didn't say, "Oh dear, wrong widow." Instead, he said to her, *"Do not fear..."* (1 Kings 17:13). Then, he told her to go and do what she had planned but to make him a little cake first before making one for herself and her son. He assured her that the Lord had said the bin of flour wouldn't waste away and the bottle of oil wouldn't dry up until He sent rain. (See verse 14.)

What a word God had given Elijah! And what a promise Elijah gave that widow! If she would do what he'd told her to do, she would not run out of food during the entire drought. She did as he'd asked, and the Bible says, *"The bin of flour was not used up, nor did the jar of oil run dry, according to the word of the Lord which He spoke by Elijah"* (verse 16). Note that this occurred *"according to the word of the Lord."*

This widow "sowed" one cake when she fed Elijah the first time, but how many meals did she reap? Suppose Elijah was with her for about three years, until near the end of the drought. That would have amounted to more than 3200 meals!

What if Elijah hadn't spoken the word of the Lord? Would the bin of flour and bottle of oil have served to provide for him, the widow, and her son? No. We don't emphasize nearly enough the importance of speaking the promises of God. We have to believe the Word, speak the Word, and act on the Word to have our needs met. And, what if the woman had said, "I'm not going to give you my cake! I have barely enough for myself"? Again, the miracle wouldn't have happened.

I'm a great believer in speaking the Word. Your tongue is the most powerful weapon and force of your life. (See, for example, Proverbs 15:4; 18:21; James 3:2–11.) So, what's going to bring you through your personal "drought" situation? The Word of God that you speak in faith in your prayer closet will bring you through.

Faith and Refining

Let me tell you another story from the life of Dr. David Yonggi Cho that shows how God refines us for His purposes. At one point, God began to give Dr. Cho a passion and a burden for Japan. Historically, the Koreans have hated the Japanese because the Japanese occupied their country at one time and were horribly cruel to them. Even today, you still hear about the cruelty the Japanese inflicted on the Koreans. In fact, Japan has issued statements of apology to South Korea for how they treated the people during colonial rule. So, when God said to Dr. Cho, "I want you to take the gospel to Japan," he was not a "happy camper."

But, in obedience, he started to learn Japanese and went on television trying to win the Japanese people to Christ. In addition, Dr. Cho's calling and gifts were in starting churches, and in doing so, he would use many "cell group" leaders. As you may know, cell groups are small gatherings of believers who meet regularly for fellowship, worship, prayer, and Bible study. Dr. Cho wanted to start cell groups in Japan to further reach the people for Christ.

Many years ago, I traveled with Wally and my mother to Dr. Cho's church in Seoul, Korea, at a time when he had 20,000 cell leaders. I learned that 19,000 out of the 20,000 cell leaders were women. When I asked Dr. Cho why, he said that the men worked in the daytime, but the women were available and wanted to be active in ministry. They were also amenable to opening their homes to others for the purpose of studying God's Word together.

Dr. Cho had learned how to enlist women to spread the gospel and disciple others, so, he took some of his top cell leaders and talked to them about starting cell groups in Japan. The woman he chose to initiate the outreach was one of his top-ten cell leaders. He told her, "I want you to go to Tokyo, and I want you to start a church. We will pay your expenses and pay for the beginning of the church for one year, but you can't come home until you have five hundred members in your church."

This poor woman was scared out of her wits about her new assignment, but she accepted it and went to Japan. Well, after we make such a decision, how are we to proceed? We are not to "rent out" our minds to the devil and live in fear, but we are to live in faith.

I think what this woman did was hilarious. God gave her a creative way to win people for Christ. Japan is an extremely crowded nation, and very few people live in houses; most live in high-rises. This woman lived in a high-rise apartment in Tokyo, and she would stand in the lobby as people came in with their children, their groceries, and their packages. She would ask them, "Can I help you? Can I carry your packages? I'll just ride on the elevator with you." She started to ride the elevators with people, and then she had them over for cookies and tea. Pretty soon, she had a church of five hundred.

> **Each of the "refining" circumstances in our lives is really part of the process by which our faith is developed.**

You see, each of the "refining" circumstances in our lives is really part of the process by which our faith is developed. In every such circumstance you experience, you need to look to God rather than focusing on your current resources, such as the widow did with the last handful of flour in her bin.

These "Zarephath" experiences are very important to your spiritual growth and for receiving your miracles. You have to be careful because, if you give in to fear and dwell on thoughts like *I don't know what I'm going to do; I just don't know how I'm going to make it,* you'll never receive the creative ideas God has for you. Living in faith is vital, especially because you don't know what you might need to believe for next. Even after the miraculous provision of flour and oil, Elijah soon had another crisis. The widow's son became sick and died, and the widow questioned the prophet, saying, *"What do you have against me, man of God? Did you come to remind me of my sin and kill my son?"* (1 Kings 17:18 NIV).

He replied, *"Give me your son"* (verse 19). Then, he carried the boy to the upper level of the house, where his room was, and laid him on his own bed. Note what he did next. He questioned God. That helps us to see that Elijah was as human as we are. Nobody has done it all right. Nobody on earth can claim the title of "perfect." So, when the enemy comes to tell you what you did wrong, you can say, "Yes, and I've repented and I'm forgiven, and God loves me."

It's what Elijah did next that's so important. He stayed in faith. He didn't say, "Well, God's blessings were good while they lasted." He didn't let fear move into his mind, and he didn't give up. When tragic things like this happen, it is easy to give way to fear, but Elijah stretched himself out on the boy three times and cried out, *"O LORD my God, I pray, let this child's soul come back to him"* (verse 21).

What was the result? *"Then the LORD heard…"* (verse 22). Does God hear your voice? In times of crisis, does He hear you? Are you praying according to His Word?

> *Then the LORD heard the voice of Elijah; and the soul of the child came back to him, and he revived. And Elijah took the child and brought him down from the upper room into the house, and gave him to his mother. And Elijah said, "See, your son lives!" Then the woman said to Elijah, "Now by this I know that you are a man of God, and that the word of the LORD in your mouth is the truth."*
>
> (verses 22–24)

The greatest miracle recorded in this seventeenth chapter of 1 Kings is the resurrection of the widow's son. We are not to go from fear to fear; we are to go from faith to faith and from victory to victory. Don't tell me that faith doesn't work. It's too late—I know how faith works! We need to keep God's Word at the forefront. *"Faith comes by hearing, and hearing by the word of God"* (Romans 10:17).

We are not to go from fear to fear; we are to go from faith to faith and from victory to victory.

When I started teaching adult Sunday school, as well as home Bible studies, a well-known evangelist came from Scotland to minister at our church, and he told me, "Of all the pastors' wives I know, you're the biggest example of a failure. You don't lead the worship, you don't play the piano, you don't have a women's ministry, you don't teach children, and you're just a failure." There will always be people who will criticize us, who will claim that what we're trying to do won't work, who will tell us we won't make it, who will remind us of those who died after being prayed for, and so on. We don't need to hear those words. Rather, we need to hear the Word of the Lord in our mouths and in the mouths of those around us.

Note how Elijah started out in 1 Kings 17. He brought a hard word to Ahab, who could have killed him, and he ended up raising someone from the dead. He went from faith to faith—not from fear to fear.

Again, fear is a deadly thing, and once it starts to process in your mind, it takes you down, down, down. But, as we have been learning, we can resist fear by speaking the Word. The Scriptures say we overcome the devil by the blood of the Lamb and by the Word of our testimony, and by not loving our lives to the death. (See Revelation 12:11.)

I encourage you to set aside a time to pray daily. Use your time in the prayer closet to speak words of faith, not fear. Pray the promises of God. Then, you will see God's power and miracles become a reality in your life.

REST STOP
ON YOUR PATHWAY TO MIRACLES

1. What special place will you designate, or have you already designated, to be your "prayer closet"?

2. Arrange your schedule to set aside time daily for prayer.

3. What area(s) do you feel God is currently calling you to pray about according to His Word?

4. Keep a written list of your prayers and their answers.

5. Enlist a prayer partner who will pray in his or her prayer closet the same scriptural promises you are praying in relation to your need.

BIBLICAL EXAMPLES AND SCRIPTURES RELATING TO MIRACLES FROM THE PRAYER CLOSET

- *Miracle healing of Miriam's leprosy*:
  Numbers 12

- *Miracle of Elijah's provisions during the drought; miracle of the resurrection of the widow's son*:
  1 Kings 17

- *Miracle of deliverance after Esther's fast*:
  Esther 3–9

- *Miracle of Jesus' spiritual strength after fasting in the wilderness*:
  Matthew 4:1–11; Mark 1:12–13; Luke 4:1–14

- *Miracle of Lazarus' resurrection*:
  John 11:1–45

- *Miracle of the "second Pentecost"*:
  Acts 4:23–33

- *Miracle of Dorcas's resurrection*:
  Acts 9:36–42

- *Miracle of Paul's recovery from stoning*:
  Acts 14:19–20

- *Miracle of the great earthquake that opened the prison doors and loosed the prisoners' chains*:
  Acts 16:16–40

Pastoring at our second building, Full Gospel Chapel. Sarah is the little one in the middle.

Thank God for Wallace Hickey in my life. God brought us together, and we married on December 26, 1954.

Teaching at one of my early Bible studies.

Taping my radio program.

We've come a long way since the early television days.
Currently, *Today with Marilyn and Sarah* has a potential global audience of 2.5 billion viewers weekly.

Receiving an honorary Doctorate of Divinity
from Oral Roberts University in 1986.

It was a miracle experience to be on the board of regents at Oral Roberts University
for twenty years, nineteen of which I served as chairman.

I was the first woman on Dr. David Yonggi Cho's board of directors for Church Growth International. Dr. Cho has enriched my life and encouraged big vision.

Speaking to Dr. Cho's cell leaders in Seoul, Korea.

Reece and Sarah beginning in the ministry and on television. Wally and I are so proud of them.

I'm a strong believer in miracles being birthed through prayer.

Distributing food on the outskirts of Manila. Later, more than fifteen wells were provided by Marilyn Hickey Ministries to supply water for 6,500 families there.

More than one-fourth of the 150,000 people in the city of Nazret, Ethiopia, attended our healing meetings in 2002.

Lahore, Pakistan, 2003.
More than 200,000 came to hear the message that Jesus loves them and wants to heal them.

Visiting with the imam, the highest-ranking religious leader in Pakistan.

His Majesty King Abdullah II Ibn Al Hussein, king of the Hashemite Kingdom of Jordan. While meeting with the king in 2005, I recalled fondly the prophecy spoken over me by Daisy Osborn years prior: "Marilyn, God is going to use you to be a world evangelist. You will affect leaders of nations, and you will have many audiences."

In an outdoor stadium in Khartoum, Sudan, in 2007, thousands flooded the field to receive Christ and the baptism of the Holy Spirit. Miracles abounded as blind eyes were opened, deaf ears received hearing, and the oppressed were set free.

At the leadership conference in Sudan, I anointed 4,000 pastors and leaders, preparing them for ministry at the evening healing meetings and for the weeks and months to follow.

At the Islamic House of Wisdom in Dearborn, Michigan, with Imam M. A. Elahi in 2009.

I was the first woman invited to speak in a mosque in over 1,400 years. Now, that's a miracle!

Wally has been my partner in life and ministry for more than fifty-five years.

CHAPTER 8

MIRACLES IN YOUR HANDS
Change the World Around You

When I became chairman of the board of Oral Roberts University, I knew the position was God's will for me, but I was nervous as I called the first meeting to order. I wanted to please Dr. Roberts and preside over the meeting properly. As I chaired more meetings, I felt more at ease, but, sometimes, I didn't agree with the decisions Oral Roberts made, and I would think, *I would do it this way.*

Then, the Lord asked me, *Which part of your body has eyes?*

I answered, "My head."

Who has the vision for Oral Roberts University?

"Oral Roberts."

That's right. Oral Roberts is the head. He has the vision for ORU.

So, during those years, I became "hands" at ORU, not only for Oral, but also for his son Richard, helping to carry out their vision for the university. I believe they were very important years for the university and for me.

The Bible says that Christ is the Head of the church and that all believers are collectively His "body." (See, for example, Colossians 1:18.) Each believer is given specific spiritual gifts by the Holy Spirit to edify others in the church. The apostle Paul used the illustration of members of the human body—the hand, the foot, the ear, and the eye—to show how the various

139

gifts work together. (See 1 Corinthians 12:7–27.) But, in a general way, all Christians can be considered Christ's "hands" on earth, in the sense that we have been called to carry out His vision and purposes in the world under His headship.

WHAT IS IN YOUR HANDS?

In the human body, hands are especially significant because they are the main instrument through which our bodies carry out what our minds want to accomplish. So, let us consider the various ways in which we function as Christ's hands to bring about miracles.

What is our first step? To recognize what God has already given us to fulfill His purposes. When the Lord appeared to Moses at the burning bush and appointed him to bring His people out of slavery in Egypt, He didn't ask what was in Moses' head. He asked him what was in his hand. It was a rod, which he used in his occupation as a shepherd. (See Exodus 4:2–5.) Moses didn't realize he held the rod that, used in God's service and power, would change the world.

Then, there was the boy mentioned in the Gospels who brought his lunch from home when he went to hear Jesus teach. What was in his hand? Five loaves and two small fish. It didn't look like much to Jesus' disciples; but, through it, Jesus would feed over 5,000 men, in addition to women and children. (See, for example, John 6:5–14.)

> **Accessing the miracles God wants to work through us requires us to take what He has given us and offer it back to Him for His purposes.**

Yes, there are miracles in our hands that we don't yet know about. Accessing these miracles requires us to take what God has given us—His Word, our physical hands, our faith, our gifts and talents, our resources, and so forth—and offer it back to Him for His purposes.

In this chapter, I want to encourage you to trust in God's power, so that you will take additional steps along the pathway to miracles by laying hands on the sick and seeing them healed, and by using what God has placed in your "hands" to effect other miracles in your life, in the lives of your family members, at your place of employment, in your community, and anywhere else the Spirit of God may lead you.

THE LAYING ON OF HANDS

Jesus said that believers *"will lay hands on the sick, and they will recover"* (Mark 16:18). Many Christians say they believe this promise, but how many actually follow it? We must do what Jesus told us to do, so that what has the potential to happen *will* happen to fulfill God's perfect will. God conveys His supernatural power through the hands of believers. The early Christians also practiced the laying on of hands when commissioning people for ministry and praying for people to receive the Holy Spirit. (See, for example, Acts 6:1–7; 8:14–17.)

One of the greatest miracles I've ever seen involving the laying on of hands was in an A. A. Allen meeting. A. A. Allen was an evangelist in the 1950s and 1960s who moved in the supernatural. My husband, Wally, and I had the opportunity to see firsthand how "miracles in the hands" work when he came to Denver to hold meetings there.

At the time A. A. Allen came to our city, Wally and I were actively serving Jesus in every way we knew how because we loved Him. We taught Sunday school and sang in the choir at our church, Calvary Temple. I was a school teacher and had home Bible studies for junior high students. We also did street witnessing. But were not yet in full-time ministry, so, in these meetings with A. A. Allen, we were "personal workers," which meant that when he gave the call for salvation, we were among the volunteers who prayed with people to receive Christ.

Approximately 5,000 people attended the meetings, and, each night, Wally and I would go backstage behind the curtain to pray with those who had come forward to receive Jesus. One night, we went back to pray with people and saw the most pitiful-looking man on a stretcher. He was skin and bones. When

I asked the people with him what was wrong with him, they said he had tuberculosis. It had eaten away at his lungs, and he most likely wouldn't live beyond a week. The doctors had given him no hope, so this man and his friends were waiting for Brother Allen to lay hands on him.

Wally and I were praying with those who wanted to receive Jesus when we saw Brother Allen walk through the area. He approached the man on the stretcher and asked, "What is wrong with this man?" The man's friends told him the same thing they had told us. Brother Allen said, "Prop him up." Then, he prayed, laid one hand on either side of the man's chest, and said, "In Jesus' name, receive new lungs." The man fell backward, and his friends caught him and put him back on the stretcher.

I asked his friends, "What is his name?"

"His name is Gene Mullenax." For some reason, even though I'm not very good at remembering names, I remembered that one.

I didn't know what had happened to the man following that meeting, but, several years later, after I became involved in radio, I was invited to speak at a church in Little Rock, Arkansas. I looked at the pastor's name on the invitation and thought, *This name sounds familiar.* But I couldn't remember why the name was memorable to me.

When I arrived at the church, I looked at the pastor and thought, *Gene Mullenax.* Then, I realized he had the same name as the man who had been dying of tuberculosis, but this man didn't look like him.

I told the pastor of my experience at A. A. Allen's meeting, and he responded, "I am the man. God gave me new lungs."

God gave Pastor Mullenax new lungs through the laying on of hands. I wouldn't say that Brother Allen was bombastic or enthusiastic in the way he prayed. He prayed a very simple prayer, placed his hands on the sick man, and commanded in the name of Jesus that he receive new lungs.

I ask you to remember, again, that it is not your name or my name that brings about miracles. It is the name of Jesus; it is His provision. We cannot just *say*, "I believe in healing." We must practice it. It must be an ongoing part of our lives.

> **We cannot just *say*, "I believe in healing." It must be an ongoing part of our lives.**

I have seen miracles occur all over the world, and I know that you will see them happen, too. Some miracles require the laying of hands, and if you are willing to lay hands on the sick, you will see those miracles. Sometimes, the manifestation of healing will be a process, and sometimes, it will be instantaneous. Thank God for whichever way He does it. Healing is the *"children's bread,"* as we read in the biblical accounts of the Syro-Phoenician, or Canaanite, woman. (See Matthew 15:21–28; Mark 7:24–30.) This means that healing is something our heavenly Father gives to us, His children.

Miracles are in your hands. They are not just in the hands of well-known evangelists but in the hands of all believers. That is what Jesus told us in Mark 16:18. And, over the fifty-plus years that I have been in the ministry, I've seen thousands of miracles happen through the laying on of hands.

I recall a specific healing of a baby whose parents attended our church. The baby's birth itself had been a miracle. The couple had been married for seventeen years and wanted to have a baby but were unable to. When they moved to Denver from Florida, they came to our church. My husband laid hands on them and believed that they would have a baby. Remember, they had been unable to have children for seventeen years. Within a year, his wife became pregnant, and she delivered a beautiful baby girl. This was an exciting event, to say the least. However, during the baby's examination, the doctors found a tumor on her back that appeared to be embedded. It would be very difficult to remove, and it appeared to be growing rapidly. Of course, the parents were very concerned, as you would be if it were your child.

The baby was scheduled to have a thorough checkup in a few days. So, at our church, we organized a special prayer line with the laying on of hands, and when we laid hands on the baby, the Lord gave me a word that there would be no tumor.

The couple took their daughter in for the checkup, and she was put through all kinds of tests. Meanwhile, the parents sat in the waiting room and silently prayed, *God, we have to have a miracle. We have waited seventeen years to have this baby, and we cannot have her die now with a malignant tumor.*

After they had waited more than an hour, the doctors came out and said, "We don't know what happened, but during the examination, the tumor disappeared." It was a miracle to the doctors as well as to the family.

This lovely girl is now eleven years old, and there is no tumor on her back. She loves Jesus, and it is exciting just to be with her. Her father is the one who set up my international ministry. When her parents accompany me on trips to some of our big international meetings, they bring her with them. During those times, I am reminded again that there are miracles in our hands. A key point for all of us to remember is that healing is not just for evangelists and preachers to practice. Healing through the laying on of hands should be practiced by the total body of Christ. We need to do "miracles in our hands."

To support and encourage this practice, our ministry has hosted several women's mentoring clinics in Denver, as well as internationally, in places such as Guatemala and Costa Rica. I love to teach people how to pray for the sick, and I love to teach them to believe for miracles.

At one of our Denver meetings, we had the wonderful opportunity to pray with and minister to about 250 women. As we usually did, we had the participants form a prayer "tunnel," or a prayer line, and invited people to walk through it as the rest of the women laid hands on them, and an interesting miracle occurred. A woman who was missing a tooth at the back of her mouth checked herself after she came through the prayer tunnel and found that she had a new tooth. She came up and testified of this miracle, which had occurred through the laying on of hands.

You have miracles in your own hands. Don't hesitate to pray and have faith in God for the things He desires to give to you and others.

"SENDING" MIRACLES FROM YOUR HANDS

One of the sweetest miracles in relation to the laying on of hands happened to me in Pakistan. The second time I went to minister in Pakistan, we went to the city of Rawalpindi. While we were there, we hosted a large dinner before the big healing meeting, with imams and political leaders as invited guests. We entertained and encouraged them, and it was a warm and wonderful evening; we showed love to the leadership of the country as much as we could and told them that we were in their country not to hurt them but to bring healing.

At the dinner, I was seated next to a leading imam who had a long beard and was wearing a long robe. Not only was he a religious leader, but he was also a very important political figure. Honestly, I was frightened that I might say the wrong thing or do something that was not a Pakistani custom and would be offensive to our guests. We hoped to hold five nights of meetings, and I could ruin our opportunity for ministry.

The imam spoke perfect English as he said to me, "I have terrible pain in my knees." That was how he began the conversation! He added, "Would you pray for me?"

I was shocked that he had asked me. However, I said to him, "I will be happy to pray for you, but I would like to pray according to the Bible. In the Bible, Jesus said that believers would lay hands on the sick and they would recover. Would you have a problem if I put my hands on your arm and send the Word into your knees? The Bible says in Psalm 107:20 that the Word heals and delivers. A second Scripture is Mark 16:18, which explains the laying on of hands. It talks about praying in the name of Jesus and sending the Word to heal, such as for your knees."

He said, "I don't have a problem with that."

So, right at the table, with the food in front of us, I put my hands on his arm, prayed in Jesus' name, and sent the Word into his knees—the Word that heals and delivers from every destruction. (See Psalm 107:20.)

For the remainder of the dinner, he didn't say anything about the pain, so I had no idea what happened. But a year and a half later, we returned to Pakistan for another meeting, this time in the city of Karachi. We again hosted a dinner, and the same prominent Muslim political leader sat beside me.

I asked him, "How are you?"

He said, "I am totally healed. I have not had pain in my knees or any problems with my knees since you prayed."

> **There are miracles in your hands right now. Pray in Jesus' name, lay hands on people, and believe God for their healings.**

I'm telling you, if you are a believer, there are miracles in your hands right now. You might say, "I'm not a very spiritual one." Jesus didn't say you had to be a perfect believer to lay hands on the sick. He said you have to be a believer, pray in His name, lay hands on people, and believe God for their healings. I encourage you as a believer to look at your hands right now and tell yourself, "I have miracles in my hands."

You can ask God to provide opportunities for you to lay hands on people for healing. One time, Wally and I were flying back from Cairo, Egypt. We had gone on a Nile cruise as part of our vacation, and I had spoken at an Anglican church and at a Bible school graduation. As we were getting on an Egyptian plane to fly to New York City, we saw a woman go through the business class section into first class. She was wearing black clothes that covered her completely, and it was evident that she was Islamic. You could tell she was in pain as she pulled the curtain back to pass through into first class, because she was crying and dragging her leg as she walked.

The Lord spoke to my heart through an inner impression and told me to go up to where she was sitting and to lay hands on her and pray for her before the plane took off.

I really argued with Him, saying, *Oh, God, You know they don't like business class passengers going into first class. They could throw me out. And another thing: she is a Muslim. I don't know that she's going to welcome my praying for her and laying hands on her in Jesus' name.*

The Lord said, *Isn't it you who says you love Muslims and Muslims love you?*

I said, *Okay, I love them; I will go.*

I got up, pulled the curtain back, and went into first class. Thank God, she was sitting by the aisle. I knelt down and talked to her. She spoke English, so that was a blessing. I told her, "I saw you walking through the business class. You were dragging your leg, and it showed that you are in such terrible pain. It touched my heart. I like to pray for the sick in Jesus' name. Would you allow me to lay hands on you and pray in the name of Jesus and believe God to heal you?"

She said, "Oh, yes."

I placed my hands on her and prayed in Jesus' name. I can't tell you I saw a big miracle happen. I just believed God. I went back to my seat and sat down feeling I had been obedient, because there are miracles in our hands. I share this story with you to tell you that I did that in faith. I don't know the end result. I can't tell you what happened. The woman did not immediately get up and dance around. She did not write me a letter to tell me what occurred. I can just tell you that I walked in the faith that Jesus gave me.

I want to share another thing we can do in relation to sending the Word through our hands. I pray on television for the sick, and my daughter, Sarah, does the same. We obviously can't jump out of the screen and lay hands on people; there is no way we can pray for the television audience in person. Our ministry also holds large healing meetings around the world, and we cannot physically lay hands on everybody, since there might be 65,000 people in attendance. No one could run out into an audience of that size and lay hands on everyone.

So, what do I do? I lift my hands, pray in the name of Jesus, and *send the Word* that heals and delivers from destruction. In the healing meetings, I then ask people to come up and share their testimonies of what God has done for them in the name of Jesus. If you could read the letters and e-mails we've received from those who have watched our television program and attended our large meetings, you would be amazed. I've had reports of dramatic miracles and could fill many books with tes-

> **Our part is to be obedient to lay hands on people and to send God's Word to them in healing power.**

timonies of people who were healed in Jesus' name. We weren't able to personally touch them, but God's Word touched them.

Again, Sarah and I are not their healers. Jesus is their Healer. Our part is to be obedient to lay hands on people and to send God's Word to them in healing power.

MIRACLES THROUGH HANDS ACTING IN OBEDIENCE

Miracles occur as we obey what God tells us to do. Of all the miracles God worked through the hands of Elisha, the one recorded in 2 Kings 3 is among my favorites, because there was so much darkness in the situation, and God used some uncommon means to bring about a solution.

The situation concerned a king of Israel named Jehoram, who was the son of Ahab and Jezebel. Politically, he was in a deep hole because of a problem with the Moabites. The Moabites were a big tribe that occupied a mountainous strip of land running along the eastern shore of the Dead Sea (modern-day Jordan). Under King Ahab, the Moabites had been forced regularly to pay a tribute of 100,000 lambs and the wool of 100,000 rams to the northern kingdom, but after Ahab died, they rebelled and refused to pay. King Jehoram decided to fight against them to get the payment. Therefore, he called on Jehoshaphat, the ruler of the southern kingdom of Judah, to help him in a battle with them. (See 2 Kings 3:4–7.)

The southern kingdom of Judah had not yet turned to idolatry, as the northern kingdom had, and Jehoshaphat was a king after God's heart. However, he had a weakness. He compromised with Jehoram because he wanted to have peace with the kingdom of Israel. (See 1 Kings 22:42–44.) Yet the people of the northern kingdom were idol worshippers, and the Bible tells us, in effect, "How can you have peace with demons?" Demons are behind the worship of idols. (See 1 Corinthians 10:19–21.)

Jehoshaphat made the mistake of not asking God if he should go to war with King Jehoram, and he told the king, in effect, "My people are as your people. Yes, we'll go fight the Moabites with you." He should not have allied himself with this idolatrous king. But Jehoshaphat brought his army and Jehoram brought his, and, along with the king of Edom, they went to war against Moab. They traveled for seven days and then found that they had run out of water. This was a very serious problem. They were about to go into battle, and they had no water for themselves or their animals. (See 2 Kings 3:7–9.)

The king of Israel and the king of Judah had two distinct reactions to the situation, and I want you to take note of each of them; they instruct us regarding what our own reaction should be to negative circumstances:

- King Jehoram said, "Look what's happening! I knew we'd have a problem. I knew God was against us." (See verse 10.)

- King Jehoshaphat said, "Is there a prophet around here? Can we get a word from the Lord?" (See verse 11.)

When a problem or crisis arises, how do you react? Do you say things like, "What's the use? Things will go down the drain, as they have for years," "I'm never going to get well," or "I'm always going to have a problem in my marriage"?

Those are the wrong words to say when faced with a negative situation. Rather, you should seek the word God has for you.

Jehoshaphat was told there was a prophet, and that his name was Elisha. He was living nearby, so the three kings went to his house and knocked on the door.

Elisha's response to their inquiry was hard-core. He asked them what they were doing there, even though he probably already knew. He even told the idolatrous Jehoram, in effect, "What do you want with me? Go and ask the prophets of your 'gods.'"

Jehoram played his ace, telling Elisha that it was the Lord who had called the three kings together.

And Elisha said, "As the LORD of hosts lives, before whom I stand, surely were it not that I regard the presence of Jehoshaphat king of Judah, I would not look at you, nor see you. But now bring me a musician." Then it happened, when the musician played, that the hand of the LORD came upon [Elisha]. (2 Kings 3:14–15)

If we're followers of God, the light in us is greater than the darkness around us.

Jehoshaphat loved God and followed Him, so, except for the fact of his presence, the miracle would not have occurred. We can be in the darkest situation, and we can even have made a mistake, but if we're followers of God, the light in us is greater than the darkness around us. Nonetheless, we are not to compromise with sin. You may say, "Well, everybody's compromising." It doesn't matter—don't you give in. Jehoshaphat had gotten into trouble, but Elisha recognized his faith, and God pulled him through. I want to tell you, God will pull you through, too.

Note that Elisha asked for a musician. His request reveals something very helpful for us in understanding the means of a miracle. The musician was someone who could lead Elisha in a time of worship, during which he could get spiritually in tune with God. They brought the musician, and Elisha got a word from the Lord. The word from the Lord was really the means by which the miracle came. I believe with all my heart that there is a means for your miracle, and it is God's Word. A specific word from the Lord can turn your situation around as you receive and hold on to it.

And [Elisha] *said, "Thus says the LORD: 'Make this valley full of ditches.' For thus says the LORD: 'You shall
not see wind, nor shall you see rain; yet that valley
shall be filled with water, so that you, your cattle, and
your animals may drink.' And this is a simple matter in
the sight of the LORD; He will also deliver the Moabites
into your hand."*   (2 Kings 3:16–18)

God told them to dig ditches in the valley. Doesn't that
sound crazy? Yet, many times, God gives us something very
simple to do. Note how this miracle came about through the
hands of the soldiers, which they would use to dig the ditches
in accordance with God's command.

In the Gospels, we read how God instructed people to do
simple actions in order to receive miracles, such as to put mud
on somebody's eyes and then tell the person to wash in the
pool of Siloam to bring about a healing, or to go fishing in order to catch a fish with a coin in it so a tax could be paid. (See
John 9:1–7; Matthew 17:24–27.) After receiving such instructions but before experiencing the miracle, it would be easy to
move out of faith and to fall into natural reasoning, thinking,
*Why should I do that? What does that have to do with any-
thing?* We need to be careful not to miss out on our miracles
as a result of not doing what God tells us to do. Just as God
told Moses to look at what was in his hand, He may tell you to
look at what is in your hand—a rod, a shovel, a certain gift or
talent—and put it to use, allowing Him to bring a miracle out
of your obedience.

The three kings obeyed God's word, given through Elisha.
God had told them to fill the valley with ditches, and they did
so. They had their soldiers digging until the job was done. It may
have seemed ridiculous to them at the time, but, in the morning, the miracle occurred. The Moabites were riding out to attack them when they saw the sun reflected on the water, and it
looked like blood to them. They thought that the kings had gotten into strife and killed one another, and so they said, in effect,
"Look at all the pools of blood. We'll go in there and take their
spoils." The Moabites roared down the hill but were overcome by

the three kings and their armies. The word from God that Elisha had spoken had come true. (See 2 Kings 3:20–24.)

I want you to notice something about miracles and never forget it. It's something that God burns in my heart with passion. This miracle came at the time of the morning sacrifice. You may ask, "Well, what's that?"

Twice a day, at the temple in Jerusalem, a priest offered a lamb for the sins of the nation. These were called the morning sacrifice and the evening sacrifice. (See Exodus 29:38–42.) What were those lambs? They represented the Lamb of God, Jesus, who would redeem the world from all sin, all curses, and all darkness. *"Behold! The Lamb of God who takes away the sin of the world!"* (John 1:29).

In chapter 2, we talked about the miracle-working blood of Jesus. All our miracles have been purchased by Jesus, the Lamb of God, on the cross, and we are to pray for miracles and claim God's promises in His name. I got excited when I realized that the miracle of the defeat of the Moabites came at the time of the morning sacrifice of the lamb, and I thought, *I'm going to go through the whole Bible and see where it talks about morning and evening sacrifices to see if there are other miracles recorded in connection with them.*

One such connection I noticed was when Elijah challenged the prophets of Baal on Mt. Carmel and said, in effect, "Let the God who is the true God answer by fire to burn up the sacrifice to Him." The prophets of Baal put out a sacrifice and then cut themselves, screamed, and cried to the point of exhaustion— but no fire came. Elijah let them try all day, and then he poured water over his sacrifice to the true God three times, saturating it (to show that it would be a true miracle if the sacrifice were to burn). He then prayed a short prayer to God. The fire fell after Elijah's prayer, and the Bible says that this occurred at the time of the evening sacrifice. (See 1 Kings 18:17–40.) When did the miracle come? At the time the priest sacrificed the lamb on behalf of God's people.

What does this example say to you and me? The miracles that we pray for in Jesus' name come because everything in heaven and earth has to bow to His name. (See Philippians 2:9–11.) He is King and Redeemer. His sacrifice *"once for all"* (see, for example, Hebrews 10:10) made the way for us to receive miracles. It's in His name that we claim the promises; it's in His name that we call in the provision; it's in His name that we heal sicknesses and cast out demons.

> **The miracles that we pray for in Jesus' name come because everything in heaven and earth has to bow to His name.**

MIRACLES EVEN AS A RESULT OF HANDS OF VIOLENCE

Sometimes, even when we make terrible mistakes, God will bring miracles from these circumstances to demonstrate His power and love to those involved. (See Romans 8:28.) I will give you an example of this type of miracle that is both sad and amazing. It's the miracle of the healing of Malchus's ear, which happened in the garden of Gethsemane on the evening before Jesus was crucified. A detachment of Roman soldiers and officers from the chief priests and Pharisees came to arrest Jesus. Peter, outraged by this situation—earnest, excitable, hotheaded Peter—raised his sword to protect Jesus and cut off the ear of a servant of Caiaphas, the high priest. Peter may have been trying to kill the man but missed. (See John 18:3–12.)

This reckless act would usher in Jesus' final public miracle. It's the first time we know of that Jesus healed a wound that had resulted from violence. Only John's gospel names Peter's victim, and only Luke's gospel records the actual healing:

> *And one of them struck the servant of the high priest and cut off his right ear. But Jesus answered and said, "Permit even this." And He touched his ear and healed him.*
> (Luke 22:50–51)

In His last miracle before dying on the cross, Jesus healed a man numbered among His enemies and provided another powerful sign to the disciples and the world that He was the Savior whom God had sent. Malchus had been attacked because he was the enemy of Jesus; yet because Jesus loved even His enemies, this servant of the high priest received a miracle of healing.

Notice that Malchus lost his ear at the hand of Peter but regained it at the hand of Jesus. Can you picture Malchus's astonishment as he underwent the trauma and pain of this calamity and then the experience of restoration? I wonder where Malchus was at the time of Jesus' crucifixion. It's impossible for me to believe he would have been crying "Crucify Him" after receiving such a remarkable miracle from Jesus.

Peter loved Jesus, but he failed to realize that the moment of Jesus' arrest had been planned before the world's creation and that Jesus was in complete control of the situation. (See Matthew 26:51–54.) Jesus demonstrated His continued submission to His Father when, after the healing of Malchus, He told Peter, "*Shall I not drink the cup which My Father has given Me?*" (John 18:11). We, too, have to remember that Jesus is in control when crises in our lives tempt us to act rashly.

BELIEVE THE WORD OF GOD

One word from the Lord can change negative circumstances to positive ones.

One person's faith and corresponding actions can bring about miracles. You may work in an office where everybody around you is an unbeliever, but you can reflect the light of Jesus in that office. You may teach in a school where you're the only teacher who is a Christian, but you can bring Jesus' light into that school. One word from the Lord can change negative circumstances to positive ones. Keep your faith in the Lord and don't give up!

In the United States and around the world—even in countries where the people are Muslim, Hindu, and Buddhist— miraculous healings are taking place in the name of Jesus. God works miracles as believers practice the laying on of hands. He works miracles as we lift our hands and send forth His Word, which does not return to Him void. He works miracles using the various resources in our hands that we dedicate to His service. He even sometimes works miracles using our mistakes.

Are you a believer? Then, believe the Word of God—there are miracles in your hands!

REST STOP
ON YOUR PATHWAY TO MIRACLES

1. What healing miracle(s) by the laying on of hands have you witnessed?

2. Write down the names of two people who are sick and then spend time praying for them in your prayer closet. Make arrangements, if possible, to lay hands on them for healing. If you are unable to do this, then "send the Word" to meet their needs, according to Psalm 107:20.

3. Memorize these healing Scriptures: Mark 16:17–18; Psalm 107:20; Malachi 4:2.

4. Offer what is "in your hands" to God to use for His purposes.

5. Ask your heavenly Father to use even your mistakes for good.

BIBLICAL EXAMPLES AND SCRIPTURES RELATING TO MIRACLES "IN YOUR HANDS"

- *Miracle sign of the rod*:
  Exodus 4:1–5; 7:8–13

- *Miracle of Samson's jawbone*:
  Judges 15

- *Miracle resurrection of Jairus's daughter*:
  Matthew 9:18–19, 23–26; Mark 5:22–24, 35–43;
  Luke 8:41–42, 49–56

- *Miracle healing of man born blind*:
  John 9:1–7

- *Miracle healing of deaf man of Decapolis*:
  Mark 7:31–37

- *Miracle healing of blind man of Bethsaida*:
  Mark 8:22–26

- *Miracle healing of crippled woman*:
  Luke 13:10–17

- *Miracles at Ephesus*:
  Acts 19:1–12

- *Miracle healing of Publius's father at Malta*:
  Acts 28:7–9

- *Miracle deliverance of Syro-Phoenician woman's daughter*:
  Matthew 15:21–28; Mark 7:24–30

- *Miracles at Samaria*:
  Acts 8:5–8, 13

- *Miracle at Gibeon*:
  Joshua 10:1–11

- *Miracle of the trenches*:
  2 Kings 3:4–25

- *Miracle of the multiplied loaves and fish*:
  Matthew 14:13–21; Mark 6:32–44; Luke 9:10–17;
  John 6:1–14

- *Miracle of coin in fish's mouth*:
  Matthew 17:24–27

- *Miracle healing of Malchus's ear*:
  Luke 22:47–51; John 18:10–11

CHAPTER 9

MOVE-YOUR-MOUNTAIN MIRACLES
All Things Are Possible with God

Everyone faces difficulties at times that seem mountainous, whether they are financial, physical, emotional, or spiritual. Yet Jesus said,

> *For assuredly, I say to you, whoever says to this mountain, "Be removed and be cast into the sea," and does not doubt in his heart, but believes that those things he says will be done, he will have whatever he says.*
>
> (Mark 11:23)

This passage tells us to speak to our mountains, which indicates to me two things: (1) Mountains must have "ears." In other words, they respond when we speak to them in faith. (2) There must be something on the other side of the mountain waiting for us that is wonderful and miraculous.

Jesus told us to command the mountains to be removed, and He told us not to doubt. I believe many miracles await us if we will begin saying the same things God says to the "mountains"—to the problems that are in front of us—and not just bowing to them.

Don't talk *about* your mountains, talk *to* them.

SPEAK TO YOUR MOUNTAIN

Many times, God calls us to do things we are not adequate to do, so that we will rely on Him and give Him the glory. We must trust Him to supply what we don't have as we fulfill His purposes.

For example, when I first became involved in television ministry, I did not think I had the physical appearance necessary. I had brown stains on my teeth, and this was an unusual type of "mountain" I needed to overcome. The stains were not from smoking or chewing tobacco. I grew up in the panhandle of Texas, and the minerals in the water there caused my teeth to become stained. The good news was that the minerals also protected me from getting cavities! I am eighty years old, and I've had only one cavity in my life.

However, I was very self-conscious about these stains when I smiled. I told my husband that I would like to have the enamel on my teeth scraped and then have the teeth whitened. He said, "No, I will not let you do this." Yet, after five or six months of my being on television, someone wrote and asked if I chewed tobacco.

So, I went to my dentist and explained to him my desperation. He said, "Marilyn, there is something new out, liquid enamel, and we could try it on your teeth. Every six months, we'll have to chip it off and start over, but we'll try it." He coated my teeth with the liquid enamel, and no one else asked if I chewed tobacco, but it was a nuisance.

Then, I claimed Psalm 37:4, *"Delight yourself also in the LORD, and He shall give you the desires of your heart,"* and I prayed, "God, my desire is that You take the stains out of my teeth." All dentists will tell you this is impossible for the type of stains I had, but, again, all things are possible with God (see Luke 18:27), and we can move mountains if we speak His words to those mountains. I began to speak Psalm 37:4 to my teeth.

About six months later, I was in the dentist's office having the remains of the liquid enamel taken off. The stains should have been noticeable. However, my dentist went out and got a mirror to show me my teeth, and when I looked, I saw that there were no longer any stains on them. To this day, I can look in the mirror and smile and say that I have Psalm 37:4 teeth.

I have been moving mountains with God's promises for many years. These same promises will work for you, but you have to be diligent to believe them, and you have to speak them to your mountains. You also have to persevere when the circumstances say it's not working or when people criticize you and tell you it won't work.

> **You have to speak God's promises to your mountain and persevere when it looks like it's not working.**

After my mother became a Spirit-filled Christian, her brothers and sisters (she was one of eleven children) considered her to be "over the top" in her beliefs, and they came against her. Yet Mom stood for the miraculous, no matter what. When she had a tumor in her breast, they all said she would die from it, but she said, "No, I will be healed." The Scriptures say, *"I shall not die, but live, and declare the works of the LORD"* (Psalm 118:17). My mother lived a long life. She died at ninety—without the tumor. The good news about her family members is that I believe most of them are born again today. Some in the older generation have already gone to be with the Lord, and many of the grandchildren and great-grandchildren are Spirit-filled and "turned on" to God.

We may have to be a light in the midst of a lot of darkness around us, but if we'll stay in faith, we'll experience the truth that light is greater than darkness. You may be saying, "I'm surrounded by unbelief; I'm surrounded by darkness," but I want to encourage you that your faith and the Word of God can bring about a miracle. The light is greater than the darkness around you. As the Bible says, *"Christ in you, the hope of glory"* (Colossians 1:27).

SEE WHAT'S ON THE OTHER SIDE

You may be facing a mountain that is overwhelming or have mountains of problems that have been around for years and don't seem to change. You can be discouraged about your mountains, or you can see what's on the other side of these mountains and discover how to move them out of the way.

You may say, "Well, I don't think I can."

Don't say that. In fact, don't imagine that in your heart, don't think that in your head, and don't speak that with your mouth, because you are called to be a mountain mover!

In the early 1990s, I spoke at a conference in Honduras, and I helped a woman who was supplying food to the Contra army, which was fighting against the communist-oriented Sandinista government in Nicaragua. Both Nicaragua and Honduras were experiencing a battle between the Sandinistas and the Contras.

The woman I was helping told me, "I sell food to the Contra army back in the Honduran jungle. They have their wives and their children with them. The women don't have anything to wear, and the children don't even have diapers. They don't let anyone else go back there, but you could go as my assistant. You could bring clothes and diapers—and you could preach. There's no one there to stop it, and I'll act like I'm in command."

I thought, *Wow, that sounds like a real God-opportunity.* So, I went.

We flew into Tegucigalpa, Honduras, and then drove deep into the jungle to the forested camp. I was naïve and didn't realize how dangerous it was to go there. We maneuvered down a road, and I saw an army on one side of the road wearing one color, and another army on the other side wearing a different color.

I said, "Whose soldiers are those over there?"

She said, "They're the Contras."

I pointed to the other side. "And who are they?"

She answered, "The Sandinistas."

"And we're in the middle?"

"Yes."

"Could they attack us?"

"Yes, a van like this was attacked about three weeks ago, and everyone in it was killed."

I thought, *Here I am, right in the middle. God help me.*

Finally, we arrived at the camp, and I got to give out the clothing and the diapers for the babies. I preached and invited people to receive Jesus. I also handed out Bibles. Until that time, the people had nothing to read, and I saw them afterward, sitting and reading their Bibles. Then, we drove back the long distance to Tegucigalpa and left the country the next day.

I had heard that the spiritual climate in Honduras at that time was not very strong. For example, a large Spirit-filled, or charismatic, church might have had seventy-five to a hundred members. Years later, I received an invitation to speak at a conference in San Pedro Sula, Honduras. When I arrived, I asked, "How many women do you expect?"

"We'll probably have five thousand; and, tomorrow night, when you speak, we'll probably have ten thousand. For the crusade in the stadium, we're expecting fifteen to twenty thousand. We've been hit with revival. Everywhere you go, people are getting saved."

What God can do in about twelve to fourteen years! What had happened in Honduras? It was because of the Bible. It was because of a revival of people reading, hearing, and believing the Bible. There had been a mountain of unbelief, but God had moved it according to His Word. Isaiah 55:10–11 says that God's Word won't return to Him void, and it didn't.

Let's review what Jesus said about the mountains in our lives:

> *For assuredly, I say to you, whoever says to this mountain, "Be removed and be cast into the sea," and does not doubt in his heart, but believes that those things he says will be done, he will have whatever he says.*
> (Mark 11:23)

How do you move a mountain? You move it with your mouth. Again, you need to talk *to* your mountain and not just talk *about* it. So many people talk about their mountains, saying things such as, "I'm sick; the doctors gave me a bad report, and I don't know if I'm going to make it." They don't talk to their bodies. They don't speak the Word to their bodies. I have more energy now than I've ever had because I daily speak the Word to my body.

What are you saying about your life? Are you talking about the mountain or to it? Remember that mountains have "ears," or Jesus wouldn't have told you to speak to them. So, if you're saying, "Wow, I'll never overcome this mountain; the situation will never improve; it'll never change," then that is what the mountain will "hear."

Instead, move the mountain by speaking words that are the opposite of those that express fear and discouragement— words of faith based on God's Word.

The word in the original Greek that is translated "*says*" in the phrase "*whoever says to this mountain...*" can mean "command." You don't just say to the mountain, "Well, I hope you will move." No, you *command* it to move in the name of Jesus.

Say it! You can't just think it. The mountain can't hear what you're thinking. Tell it, "*Move*, and be cast into the sea. Devil, you're not going to break up my marriage, you're not going to destroy my children, you're not going to ruin my health, and you're not going to send me into bankruptcy. I'm telling you loudly, I'm commanding you, *move*! I have authority, because Jesus who is in me is greater than you who are in the world." (See 1 John 4:4.)

The next part of Jesus' statement about speaking to your mountain is "*...and does not doubt in his heart, but believes that those things he says will be done...*" (Mark 11:23). What you say to the mountain must be based on your faith.

The verse concludes, "*...he will have whatever he says.*" In the King James Version, "*says*" is translated from a different word in the Greek than the one at the beginning of the statement. This second word refers to building systematically. In other words, you keep saying it, and saying it, and saying it, so that it builds until the words have such power and force that they push the mountain into the sea.

It is amazing what happens when you speak God's Word in faith. If you will command out loud and build your faith through consistently speaking to your mountain, that mountain will move.

> **You keep saying it until the words have such power and force that they push the mountain into the sea.**

WHEN MOUNTAINS STILL DON'T SEEM TO MOVE

What about certain cases, however, when mountains still don't seem to be removed? Let me tell you about one of my experiences with such a mountain.

In 1983, Ethiopia was experiencing very bad times. First, the country was in a challenging period of famine, and many thousands of people were starving to death. In addition, its government had become Communist, and it was almost as though the very life of the nation was being squeezed out of it. I remember reading a newspaper account of the things that were going on in that country and being deeply touched by it. Through this experience, God led me to minister in Ethiopia, and He showed me that He is able to move any mountain in my life. Before I tell you how He did this, I want to give you a little background to the country and its people.

First, I'd like to say that I love Ethiopians; they are precious people. And they are unique-looking. I have been in seventeen countries in Africa, and I've noticed that Ethiopians have a different appearance from all other people I've seen on that continent. The book of Jeremiah indicates that you can tell an Ethiopian by his looks. (See Jeremiah 13:23.) That book was written more than 2,400 years ago, and what it says is still true. Once you catch on to the way Ethiopians look, you can recognize them anyplace. I notice Ethiopians when I go to the airport in Denver, and I see many of them in Washington, D.C., and in Los Angeles.

The Ethiopian people also have a long history. They are descendants of Cush, one of the grandsons of Noah. Ethiopia is mentioned a number of times in the Bible. David wrote, *"Envoys will come out of Egypt; Ethiopia will quickly stretch out her hands to God"* (Psalm 68:31). And, according to the Ethiopians, they were the first group of Gentile peoples to become Christians. In the New Testament, we read that a eunuch who was a minister of Candace, Queen of Ethiopia, and was in charge of her treasury, was traveling from Jerusalem to Gaza. God directed the apostle Philip to him, and Philip heard him reading from the book of Isaiah. Philip shared the gospel of Jesus Christ with him, and he believed and was baptized. (See Acts 8:26–39.) And this eunuch is traditionally considered to be the first Gentile convert and the founder of the Ethiopian church.[8]

With this background, I want to share with you the miracle I experienced in Ethiopia and how God still moves mountains when they don't seem to be budging an inch.

After I had heard about the Ethiopians' plight in 1983, God spoke to me to do something major. He told me to take 10,000 Bibles into Ethiopia and $10,000 worth of food for the children. This was a huge step of faith for me; I had never done anything like it before. I called the ministry of affairs at the Ethiopian embassy in Washington, D.C., to see if it would be possible to obtain visas for me, a staff assistant, and a videographer, who would record the trip.

The man at the embassy was very positive. "Yes," he said, "it's possible." I asked if he was certain we could get the Bibles in, and he assured me we could and that, of course, the food would be most welcome.

I then contacted Paul Cole, the son of Ed Cole, and asked him if he would do the videotaping, and he said he would. I also arranged to take along a staff person. Both Paul Cole and the staff person received their visas, but mine did not come. Three days before I was scheduled to leave, my visa still had not arrived.

---

8. Eusebius, hist. Eccl. 2.1.13e, http://www.ccel.org/ccel/schaff/npnf201.iii.vii.ii.html.

Our ministry staff was in quite a panic over it and asked me, "What are we going to do?" We had 10,000 Amharic language Bibles ready to go, as well as $10,000 worth of food. The food could go to another destination, but the Bibles could go only to Ethiopia. What would we do with 10,000 Ethiopian Bibles? My heart wanted to panic, too. It looked like the trip would never happen, and I needed to exercise much faith.

In the meantime, a woman from Ethiopia had been saved at our church. I phoned and asked if she would come talk with me. When we met, I told her what I wanted to do, and she asked me, "Who are you calling in D.C.?"

I told her the name, but I could not pronounce it correctly. She said, "Let me call him for you." As we sat in my office, she called the man and began speaking to him in Amharic. She was laughing and talking, and laughing and talking, for about fifteen or twenty minutes. Then, she hung up the phone and said, "You will have your visa tomorrow."

I asked, "How did you get the visa?"

She replied, "He is my old boyfriend."

I learned that when God wants to do miracles, He can even use old boyfriends.

When I arrived in Ethiopia, I could see that the country was under tremendous oppression. The government officials were hard and harsh, and everything had to go through them. They confiscated all of my video equipment, but they allowed me to keep the food I had brought, plus the additional food that would arrive soon. They told me defiantly that the food would go to the children. They felt I was a spy, and they wanted to call me in for questioning. There I was with 10,000 Amharic language Bibles, and I didn't know if they were angry with me for bringing them.

I'll never forget the day they called me in for questioning. An Ethiopian Christian woman sat beside me as they

They felt I was a spy, but God spoke to my heart, *Don't give up. This mountain will move.*

asked many questions along the lines of, "What is your real purpose for being here? Who sent you here?" However, God spoke to my heart, saying, *Hold on; don't give up. This mountain will move.* All at once, a man came into the room. He appeared to be another secretary, and he whispered to the man who was questioning me. Then, they called over the woman who'd been sitting beside me to talk to her privately. After the three had spoken, the man doing all the questioning said to me, "All right, instead of believing you are a spy, we are going to send you as our guest along with seventy-two American congressmen who want to see the drought area where the famine is the worst. We are taking them in our own plane, Ethiopian Airlines, to Gondar, which is our ancient capital. We are going to take you as a guest of our government."

Something dramatic had happened in that room!

Afterward, I asked the Ethiopian woman who had been sitting beside me how the conversation had gone and what the head man of the committee had said.

She answered, "He told me and the secretary that you are an evil woman and that you are part of a spy group. So, I said to him, 'No, she is not an evil woman. She just wants to feed babies and is concerned about our country.' He said, 'Okay, she's probably just some dumb woman who can't do anything, so let her go ahead.'"

They gave me back my video equipment and allowed Paul Cole to go with me into the drought area.

If you've never seen starving people, it is not a good experience, but it is an unforgettable one. When we arrived in Gondar, they had a Russian helicopter there, which took us and three different companies into the drought region. I have video footage of our arrival by helicopter and what we witnessed. It was a horrific sight. I saw emaciated and pitiful-looking African people with gray skin and gray hair. Of course, my heart went out to them.

The Ethiopian government lavishly entertained the American congressmen. Because I was included in the group, I was entertained, too. We stayed in the nicest hotel there and saw various ancient sites related to Ethiopia's history. However, during this time, I thought, *Who will distribute my Bibles?*

An Orthodox Ethiopian priest was recommended to me, and he was delegated to distribute the Bibles. I met with Father Habt Mariam, who had been imprisoned by the Communists for ten years. He wanted to restore the church around the capital city of Addis Ababa to some kind of normalcy and bring the congregation back together, which had been scattered by Communism, and he was thrilled to receive the Bibles. He became a friend and encouraged me that God could move in Ethiopia in wonderful ways.

While I sitting in the lobby of the Hilton Hotel waiting for the Communists to take me to the next meeting, the Lord spoke to my heart and said, *I want you to come back and have a healing meeting in Ethiopia.*

I thought, *Oh, Lord, I've never had a healing meeting, much less in Ethiopia, a Communist country. How would I do that? The government is so controlling and so anti-anything to do with God.*

However, I asked the Communist leaders before I left if it would be possible for me to come back and bring food and Bibles and also have a healing meeting in the city of Addis Ababa. They laughed and laughed. Then, they said, "We don't even believe in God. Yes, you can come back with food; and, yes, you can come back with Bibles; but no healing meeting."

The Orthodox priest worked with me, and, within a year, I again got 10,000 Amharic language Bibles together and $10,000 worth of food. I spoke with the government, asking if I could come another year and have a healing meeting. "Absolutely not," they told me. "We are a Communist government; we're atheist. We don't believe in God, and you cannot have a healing meeting." But, once again, they allowed me to bring in 10,000 Bibles and to go by helicopter to the hard-core starvation areas of the country and distribute food.

Believe me, the people were clamoring to get Bibles in their own language, and it was a great blessing to the Orthodox church at this time. There were also underground evangelical and Spirit-filled churches there, but if I had contacted them, I could have endangered the believers' lives.

Before I left, I asked again about having a healing meeting because I wanted to *move that mountain*. God had spoken to me about having a healing meeting in Ethiopia, and I believed it would happen.

But the mountain didn't move. The officials again said, "No, we are atheist. You cannot have a healing meeting." So, I went home and prayed.

In 1987, I went back again with food and Bibles, and I asked the Communist government once more if I could have a healing meeting. They said, "Absolutely not. You can't have a healing meeting here. We are atheist." It appeared that it was just not going to happen.

> **We must move mountains. We cannot allow the mountains to move us.**

Yet, we must move mountains. We cannot allow the mountains to move us. So, I continued to speak in faith and to trust God that I would have a healing meeting in Ethiopia.

In 1994, the Communist government in Ethiopia was overthrown, and a democracy was set up. I went back again, working in any way I could with the evangelical churches, the Spirit-filled churches, the Orthodox church, and desiring to help with Bibles. I asked the new democratic government if I could have a healing meeting, and they said, "Yes, you can, but you have to get a group who will back you." I thought, *That won't be a problem.*

I had assumed the Pentecostals or charismatics would help, and perhaps even the Lutherans, because I knew a Spirit-filled Lutheran pastor there, but no one was willing to sponsor me. They said, "We have never had a woman speak in a stadium, and that will never happen. We are not going to sponsor you. We like you, we think you are a real Christian, we appreciate the Bibles and the food and your concern for our country, but we are not going to sponsor you."

Now, I'm going to be very honest with you. You can get very discouraged speaking to mountains, especially when it takes a long time to move them.

In 1997, I decided to send one of our staff members to Ethiopia to talk with the government and see what they would do to facilitate a healing meeting. The staff member went to Ethiopia and spoke with various religious leaders, but they said, "Tell her not to keep asking and knocking at the door. No woman will ever speak in a stadium in Ethiopia. It will never happen."

I became disheartened about this situation. Then, my daughter, Sarah, asked me, "Mom, have you given up on Ethiopia? Do you not live what you teach?"

What she said really shook me, and I thought, *Yes, I have given up. I am going to repent and start again. I believe God will give me a healing meeting in Ethiopia.*

Finally, in 2002, we had healing meetings in a stadium in Nazret, Ethiopia! We had a wonderful meeting with over 40,000 people in attendance. And, on the last day, we had over 10,000 in our day ministry training school. It was an awesome time. Many people were healed, and thousands of people received Jesus as their Savior.

You may not be aware that, in Ethiopia, there are not only evangelical, Pentecostal, and Orthodox churches, as well as other denominational churches, but there are also Muslims. A high percentage of Ethiopia is Islamic. Muslims came to the meeting in Nazret and were wonderfully healed and saved. Many of the leaders who attended the daytime meetings were baptized in the Holy Spirit. Because the meeting went so well and we received such positive promotion over the radio and from various news outlets, the president of Ethiopia invited me to come and have tea with him at the palace. He is a wonderful, gentle man and an Orthodox believer, and he allowed me to pray with him at the tea.

It took from 1983 to 2002 before the miracle of the stadium healing meetings came to pass. Mountains don't always move the first time you talk to them, or even the second time. I had to keep my faith for nineteen years and not give up on what

I believed God had spoken to me. God is faithful. He did it; it happened. I still experience joy when I remember those wonderful meetings and recall the testimonies of the people there. My heart rejoices over the healings that occurred.

Sometime later, Sarah went to Ethiopia twice and held meetings in Gondar by the leading of the Holy Spirit. She has a great passion for Ethiopia. Little did I dream that this development was also on the other side of the mountain.

I want to encourage you, if you have a mountain that has been there for a long time—such as a physical need, a financial need, or a relationship need—never forget that Mark 11:23 says, *"Whoever says to this mountain, 'Be removed and be cast into the sea,' and does not doubt in his heart, but believes that those things he says will be done, he will have whatever he says."* Don't give up. Keep speaking the promise. God is faithful, and we have to be faithful to our part, too. Let me say that, in those nineteen years, although I was waiting for that particular miracle, I continued to step out in faith and serve God. I prayed for the sick and visualized a beginning of miracles, a beginning of people being healed—coming out of their wheelchairs, having their limbs lengthened, and having their deaf ears opened.

BE A MOUNTAIN MOVER

> **Your pathway to miracles will open before you as your faith grows and as your experience in God increases.**

God is always moving in our lives. Your pathway to miracles is a process. It will open before you as your faith grows and as your experience in Him increases. God truly does take you from faith to faith, from glory to glory, and from strength to strength. We have to keep talking to our mountains and not just let our mountains talk to us. As we persevere in speaking to our mountains in faith, God will give us what is on the other side of them.

Your marriage may be falling apart. You may be facing bankruptcy. You may battle with a weight problem. You may struggle with drug addiction. You may have unsaved loved ones. Perhaps you have a chronic health condition, and you say, "I've had this for years, many have prayed for me, and I'm worse than I was before." Any of these situations may seem impossible to overcome. But, I'm telling you, God can do anything.

Do you want to see the impossible become possible? I believe God can give you supernatural faith, which can bring the miraculous into your life in extraordinary ways. I hope you've been reading the Bible references listed at the end of each of the chapters in this book. Read several of them daily. Doing so will lift the level of your faith for miracles.

No mountain-sized problem is too big for God, and no nation or city is too hard for Him to reach. So, let me ask you: Are you speaking to your mountains according to the Word of God, or are you complaining about your mountains? Are you walking in faith and not letting the mountains crush you? Are you commanding the mountains in your life to move, in Jesus' name?

God has great miracles with your name on them! Don't just talk about your problems; speak God's Word to them. Talking about a problem does not move God, but if we speak the promises to the problem, His provision will move the mountain. If you could see what God has for you on the other side of the mountain that stands before you, you would speak to it boldly.

Today, become a mountain mover!

Rest Stop
on Your Pathway to Miracles

1. What do you think is on the other side of the mountain you want removed? Pray about it, write down what you think God is saying, and then record promises that speak to the problem.

2. In the past, have there been any mountains in your life that you felt were unmovable and therefore gave up on trying to remove? If you can't think of any such instances, ask the Holy Spirit to reveal any you may have forgotten. If you do recall some, repent for any lack of faith and perseverance, receive God's forgiveness through Jesus, and then repeat question 1 if these mountains still need to be removed.

3. Read some biblical accounts of those who were held prisoner, such as Joseph, Paul, and Peter. What do these situations have in common, and what can you learn from them?

4. Memorize Mark 11:22–24.

5. Write down five Scriptures that describe God's faithfulness.

6. Are there people with whom you can pray to help build their faith to move mountains in their lives? Write down their names and begin to pray for them in your prayer closet. Then, contact them and offer to pray with them.

Biblical Examples and Scriptures Relating to Move-Your-Mountain Miracles

- *Miracle of the parting of the Red Sea*:
  Exodus 14

- *Miracle of the bronze serpent*:
  Numbers 21:4–9; John 3:14–18

- *Miracle of Jesus calming the storm*:
  Matthew 8:23–27; Mark 4:35–41; Luke 8:22–25

- *Miracle deliverance of Gergesene/Gadarene demoniac*:
  Matthew 8:28–34; Mark 5:1–20; Luke 8:26–39

- *Miracle deliverance of demon-possessed boy*:
  Matthew 17:14–21; Mark 9:14–29; Luke 9:37–43

- *Miracle deliverance of synagogue demoniac*:
  Mark 1:23–28; Luke 4:33–37

- *Miracle healings of paralytics*:
  John 5:2–9; Acts 9:32–35

- *Miracle healing of man crippled from birth*:
  Acts 14:8–10

- *Miracle of Paul's vision at Troas*:
  Acts 16:6–15

CHAPTER 10

MIRACLES OF FAVOR

God Surrounds You like a Shield

Favor takes various forms and is just as much a miracle blessing as material provision or physical healing. God loves to show favor to His people. I encourage you to make Psalm 5:12 your confession: *"For You, O LORD, will bless the righteous; with favor You will surround him as with a shield."* The Hebrew word translated *"favor"* in this verse means "delight," "goodwill," and "acceptance." It's derived from another word meaning "to be pleased with."

I have lived by Psalm 5:12, and I claim this Scripture every day. Right now, I particularly desire favor with the younger generation. I mentor a group of young ministers who are under the age of thirty. I need this favor because I want to share my experiences and pass along the knowledge and insights God has given me over the years. I also claim favor when I need to interact with people in a political arena, when I travel to other nations to preach the gospel, and when I share the Word of God with atheists, Buddhists, Hindus, and Muslims.

God does surround the righteous with favor like a shield, and you can apply this Scripture mightily in your own life. You can confess it with your spouse, your children, and your employer or employees, and in regard to all kinds of relationships. You can pray it for your church and your community.

THE MIRACLE OF FAVOR IN HIGH PLACES

Sometimes, God's favor comes in the form of open doors with presidents, kings, and other influential leaders. I once

177

received an invitation from President Reagan to come to a gathering in Washington, D.C. I was one of thirty women who received this honor, and, at the event, I was able to distribute my Bible study program to everyone in attendance. The miracle of favor in "high places" can bring many opportunities for ministry and personal blessing. Let me give you some other examples...

Favor with a Chinese Leader

While on a ministry trip to China, I had a wonderful experience with a brilliant Chinese leader who is in her early forties and is quite well-known in that country. This woman handled all the logistics for our trip, which were extensive, but she was very cold about spiritual things. She spoke English perfectly, and she told me she was an atheist.

We had gone to China to conduct healing services in a Three-Self church,[9] and we held two nights of meetings with 3,000 people in attendance. Before the first service, I invited this leader to have coffee with me. Her reply was, "No, I don't want to have coffee with you."

But I didn't give up. I claimed Psalm 5:12.

I asked her to join me for lunch. She said, "No, I don't want to have lunch with you."

I invited her to the meeting. She told me, "No, I'm not coming."

But she came the first night. When I saw her the next day, she let me know she had been very touched by the meeting, even though she had remained in a separate room while it was going on. She also said that she had seen the DVD of our ministry trip to Pakistan and that it had affected her. I again asked her to have coffee with me, but she said no.

So, I said, "Please come to the meeting tonight."

She replied, "No, I'm not coming."

---

9. Three-Self churches are state-approved Protestant churches in China. The official name of this association of churches is Three-Self Patriotic Movement (TSPM).

I didn't see her in the meeting that evening, but I continued to claim favor with her, according to Psalm 5:12. Then, as we were about to leave by van to go back to the hotel after the meeting, she ran up to my window and knocked on it. I got out to speak with her, and I could tell by the expression on her face and in her eyes, and by the way she carried herself, that God had touched her.

"I came to tell you good-bye," she uttered.

The Lord said to me, *This is your opportunity.*

I asked her if she would like to have Jesus in her heart. "I really would," she answered, and she prayed to receive Jesus.

That was one of the most precious moments of my life, standing there on that hot evening and leading this woman in prayer with our heavenly Father. I cried all the way back to the hotel. Even now, when I tell this story, I sometimes cry. She had said she was an atheist, but we can have favor with atheists, even those who have positions in high places. Favor is powerful and can have an important role in fulfilling God's purposes.

> **Favor can have an important role in fulfilling God's purposes.**

Favor with the President of Ethiopia

In the previous chapter, I wrote about how we had tried for nineteen years to have a healing meeting in Ethiopia and how, after we were finally able to hold healing meetings in Nazret, I had met with the president of Ethiopia. Let me give you some background to that meeting because it illustrates how we can receive God's favor if we hold on to His Word.

When we'd first arrived in the country for the meetings, I'd attempted to get an appointment with the president in Addis Ababa, the nation's capital. I like to pray with leaders of nations, but I was told that his schedule was full. After the meetings, we went back to Addis Ababa for one day. When I awakened on that last day, the Lord said to me, *You will see President Girma today.* The message was so strong in my spirit that I called

Stephen Kiser, the global director for Marilyn Hickey Ministries, and said, "Today, I will see the president." He said, "No, they will not set up the meeting." I reiterated, "Yes, I'm sure I'll see him today."

Stephen said, "Okay, I will contact them again and see." He called me back and told me the contact had said there was no way.

I continued to say, "I will, because the Lord told me."

I knew I would see the president of Ethiopia, and, sure enough, while we were out shopping, someone from his office called my cell phone and said they would like for us to come.

We went to the palace with our video equipment and had tea with the president. Although it is apparently not customary to pray with a leader who is Orthodox, I prayed with him, and he was receptive. He told me he had invited me because he had heard about the healings and miracles we'd had at Nazret. He was warm and open, and he invited us back. And, as I wrote earlier, Sarah has been to Ethiopia twice since then.

Favor with the King of Jordan

In 2005, God opened a door and gave me favor to speak with the king of Jordan, His Majesty King Abdullah II. This came about because God had given me favor with a Jordanian man who had access to the king. What do you say to a king? You are not given a long audience to visit with him, so I realized that I needed the Holy Spirit to show me what his need was and to give me the wisdom to know what I could share with him.

The Bible says, *"A man's gift makes room for him, and brings him before great men"* (Proverbs 18:16). When Stephen Kiser and I went to see the king, we presented him with a special gift. Then, I said to him, "I would like to pray for your sick relatives, because I'm here in Jordan to be a blessing. I'm here to pray for the sick in the name of Jesus, and I believe God has special miracles."

The king told his assistant to write down the names of his family members, because he wanted to see them healed.

God gave me favor through the vehicle of healing. I have found that a miracle of healing has an impact on anyone, no matter who he or she is. We must have favor in order to speak what God wants us to speak and favor to walk in the wisdom and power of His anointing.

> **We must have favor in order to walk in the wisdom and power of God's anointing.**

While we were in Jordan, we held a healing meeting in a hotel ballroom in Amman, which is a hilly area located in the northwest part of the country. There were about 2,000 people at this meeting, and many were healed and received Jesus. A woman who'd been blind in one eye and who'd also had a troublesome knee was healed, and both of her daughters came forward to receive Jesus as Lord and Savior.

Favor is awesome, so use it in the name of Jesus. Use the Word and watch God do the miraculous in your life!

ESTHER'S SEVENFOLD FAVOR

The biblical account of Esther, or Hadassah, her Hebrew name, is a favorite of many people, including myself. As her story unfolds in the book of Esther, we can see favor exhibited seven times in her life as she fulfilled God's purpose, even though she also experienced major challenges. Favor is especially needed when times are difficult or we need a breakthrough in a situation. Let's look at these seven instances of favor in Esther's life.

1. With Mordecai, Her Cousin and Guardian

Esther lived with her cousin, Mordecai, in Shushan, the city where the Persian kings spent their winters. Mordecai was of the tribe of Benjamin, and he was the nephew of Abihail, Esther's father. When Esther's parents died, Mordecai showed her much favor, raising her as his own daughter. Without Mordecai's support and tutelage, who knows where Esther would have wound up?

2. With Hegai, the Overseer of the King's Harem

When Esther was a young woman, the Persian king Ahasuerus held a great celebration for his officials, his nobles, and the princes of the 127 provinces over which he ruled. This celebration highlighted the king's wealth and influence, and it for lasted six months! Then, he held a seven-day feast for the entire city of Shushan. On the seventh day of the feast, when the king had had a little too much to drink, he commanded that his queen, Vashti, come before him, his officials, and the people, wearing her royal crown. He wanted to show her off, but she refused to come. He was furious, and after consulting his advisers, he sent Vashti away and held a contest for a new queen. A summons went out into all the provinces to gather beautiful women as potential brides for the king, and Esther was taken to the palace as part of this search and placed under the care of Hegai, the king's eunuch. The Scriptures say,

> *Now the young woman pleased* [Hegai], *and she obtained his favor; so he readily gave beauty preparations to her, besides her allowance. Then seven choice maidservants were provided for her from the king's palace, and he moved her and her maidservants to the best place in the house of the women.*
>
> (Esther 2:9)

Esther got the VIP treatment, and she was an orphan gal from Shushan! This is the first time the word "*favor*" is used in the book of Esther, although Mordecai had shown favor to Esther by raising her as his daughter. The Hebrew word translated as "*favor*" in the above verse is *chesed*, and it means "kindness," "goodness," and "faithfulness."

One Hebrew word translated as "*favor*" is *chesed*, and it means "kindness," "goodness," and "faithfulness."

All the young women underwent a full year of beauty treatment, and when they had completed their preparations, they began to be paraded before the king one by one. During that year, Mordecai had been outside the palace daily, pacing up and down and inquiring about Esther. He continued to watch out for her. He had also previously told her also not to let anyone know that she was a Jew, for her protection.

When it was about time for Esther to go before the king, she prepared herself according to Hegai's advice and again received favor from him and *"all who saw her"*:

> Now when the turn came for Esther the daughter of Abihail the uncle of Mordecai, who had taken her as his daughter, to go in to the king, she requested nothing but what Hegai the king's eunuch, the custodian of the women, advised. And Esther obtained favor in the sight of all who saw her. (Esther 2:15)

The word *"favor"* in this verse is translated from a different Hebrew word than the one in verse 9. This word is *chen,* and it has the meaning of "grace" and "charm."

3. With King Ahasuerus, as His Choice for Queen

The Bible says that Esther went in to see the king in the tenth month. If it was the tenth day of the tenth month, it would have been a holy day of minor fasting for the Jews. "Minor" fasting means they fasted from sunrise to sunset. Perhaps this was another reason for the favor she obtained that day. Esther may have been fasting, as well as Mordecai.

And what do you think she received when she went before the king? Well, favor, of course!

> The king loved Esther more than all the other women, and she obtained grace and favor [chen] in his sight more than all the virgins; so he set the royal crown upon her head and made her queen instead of Vashti. (Esther 2:17)

4. With King Ahasuerus, at Esther's First Special Request

Favor rained on Esther once again when she approached her husband, King Ahasuerus, at his court without being summoned. She had done so at Mordecai's urging because a crisis had arisen for the Jews, even though such an action could be punishable by death. One of the king's high officials, the proud Haman, was angry because Mordecai would not bow or defer to him. So, he had devised a plot in which he had gotten the king to sign a decree that all the Jews in every province of the land should be attacked and killed on a particular day.

Esther was frightened about going into the king's presence without having been summoned. So, before she went, she fasted for three days and nights, as did her maids, Mordecai, and all the Jews in Shushan. Then, Esther put on her royal apparel and approached the king.

> *So it was, when the king saw Queen Esther standing in the court, that she found favor [chen] in his sight, and the king held out to Esther the golden scepter that was in his hand. Then Esther went near and touched the top of the scepter.* (Esther 5:2)

The extended scepter signified her right to live. That's favor!

King Ahasuerus then offered her half his kingdom. But, rather than accepting it, Esther invited him to a banquet—along with Haman, the perpetrator of the plot to obliterate her people.

5. With King Ahasuerus, at Esther's Second Special Request

It gets even better. They have the banquet, just the three of them, and the king asks her what her petition is. In other words, he's not fooled. He knows she wants something.

Esther puts him off by answering,

> *If I have found favor [chen] in the sight of the king, and if it pleases the king to grant my petition and fulfill my request, then let the king and Haman come to the banquet which I will prepare for them, and tomorrow I will do as the king has said.* (Esther 5:8)

What, you say? She's asking for favor? Yes, but you can bet she was listening to God's Spirit as He directed her, because she and all those people had prayed and fasted. Well, Esther indeed found favor in the king's sight, and he agreed to the second banquet.

But between these banquets, Mordecai was honored by the king for his past service of saving the king's life. Haman had wanted Mordecai hanged on the gallows but was humiliated when the king asked him to be the one to lead a procession honoring Mordecai. So, now, Haman dreaded going to the upcoming feast. He knew that he might be the one who would be "cooked."

6. With King Ahasuerus, as Esther Pleaded for Her People

Previously, Esther had both received favor and petitioned for it, and now she used the favor she had been granted for God's purposes of protecting His people. As she, the king, and Haman were at dinner, the king asked her again, "What do you want?" (I love the fact that he didn't give up.)

> Then Queen Esther answered and said, "If I have found favor in your sight, O king, and if it pleases the king, let my life be given me at my petition, and my people at my request. For we have been sold, my people and I, to be destroyed, to be killed, and to be annihilated. Had we been sold as male and female slaves, I would have held my tongue, although the enemy could never compensate for the king's loss." (Esther 7:3–4)

The king promptly asked, "Who is this man?"

Esther replied, "Haman."

Can you imagine how Haman felt when he heard his name spill from the queen's lips?

The king was so enraged that he left and went out into the palace garden. Meanwhile, the intrigue continued as Haman proceeded to plead with Esther for his life. Unfortunately for him, King Ahasuerus returned just as he was falling upon the couch where Esther was seated. Then, the king ordered that Haman die on the very gallows he'd built and intended for Mordecai.

7. With King Ahasuerus, in Counteracting the Decree against the Jews

That was the end of Haman, but it isn't the end of the story. Esther begged King Ahasuerus to prevent the scheme planned by Haman. Since the decree bore the king's seal, which was irreversible, there was only one way to counteract it—to again obtain favor with the king. Esther said to him,

> *If it pleases the king, and if I have found favor in his sight and the thing seems right to the king and I am pleasing in his eyes, let it be written to revoke the letters devised by Haman, the son of Hammedatha the Agagite, which he wrote to annihilate the Jews who are in all the king's provinces. For how can I endure to see the evil that will come to my people? Or how can I endure to see the destruction of my countrymen?*
> (Esther 8:5–6)

The king could not reverse his original order, but he issued another decree that the Jews could defend themselves, and on the day set for their destruction, they were victorious over their enemies in all the provinces. So, Esther had again reminded the king of her favor, used it as a premise for her petition, and preserved the lives of the Jews living in the Persian Empire.

Your talent, your natural and specific ability to do something well, is your beauty.

Favor carried Esther from being adopted by her cousin to becoming queen of Persia to being the vessel God used to save His people from destruction. Her beauty was given to her for a purpose—but so is ours. You may say, "I'm not beautiful." Yet you are. Your talent, your natural and specific ability to do something well, is your beauty. As Mordecai proclaimed about Esther, you are alive in God's service today *"for such a time as this"* (Esther 4:14).

"But I don't know what my specific ability is," you may say. Then do what I have done and continue to do—follow God. The Holy Spirit will lead you, and the guidance you receive may be a small thing at first. Follow that inkling. It may lead you to palaces, and it may not. But wherever it takes you, you'll be living in God's favor and fulfilling His purposes.

FAVOR WITH AUDIENCES AND CROWDS

Sometimes, we need favor when going before large audiences and crowds. Just as healing causes individuals to be receptive to God, it causes groups of people to be receptive to Him. Some of my earlier stories have illustrated this, and I'd like to share two others with you.

A Stellar Night with a Hungarian Audience

I was in Budapest, Hungary, on a ministry trip, and I preached at Faith Church, which has more than 100,000 members. I love that church. In Hungary, there are also what are called "country" churches, which are large congregations that meet in theaters. I went to one of these churches to preach and found it crowded with people. The worship there was wonderful, and then, as I stood to speak, the Lord said to me, *Before you begin to preach, I want you to pray for people with lung problems.*

I thought, *This is really strange to start out this way, because probably a lot of them are not born again.* However, I have found that if you listen to the Holy Spirit, He will lead and guide you. Now, when you have only one night in which to minister in a particular place, you have a passion in your heart to do everything. I had prayed Psalm 5:12 beforehand, saying, "God, give me great favor with this audience, so that people will really experience Jesus—so that they will be born again, Spirit-filled, delivered, and have their needs met." Because I had prayed that prayer, I listened to the Holy Spirit when He said, *Pray for people with lung problems.*

So, I asked people who had lung problems, pain in their lungs, or breathing problems of any kind to stand. Approximately one hundred people stood. I was very bold, saying, after praying for them, "Check yourself. See if you are better. If you show a dramatic difference, I would like you to come up to the platform and share your testimony."

Eight or nine people came up to share, and one of them was the mayor of the town, who appeared to be about forty years old. Minutes earlier, he had presented me with a special gift for visiting his town. The mayor said that he had come to the service knowing that he had pneumonia, and he had been sitting in great pain. He testified, "I have no pain in my lungs. I am totally all right."

Of course, the people clapped and were thrilled. That night, the mayor also gave his heart to Jesus. The greatest miracle of all is when people are born again. That's when you see God move in the most wonderful, unusual ways.

It was a stellar night. People got saved, and backsliders came back to Christ. Businessmen were really blessed because I prayed for financial wisdom and breakthroughs in their lives. When you think of Hungary, you might think of it as more of a conservative country, spiritually speaking, but they are having dramatic revivals.

A Unique Opportunity in Bethlehem on Christmas Eve

Psalm 5:12 is truly a powerful Scripture to speak into your life. It is the prayer for the miracle of favor, and therefore I want to share another "Psalm 5:12 miracle" with you. It will encourage you to pursue God's favor in your own life, as I experienced when facing a large, diverse crowd overseas.

In 2010, we were in Bethlehem at Christmastime, and we stayed on the Palestinian side rather than the Israeli side. Palestinians are not as accustomed to tourists. For more than fifteen years, tourists have chosen to stay in Israel and not even go to Bethlehem because they do not feel safe. However, I felt totally safe. I took a group of forty-five travelers with me, and I felt comfortable and secure.

> **Psalm 5:12 is truly a powerful Scripture to speak into your life. It is the prayer for the miracle of favor.**

We wanted to be a blessing to the people, and I wanted to have favor with the Palestinians—the Christians, as well as the Muslims (a large part of the population in Bethlehem is Muslim). We asked if I could have an opportunity to speak at the Christmas Eve service in Manger Square, which holds around 90,000 people.

The committee organizing the Christmas Eve event had set up a large platform for the evening, and live music was featured. People were singing and worshipping, which was a good thing, although it was not a very spiritual environment. The overall atmosphere felt more like a New Year's Eve party.

I was told that Christian music groups were scheduled from five in the evening until one in the morning. They would sing Christmas carols, for the most part. I asked if I could speak, and they said, "Yes, but we have other speakers scheduled. You can speak for only twenty minutes."

At one end of Manger Square is a huge Greek Orthodox church. It is supposed that this is the site where Christ was born. Beside it is a big Catholic church and seminary. At the opposite end of the square is a huge mosque, and on both sides are shops and restaurants.

Around us were vendors of various types and families with children: Muslim and Christian families, including Orthodox and Catholic. It was a cross-section of cultures. People had come from all over the world to celebrate Christmas in Bethlehem.

I was reminded that I had only twenty minutes to speak. But then, when I stood up to begin preaching, something interesting happened. The Muslim call to prayer sounded. That call is so loud that there is no way you can talk above it, and it lasts about five minutes. You just stand there and wait for it to finish.

While I waited, the Lord impressed upon my heart, *You can 'turn lemons into lemonade.' Be sensitive to what I can do here.*

At the end of the Muslim call to prayer, I said to this huge audience, "I'm very comfortable with the Muslim call to prayer because I go to Muslim countries all over the world. I love Muslims, and Muslims love me."

When I said that, the people roared with enthusiasm. They clapped and threw flowers on the platform.

Now, before all of this, I had prayed that God would give me favor, according to Psalm 5:12, and there was no question that I had favor. I was ready to speak on hope—hope for Bethlehem, and hope for the people's futures, families, and finances. And who is hope? I told them Jesus Christ in us is the hope of glory. I told them it is not knowing about Him but having Him inside us that matters. How do you get Jesus, the hope of glory, the hope of Bethlehem, inside you? You invite Him into your heart. I told them how I had invited Jesus to come into my heart—how I had repented of my sins, asked Him to be Lord of my life, and thanked God that Jesus had saved me. Then, I said, "I am now seventy-nine years old, and Jesus is still with me. What a miraculous life He has given me. He is in me, the hope of glory. I want you to have Christ in you, the hope of glory. I'm taking this opportunity to have all of you pray the same prayer I prayed at age sixteen, which is still working in my life. Ask Jesus to come into your heart and be Lord of your life."

Then, I led them in the sinner's prayer. It was dark, so I don't know how many people prayed, and I don't know how many people meant it. I just know that they had an opportunity to receive Jesus. I also know I had favor with that audience. God brought to pass the prayer I had prayed: "Lord, surround me with favor; protect me and be a shield to me."

I encourage you to pray Psalm 5:12 and to believe for miracles of favor. Speak favor. Don't say negative things, such as "I can't do this," "People don't like me," "People don't want to hear what I have to say," "I have the wrong background," or "I'm too old." That is ridiculous. God made you the way you're supposed to be, and He can give you favor in any situation or circumstance. I believe in the miracle of favor!

> **God can give you favor in any situation or circumstance.**

FAVOR OF OPEN DOORS
WITH BOTH THE ISRAELIS AND THE PALESTINIANS

Another time, I was in Israel, and I wanted to go into the Gaza Strip. The leadership of Gaza is Hamas, which, as you may know, is a radical Islamic group. Almost no one gets into Gaza because this disputed area is such a high-level issue between the Palestinians and the Israelis, and the Israeli government doesn't want travelers to go there.

I love Israel and its people, and I have gone to Sderot, which is a town that the Palestinians have targeted with missiles. The Jewish people in Sderot live in fear all the time because of this constant barrage of missiles. Usually, the missiles come at a time when school is out, so many of the children have been maimed by them. Our ministry has done a lot to help these children, and we have also built bomb shelters for the people. The rabbi there has been very open to our help on every level.

However, I desired to hold a healing meeting in Gaza, but I could not get the Israeli government to give me permission to go there, and I had no way to contact Hamas. The last time I was in Israel, God opened the door for me to meet some of the Hamas leadership; the government gave me permission to go in for two hours. This was a great miracle, and I am still seeking an opportunity to go and have a healing meeting there. I believe the two-hour visit I had will help open a future door.

On the whole, I have many opportunities with the Orthodox Jews in Israel, and our television show, *Today with Marilyn and Sarah*, is broadcast there twice a day. About six years ago, I met a Jewish leader in Israel who told me he believed that Jesus is the Messiah, but he was not going to invite Him into his heart because his adult children would reject him. I told him that he was trying to play the part of God and encouraged him, saying, "How do you know your children would reject you?" However, he turned down my offer to pray with him.

Six months later, he came to the United States and visited our church in Denver, and I gave him a card with the sinner's prayer on it to pray in his room that night. I later learned that he did not do so.

About a year later, I went to Israel and had lunch with him and his new wife, a Jewish woman from the States. They both had received Jesus and boldly told me how wonderful it was to have Him in their hearts. This news was so exciting to me. After that, they both came to a meeting at a large church in Boston where I was teaching, and they were filled with the Spirit. I hear from them regularly by e-mail, and there is some interest among their adult children to receive Jesus.

FAVOR WHILE WITNESSING TO FELLOW TRAVELERS

Previously, I've discussed how I share Jesus with people when I travel by plane. I feel the Lord gives me special favor with my fellow voyagers. If you want your experience with Jesus to be continually fresh, be a soulwinner. Always keep in mind that, with God, the most important thing is people. *"For God so loved the world that He gave His only begotten Son, that whoever believes in Him should not perish but have everlasting life"* (John 3:16). When you die, you can't take your car, your house, or your clothes with you. But you can "take along" people whom you've led to Christ.

> **If you want your experience with Jesus to be continually fresh, be a soulwinner.**

Once, when I was flying to Buffalo, New York, I prayed according to Psalm 5:12: "God, give me favor on this plane. Give me favor with the person who sits beside me." A nicely dressed, middle-aged businessman settled in beside me. We began to talk, and I found out that he was a rancher from Colorado. Then, he asked me, "What do you do?" Again, when people ask this question, it is a perfect open door. I said, "I am married to a pastor. My husband pastored for years, and I teach the Bible on television. I go all over the world. I go to Hindu countries, Buddhist countries, and Muslim countries."

He said, "Well, I'm so glad to hear that because when I was raised in church, they said the only way to God is Jesus. I'm glad that you go to the Hindus, the Muslims, and the Buddhists, because there are many ways to God, as long as they are sincere."

I thought, *Oh, no.* I get this response so much, and it bothers me, because when I begin to tell people what the Bible says—that Jesus declared, *"I am the way, the truth, and the life. No one comes to the Father except through Me"* (John 14:6)—they turn me off. Or, they want to argue with me. I argue back, and then I feel like I've failed God. I don't reach people; they're just upset. So, I prayed, *Lord, help me with this. I want to have favor with this man, but, more than anything, I want him to know Jesus.*

I know the Holy Spirit gave me the answer, because this is how I responded: "Well, I don't want to get into an argument with you about what the Bible says, but could I tell you my experience with Jesus?"

He said, "Yes, you can."

I gave him my testimony, saying, "When I was sixteen, I invited Jesus Christ to come into my heart, and He has never left me. I simply repented of my sins and invited Him to be Lord of my life. I told Him I had faith in His blood to cleanse me from sin, and I thanked Him for saving me." I didn't know how the man would react to this, but he began to weep.

Then, he said, "I was supposed to sit next to you. I've just been diagnosed with cancer."

A hushed moment slipped by between us.

He said, "What is that prayer?"

His heart was so open and tender. I like to pray the sinner's prayer out loud with people, if I can, but if they're not comfortable doing that, I give them one of my cards with the sinner's prayer printed on it. I gave him the prayer card, and he received Christ as his Savior. It was a wonderful experience.

I rejoice because I know our encounter was a "setup" from God, and that it was favor, with the power of the Holy Spirit at work. A man received Jesus as his personal Savior!

> **Our encounter was a "setup," with the power of the Holy Spirit at work.**

I encourage you to love "sinners" and to share Christ with them. Tell yourself, "I love sinners, and sinners love me." Pray according to Psalm 5:12—"I'm surrounded by God with favor like a shield"—in preparation for your God-ordained encounters with individuals, groups, and crowds of all kinds who need to hear about Jesus' love and His sacrifice on the cross for them.

REST STOP
ON YOUR PATHWAY TO MIRACLES

1. Be sure to commit Psalm 5:12 to memory, because it is key to receiving the miracles of favor God wants to do in your life.

2. Has God spoken to you by His Holy Spirit about praying for someone? If so, have you followed through? Write down some instances of when you have.

3. To open the door to the gospel for others, pray about two people whose lives God wants to touch, and then pray about giving them a specific gift that would bless them. When you sense God prompting you to do so, give these gifts, and then follow the Holy Spirit's leading in sharing Christ with them.

4. How are you preparing for times when you find yourself in one-on-one conversations with people who need Christ? If you have not done so already, determine your plan. For example, think through your own testimony and be ready to give it. As the apostle Peter wrote, *"In your hearts set apart Christ as Lord. Always be prepared to give an answer to everyone who asks you to give the reason for the hope that you have. But do this with gentleness and respect"* (1 Peter 3:15 NIV). Also, do you have a "sinner's prayer" readily available for praying with people? You can carry cards with such a prayer among your credit cards so that you can give them to those you meet who are open to the gospel. Or,

you can memorize the prayer and tell it to others. Refer to the end of chapter 14 of this book for an example.

5. When you are in a situation in which you might have an opportunity to witness to someone, speak Psalm 5:12 and then trust God to work.

BIBLICAL EXAMPLES AND SCRIPTURES RELATING TO MIRACLES OF FAVOR

- *Miracle of Enoch's translation to heaven*:
  Genesis 5:23–24; Hebrews 11:5

- *Miracles of blessing and favor for Abraham*:
  Genesis 17:1–8; 15–22; 18

- *Miracles of water brought out of rocks in the desert*:
  Exodus 17:1–6; Numbers 20:7–13; Nehemiah 9:15,
  20; Psalm 78:16; 105:41.

- *Miracle of manna*:
  Exodus 16; Nehemiah 9:15, 20; Psalm 78:23–25;
  105:40; John 6:22–58

- *Miracle healing of the waters at Marah*:
  Exodus 15:22–27

- *Miracle of the budding of Aaron's rod*:
  Numbers 17:1–11

- *Miracle of Moses being taken by God at death*:
  Deuteronomy 34:1–7

- *Miracle of crossing the Jordan River*:
  Joshua 3:7–17; 4

- *Miracle appearance of the Commander of the army
  of the Lord to Joshua*:
  Joshua 5:13–15

- *Miracles of favor and approval for Esther:*
  Book of Esther

- *God the Father's words of approval at Jesus' baptism:*
  Matthew 3:13–17; Mark 1:9–11; Luke 3:21–22

- *The transfiguration of Jesus with God the Father's words of approval:*
  Matthew 17:1–9; Mark 9:2–9; Luke 9:28–36;
  2 Peter 1:16–19

- *Miracles of post-resurrection appearances:*
  Matthew 28:1–10, 16–20; Mark 16:9, 12, 14;
  Luke 24:13–53; John 20:11–21:14; Acts 1:3; 9:17;
  1 Corinthians 15:3–8

- *Miracles at Malta/kindness of the inhabitants:*
  Acts 28:1–10

CHAPTER 11

GIANT MIRACLES
Extraordinary Miracles, Signs, and Wonders

There are times when God's people don't need just a little miracle; they need a *big* one. Examples of "giant" miracles are evident throughout the Bible. We have discussed some of them in previous chapters, but I will list just a few here to illustrate: the parting of the Red Sea, the drowning of the Egyptian army that was pursuing the Israelites, the sun standing still at Joshua's command, the miracles of Elijah and Elisha, and the miracles of Jesus, such as the feeding of the 5,000, the calming of the storm at sea, and the raising of Lazarus from the dead. These were all dramatic miracles. Giant miracles address big needs, and we shouldn't expect less from our glorious, all-powerful God.

Spectacular miracles are happening in the church worldwide. I want to talk about dramatic miracles that I have experienced and those I believe God has for you in your times of need.

GIANT MIRACLES OF PROTECTION
"Disguised" by God

China has the largest population of any nation in the world (approximately 1.3 billion), and the country is experiencing a great revival. For many years, the church in China has been underground, but there are millions of believers. These believers have been persecuted, and many have been martyred for the faith.

Several years ago, I was invited to go to China to teach underground leaders. This could have been very dangerous for them. If they had been caught with a Westerner, they could have gone to prison for at least two years. I prayed intensely about how to teach them and what to minister. I also prayed for protection for them and for me.

Our youth pastor, Mike, accompanied me on this trip. We flew into Anhui province, on the eastern side of China, across the basins of the Yangtze and Huai rivers. From there, we were driven six hours to a remote farm.

There were perhaps 150 Christian leaders gathered at this farm, and I had an opportunity to minister to them during three days and nights. When it was time to depart, we left at four in the morning in a large van that had three rows of seats.

Mike and I were in the last row. They had provided blankets for us, as well as some hot tea. We had another six-hour drive to get back to Hefei, the capital of Anhui province, and we were tired, cold, trying to sleep, and somewhat fearful.

Yet, before we had gone very far, the van stopped, and we heard the Chinese believers at the front of the van communicating with someone. Then, the person got into the van.

Mike had been sitting up when the van stopped. The new passenger turned out to be a soldier who was hitchhiking (the citizens of China are required to give rides to soldiers). Mike told me that the man had looked him in the eye but hadn't seemed to see him. Under normal circumstances, there would have been no question from Mike's appearance that he was a Westerner, but the soldier's vision had been blinded to him.

For five hours, we remained under the blankets, praying in the Spirit that these dear, sweet people would not be caught.

For five hours, we remained under the blankets, praying in the Spirit that these dear, sweet people would not be caught. Finally, about an hour from Hefei, the soldier told them to stop the van. He departed, never realizing our presence. God's "disguising" us that day was a giant miracle to me.

As I got on the plane in Hefei to fly to Hong Kong, I was exhausted. I hadn't had a shower in three days, and I looked terrible. But, inside, I was on fire. I had seen the underground church. Many of the young men and women leaders whom I had ministered to at that farm had 10,000 to 20,000 people in their churches. And many had spent time in prison for their faith.

I love China; the country has always been a passion of mine. I have been there thirty times now, and the majority of my visits have been with the underground church. I usually traveled there during their cold-weather season, because I could be wrapped up and not be as noticeable as a Caucasian. I have smuggled in Bibles during my visits, because hardly any of the believers I've ministered to owned one. It was difficult for them to get Bibles in the first place. Plus, if they had been able to buy a copy of the Scriptures, the government would have kept a record of the purchase, and they could have been harassed, persecuted, and sent to prison.

Kept Safe While Ministering to Underground Leaders

On another trip, our ministry team went to a city in Qinghai province, the largest province geographically. It lies in the northwest part of the country and borders Xizang, or Tibet.

Two of us met with an underground Christian and drove almost three hours to a place where 150 underground leaders had gathered at a farm with a tall brick wall around it. Some of these leaders had as many as 10,000 people under them, and they spiritually fed their churches through home cell groups.

These believers prayed and testified like nothing I've ever seen. In the morning, they would be up at about four thirty, praying. We would teach them almost all day, and, in the evening, they would pray again.

When you meet with the underground church, you don't stay at the Hilton Hotel; you stay on the farm where the people stay. It was bitter cold, and they didn't have heat. Often, rats ran inside their ceilings. But the people were warm and very gracious.

Four of us from our ministry were staying in one room. The first night, some of the Chinese people came in to us before we went to sleep and bathed our feet in hot water. They also gave us something to brush our teeth with. Then, they rolled each of us up in a blanket, almost like a hot dog, and put a bottle of hot water at our feet so that we would be warm during the night.

Even though we were having daylong teaching meetings, those of us from America were kept separate from the Chinese underground leaders as much as possible. If someone were to come to that farm and see a Chinese person with a Westerner, that person, again, could go to prison for two years. So, everything was conducted with much caution.

While I was teaching on the second day, the pastor who was with me said, "Marilyn, get on the floor, get on the floor." As I did, all the people stood up and sang.

They told me afterward that a man had come in to read the meter. The people were very concerned that he might have seen me before I'd gotten on the floor, and they told me that they would come to get us at midnight to take us to another location. They had decided to move everyone else, as well.

At midnight, they awakened me and said, "Don't worry about your luggage. We will take care of your luggage." They took us in the dark to a van they had hired. We got in the van through the back door, and then we were covered up. They drove us almost three miles and then let us out. However, they did not let us out at our destination. We had to walk another two miles, in the cold, to a different farm.

I was frightened, and I prayed, *God, please have someone pray for me tonight, that I will be safe and will not cause any of these wonderful Chinese Christians to go to prison.*

We finally got to the next farm and went through the ritual again. They bathed our feet with hot water, brushed our teeth, and wrapped us up like hot dogs. By the next day, all of the believers had been moved there from the first farm, and, throughout the day, there was teaching, praying, and testifying.

I'll never forget one woman who shared her testimony through an interpreter about how she had been preaching and had been imprisoned, separating her from her husband and two children. The prison guards tried to break her legs, but they wouldn't break. They used electric prods on her, but that didn't work. They took away her food, but she gained weight. Gradually, she began to win people to Christ—not only the prisoners, but also the prison guards. She was originally to have been there for two years, but they kept her for an additional six months, telling her, "We don't want you to leave, because you help the attitude of the prisoners."

Well, of course, she was getting them all saved. She told how almost all of the prisoners were now born again and Spirit-filled, "turned on" to Jesus Christ. The prison officials had kept her for two-and-a-half years, and she had just been released. This was only her second day out of prison. She told us that her husband had done well on his job, and that he had been given a raise, so, financially, they were prospering. She explained that her mother had moved into their house and done the cooking for the family, and that her children were fine.

As she told us these things, her face shone like an angel's. She was still living in the glory of what she'd experienced in that prison. Those were giant miracles, "miracles of miracles."

Her face shone like an angel's as she lived in the glory of her miraculous experiences in the Chinese prison.

I am sure that if you were to speak with the people of the underground church in China, they could talk about giant miracles all day. They could tell you of miracles that were "out of this world."

Signs and wonders bring people courage. People often say to me, "You know you could be killed when you go into these other countries."

Yes, I know.

"Doesn't it worry you a lot?"

There have been times when I've had horrible fear. I've stood on the platform at a stadium, looked at the thousands and thousands of people sitting in the seats, and thought, *Any of these people could kill me. They could just shoot me here and kill me.*

Yet, I didn't have a problem because, every time I entered into a situation like that, God showed Himself strong on my behalf, and it gave me courage for the next situation. And, what if I did get killed? I would go to heaven.

Miraculous Escapes

The Bible describes times when Jesus had miraculous escapes from His adversaries. These were giant miracles—possible by the hand of God alone. For example, when Jesus was still a child, probably about a year old, King Herod sought to kill Him because he had the mistaken idea that Jesus might usurp his throne as king of Judea. An angel of the Lord appeared to Joseph and told him to take Jesus and His mother, Mary, and flee to Egypt. This action resulted in two things: (1) it protected them from harm, and (2), it fulfilled the prophecy, *"Out of Egypt I called My son"* (Hosea 11:1), when they returned to Israel after the death of Herod. (See Matthew 2:13–15, 19–21.)

Years later, after Jesus had begun His ministry at age thirty, He slipped through an angry crowd that sought to kill Him after He preached His first sermon in His hometown. The people had taken offense that He had put Himself (in their minds) in the same class as the prophets Elijah and Elisha and proclaimed that "heathens," whom they hated, had been singularly blessed by God. (See Luke 4:24–27.) This is what resulted:

> So all those in the synagogue, when they heard these things, were filled with wrath, and rose up and thrust Him out of the city; and they led Him to the brow of the hill on which their city was built, that they might throw Him down over the cliff. Then passing through the midst of them, He went His way. (Luke 4:28–30)

Jesus was no stranger to peril. Other accounts (see John 8:57–59; 10:30–39) describe people's attempts to stone Him when He proclaimed His deity. These miraculous escapes kept Him alive until the God-appointed time for Him to die on the cross for our sins. (See, for example, Matthew 26:45–46.)

Miraculous escapes kept Jesus alive until His God-appointed time to die on the cross for our sins.

God has enabled me to escape miraculously from dangerous situations, also. For example, I'd always wanted to preach in Vietnam, but it is a Communist country, as well, and they are not open to having anyone come and preach there. However, I was told that there was a big, underground revival going on among the rubber plantation workers and that I could minister there secretly. "We can take you out to a rubber plantation at night. It will be outside of Saigon, maybe a three-hour drive, and then we will get on motorcycles and travel for thirty minutes into the interior of the plantation. Many will be seated on the ground, waiting for you to preach. You will not have a microphone; only your interpreter will."

I was to preach late at night so other people in the area would not be as aware of what was going on. We got to the motorcycles at about ten thirty in the evening. When I finally arrived at the plantation, I was shocked to see there were at least a thousand people seated on the ground waiting—waiting—waiting for Jesus.

I thought, *While I'm here, I'm going to do it all. When will I ever have another opportunity like this?* These Vietnamese plantation workers were born again, but I gave them the whole gospel: I preached Jesus as Savior. I preached Jesus as Healer. I preached Jesus as the One who baptizes in the Holy Spirit.

Just going and ministering there was a giant miracle. Then, when it was over at about two thirty in the morning, we went back on the motorcycles to the van, which had waited for us. When we got to the van, one of our staff people said, "Marilyn, we need to get out of here, and we need to get out of here right away. I just have a feeling we cannot sit here at all." We jumped in the van and drove back.

Later, we heard that the police had been informed there was a van with American Christians on the plantation. Police officers had come up to the driver and asked, "Where are they?"

He had responded, "They are in the rubber plantation."

They had said they would wait until we came back out. (We were further into the plantation because we had ridden the motorcycles into the interior.) They waited and waited, but we didn't come out. About two o'clock in the morning, they got hungry and decided that they would get something to eat and come back. By the time they did, we were gone.

Our ministering at that rubber plantation was a miracle opportunity, and our protection from the Chinese police was a giant miracle. Why? Because we have a "giant" God who does big things. He does miracles today in America, in China, in Vietnam, and all over the world.

GIANT MIRACLES OF SIGNS AND WONDERS

The Bible says signs and wonders will follow those who believe. (See Mark 16:17.) Signs and wonders reveal the nature of God and His attributes. I don't follow after signs and wonders; I follow after God and His Word, but signs and wonders chase me down. I have traveled all around the world, and I have seen the name of Jesus bring signs and wonders. Others have seen signs and wonders as they have ministered, as well.

A Sign Through a Snake

As I mentioned earlier, Daisy and T. L. Osborn were used mightily by God as world evangelists. Daisy related something that happened, as far as I remember, in Togo, West Africa. She went there to set up a large healing meeting, and, when she arrived, she met with some of the Christians and found that most of the country worshipped snakes. Almost every family had a snake house in front of its abode.

The leaders of the city met with her, the local believers, and other residents in a large circle. The witch doctors brought out a snake, and it was passed it around from person to person. As Daisy stood in the circle, she knew they would hand her the snake. Well, you know how much most women hate snakes! However, she was praying, and when she touched the snake, it became a rod in her hands, similar to what happened with Moses' rod. (See Exodus 4:1–5.) When she passed it to the man next to her, who was a Christian, it remained a rod. As long as a believer held it, it remained a rod, but when it went back into the hands of an unbeliever, it became a snake again. God was showing the people that He was greater than their "god."

> **When she touched the snake, it became a rod in her hands, similar to what happened with Moses' rod.**

That night, the Lord awakened Daisy and said, *Get out of here. They're coming to kill you.* She was staying in a small house, and the believers who owned it were asleep on the ground outside, so she arose and went to them. "Get up," she whispered in their ears. "We have to get out of here."

They went out into the jungle, and she found a driver who had an old, beat-up taxi. The others fled, and she offered the driver money if he would get her out. By sunrise, she had arrived at the country's border. Later, she heard that a whole group of people had come to kill her and the Christians who were with her, but they were no longer there.

That's an example of a sign and a wonder. God loves to reveal His power because that's who He is: He is all-powerful. The devil desired the power of God, but he completely missed the point, because God is not just power. He is, in essence, love (see 1 John 4:8, 16), and power is an expression of His love. Manifestations of signs and wonders are one way He shows His care for His people. We don't worship the signs and wonders; we worship Him, because He loves us so much that He does these signs and wonders on our behalf.

The Sign in the Sun

Signs and wonders also serve to expose people's sin and to bring them to repentance through the work of the Holy Spirit. When people see God moving in a wonderful way, many of them will say, "I want this God. I'm sorry for my sins." And when believers see God manifest Himself with power as they serve Him, many of them will be filled with awe and think, *Who am I that God would be so good to me? Who am I that God would use me?*

About 1997, I felt a strong call to go to Sudan and have a meeting in the capital city of Khartoum. God had given me a warm feeling for Sudan when I'd started praying for the nations one by one, a practice I wrote about earlier. Sudan is a radical Muslim country, and, historically, there have been tremendous problems with Christians being killed in the south. In July 2011, the southern region became an independent nation, South Sudan.

The Sudanese leaders were not looking for Christians to come into their country to preach, and I was certain they were not looking for women to do so. So, I wondered how I could get into Sudan. One day, I spoke openly in a meeting at Billy Joe Daugherty's Victory Christian Center in Tulsa, Oklahoma, and said I would like to get into Sudan to hold meetings. I told them I had no contacts.

Afterward, someone sent me a fax saying he knew a Sudanese man who served in the Egyptian parliament. He said the man was a Christian, although he was backslidden, and he offered to give me his name and tell me how to reach him.

I contacted this man and asked if there was any way I could come to Khartoum and hold healing meetings. It took a period of time, but, eventually, he said yes, and we received permission. We put together a team of nine people. We invited pastors and leaders to the morning sessions, where we would teach them, provide lunch, and anoint them. We would also hold meetings in the early afternoons at a polo ground. In addition, since we always provide books in the languages of the countries we visit, we printed books in Arabic for them.

When we arrived in Khartoum, one of the pastors on our team said to me, "I don't know what this means, but a twelve-year-old girl in our church had a dream in which she saw the sun, three times, with a dark ring around it. Each time the dark ring appeared, it was like a palm tree, and part of the palm tree was cut down. What do you think this means?"

> **A twelve-year-old girl had a dream in which she saw the sun, three times, with a dark ring around it.**

I didn't have any idea what a dark ring around the sun meant. The pastor shared this dream with the rest of the team, as well. Sarah was with me at this meeting, so we prayed about it.

There were about 500 leaders in attendance at the daytime meetings, and, during the break after the morning session, they would go out from under the tent to drink hot tea. Even though the weather was very hot, people still drank hot tea.

The first day, I had gone back to my hotel room after teaching the early session. However, Sarah was teaching the day's remaining sessions, so she was drinking tea with the people during the break. All of a sudden, some of the people began to get excited. As I said earlier, in Africa, when the people get excited, they ululate.

Sarah asked one of the men, "Why are they ululating?"

He said, "Look at the sun."

Sarah looked and saw a dark ring around the sun.

"What do you think this means?" she asked.

"I don't know," he answered, "but I think it is something from God."

I did not see this sign, but Sarah told me about it later, saying, "Mom, God is cooking. Something is going on here."

We continued to pray and proceeded with plans for our first meeting at the polo grounds, but then everything seemed to fall apart. The buses that were supposed to pick up the people didn't show up. Some of the leadership we had depended on didn't come through. The leaders feared that if they came to our meeting, they could be killed. It was a challenging time.

When we got to the meeting, it was very hot, because we were sitting directly in the intense sun. There were not very many people in attendance, but when I got up to preach, I preached as if there had been 10,000 people there. I preached Jesus Christ and His healing power, and we saw some wonderful miracles.

Five afternoons of healing meetings had been scheduled. So, the next afternoon, I preached again, but while I was preaching, the people stood and began to run down the polo grounds for no apparent reason. They were ululating and falling down on the ground. I had totally lost their attention, and I thought to myself, *What is going on?*

I sent one of our staff members into the audience, along with an interpreter, to investigate what was happening. He came back and said to me, "The people saw a dark ring around the sun, and they saw Jesus' face in the sun."

What do you do at such a time? You have an altar call. You invite people to come forward and receive Jesus into their hearts. Who came? It seemed as if everyone came. We began praying for the sick, and, again, we saw dramatic miracles. By the fifth afternoon, approximately 15,000 people came.

Twin boys who had been born deaf were healed. There was a woman in a wheelchair who had arrived at the meeting with just enough money to pay her taxi fare; she had no money to get home. Jesus healed her at this meeting, so she did not need taxi money. She could walk home.

Even though God did remarkable miracles, I knew that the third ring had not yet appeared around the sun, as had happened in the dream. After we left, I was thinking that we should come back and hold another meeting in Khartoum.

The sign of Jesus' face in the sun had brought the people to repentance. Do you remember the biblical account of when

Peter had fished all night long but hadn't caught anything? (See Luke 5:1–11.) Jesus told him to go out into deep water and let down his net, and Peter and his fellow fishermen caught so many fish that the nets began to break and the boats began to sink. What was Peter's response to this phenomenon? He said, *"Depart from me, for I am a sinful man, O Lord!"* (verse 8).

Some people think that God hates sinners, but just the opposite is true. He wants to reveal Himself to people and bring them to repentance, not bash them to shreds. Yes, we know God will bring judgment, but, more than judgment, He wants to bring mercy. Mercy comes first. When people begin to see the manifestation of the power of God, they come to repentance by the thousands, as we saw in these incidents in Khartoum. God's revelation drew the people to Him.

> **When people begin to see the manifestation of the power of God, they come to repentance by the thousands.**

For ten years, I tried to return to Sudan, but it looked as if it would never happen. Finally, in 2007, we were able to return. We had an open healing meeting in Khartoum, and the vice president of Sudan attended every evening meeting. This time, 37,000 people attended on the first night, and more than 65,000 people came on the fourth night. Each night, about 8,000 people came forward to receive Jesus.

I remember one man in particular who had not been able to hear for twenty-three years, and God healed him. There was a woman who had not been able to bend over or move about for years who received complete mobility. Another woman had a huge growth on her arm, and the growth instantly disappeared during the meeting.

Although it was a great meeting, we had to have lots of security. I'm sure it was a miracle that I came home, and not in a box. Just as the Lord had protected me in China, He had protected me in Sudan. He has protected me wherever I have gone, and these instances were giant miracles to me.

I believe I will go to Sudan again and hold additional meetings, because the sign of the third ring around the sun has not yet occurred.

GIANT MIRACLES OF YESTERDAY, TODAY, AND FOREVER

The God of the Bible is also the God of our present day. The God who worked giant miracles when Jesus called Lazarus from the grave and fed more than 5,000 people by multiplying five loaves and two small fish, is the same *"yesterday, today, and forever"* (Hebrews 13:8). He is moving in our lives, and He moves in power.

In the account of Jesus turning water into wine at the wedding in Cana, we read, *"This beginning of signs Jesus did in Cana of Galilee, and manifested His glory; and His disciples believed in Him"* (John 2:11). Signs and wonders reveal the glory of God and cause many people to have faith. Note that it says *"...and His disciples believed in Him."*

The miracle at Cana, which was the first Jesus performed on earth, is amazing, isn't it? The groom had run out of wine, and Jesus' mother said to the servants who were waiting on the wedding guests, *"Whatever He says to you, do it"* (verse 5). Six stone waterpots stood close by, and Jesus told the servants, *"Fill the waterpots with water"* (verse 7). After they had done so, He told them to draw out some of the liquid and take it to the master of the feast. When they did, it was no longer water but high-quality wine. (See verses 8–10.)

I've meditated on this miracle recorded in the gospel of John many times, and it is interesting to me that it wasn't the bride, the groom, or the master of the feast who was involved in this miracle. It was the servants.

If someone told you, "Fill up these pots with water"—with twenty to thirty gallons in each pot—you might say, "What for?" But they did it. And they were the ones who drew out the "water," who served it to the master of the feast, and who knew where the wine had come from when they served it to the guests.

When people see the power of answered prayer, the power of the manifestation of God's Word, they want the Lord because they understand that He's real, personal, and wonderful.

We can be people of faith, saying what God says. We can line up our expectancy with God's Word in order to move mountains and turn situations and circumstances around.

My cousin and his wife had twin daughters, and one of the girls was brain damaged and had never walked. The doctors had confirmed that she would never walk. But there was a big healing meeting going on Denver, Colorado, and the girls' grandparents (my aunt and uncle) drove almost 450 miles from Dalhart, Texas, to go to it. During the meeting, which was attended by about 5,000 people, the evangelist pointed to my aunt and said, "The woman in the red hat. You have a granddaughter who has never walked. When you go home, she will be walking."

> **We can line up our expectancy with God's Word in order to turn situations and circumstances around.**

They drove all the way back to Texas, went to their son's home, and knocked on the door. Their daughter-in-law answered it, and she was crying. "I don't know what has happened, but Gerry is walking," she said.

REMEMBER AND BELIEVE

It says in the Psalms, *"All Your works shall praise You, O LORD, and Your saints shall bless You"* (Psalm 145:10). It is good to look back at what God has done for you in the past because it encourages you for the present and for the future. I believe God wanted the Israelites to remember the various miracles He had done for them so that, as their faith in Him grew, miracles would increase. For example, He instructed Joshua to build a memorial so the Israelites would never forget the miracle of their crossing the Jordan River into the Promised Land. The crossing took place in the spring, when the river was at flood stage. Yet, the moment the priests who carried the ark of the covenant stepped into the river, the water upstream stopped flowing, and they were able to pass through to the other side on dry ground. (See Joshua 3–4.)

We have a great God who does giant miracles! In the Scriptures, we read about many miracles He has done for His people; and, in our lives today, we experience His miracles. These miracles serve as memorials for us, as well, to build our faith for additional giant miracles to come.

REST STOP
ON YOUR PATHWAY TO MIRACLES

1. Have you experienced any "giant" miracles? What were they?

2. In order to build your faith, read about one or two miracles referenced in this book every morning and evening.

3. Memorize Matthew 19:26 and other Scriptures about God's power.

4. Write down a giant miracle you need God to do and begin to pray about it and believe for it.

BIBLICAL EXAMPLES AND SCRIPTURES RELATING TO "GIANT" MIRACLES

- *Miracle of the flood*:
  Genesis 7:1–8:19

- *Miracle of languages at Babel*:
  Genesis 11:1–9

- *Miracle of destruction of Sodom and Gomorrah*:
  Genesis 18:16–33; 19:15–25, 27–29

- *Miracle of Lot's wife becoming a pillar of salt*:
  Genesis 19:26

- *Miracle signs of Moses*:
  Exodus 4:1–17, 27–31

- *Miracle signs of the plagues in Egypt and the first Passover*:
  Exodus 7:1–12:36

- *Miracle of the pillars of cloud and fire*:
  Exodus 13:21–22; 14:19–20; 40:34–38

- *Miracle of the parting of the Red Sea*:
  Exodus 14; Psalm 106:7–12

- *Miracle of the victory over Amalek*:
  Exodus 17:8–16

- *Miracles at Sinai*:
  Exodus 19:16–25; Deuteronomy 5:4–22; 9:8–11, 15

- *Miracle of the journey through the wilderness*:
  Numbers 10:11–27:23; 31:1–33:49; Deuteronomy 8:2–4

- *Miracle of the sun standing still*:
  Joshua 10:12–14; Isaiah 28:21

- *Miracle of water turning into wine at Cana*:
  John 2:1–11

- *Miracles of Jesus' escapes from death*:
  Matthew 2:13–15; Luke 4:16–30; John 8:57–59;
  10:22–39

- *Miracle of mass healings*:
  Matthew 8:16–17; Mark 1:32–34; Luke 4:40–41

- *Miracle of feeding the 5,000*:
  Matthew 14:13–21; Mark 6:32–44; Luke 9:10–17;
  John 6:1–14

- *Miracle of the withered fig tree*:
  Matthew 21:17–22; Mark 11:12–14, 20–24

- *Miracle of Lazarus' resurrection*:
  John 11:1–45

- *Miracle of Jesus' resurrection*:
  Matthew 28:1–10, 16–20; Mark 16:1–18; Luke 24:1–
  49; John 20:1–21:14

- *Miracle of Jesus' ascension*:
  Mark 16:19–20; Luke 24:50–52; Acts 1:1–11

- *Miracle of Peter's shadow bringing healing*:
  Acts 5:12–16

- *Miracle of Herod's tragic death*:
  Acts 12:20–24

- *Miracle of salvation through Christ*:
  Romans 8:1–4; Ephesians 2:1–9; Colossians 2:11–15

CHAPTER 12

YOUR MIRACLE PACKAGE
Every Good and Perfect Gift Is from Above

Packages come in different shapes, sizes, and trappings. Some are beautifully decorated but contain objects that are not as glamorous as might be expected from the way they look on the outside. Others are plainly wrapped but hold items that have great value and are highly desired.

God's "miracle packages," which are always wonderful, come in different shapes and sizes, too, and they are delivered in a variety of ways. For example, some come in big "boxes," through the ministries of large organizations, while others come in small, plain "parcels," delivered in unexpected ways. Regardless of how your miracle packages come, they will affect not only you, but others, as well, sending ripples and waves of grace throughout your family, your community, your nation, or even the world.

MIRACLE PACKAGES THROUGH LARGE MINISTRIES

Thousands of people are in ministry today because of miracles that have come about through the direct involvement or lasting influence of large ministries, such as the Oral Roberts Evangelistic Association and Oral Roberts University. It seems as if everywhere I go in the world, I encounter graduates of ORU.

I wrote earlier about how I went on ministry trips to the former Soviet Union after the Iron Curtain fell. At one point, I had an opportunity to go Kiev, the capital and largest city of

Ukraine. First, I went on a preparatory trip—taking with me Mary Smith, my administrator—to make plans to take a whole team there later for healing meetings. The only contacts we had in Kiev were three young men who were ORU students on a mission there.

When we arrived, the students met us at the airport, and we got into a large cab to go to the hotel. It was dark, we were in a strange country with strange smells, we had traveled a long time and were both extremely tired, and we looked forward to eating and going to bed. But one of the students asked, "Would you mind if we went to pray for a demon-possessed girl before we take you to the hotel?"

I thought, *I don't feel spiritual, and maybe she doesn't even have demons.*

The students explained that they had been witnessing on the street when they'd come across a seventeen-year-old girl and her grandmother. The girl was crying because she had been to a fortune-teller, and she and her grandmother were sure this person had put an evil spell on her because she would cut her flesh and bleed, and the evil spirits would say to her, "I'm going to kill you."

After hearing this, there was no question in my mind that the girl was demon possessed. I asked, "Can we pray for her in the morning?"

> **I said to the Lord, *I'm tired.* He replied, *I am not.***

They said, "No, this is our only opportunity."

I said to the Lord, *I'm tired.*

He replied, *I am not.*

Who was going to deliver her? The Lord was, and He was not tired. So, we went to where the girl and her grandmother were. They had been watching a Jesus film in Russian.

This beautiful blonde girl named Natasha sat with her head on her knees, crying. Her grandmother looked confused.

Neither one spoke English, but we had a good interpreter, and I began to read Scriptures about Jesus and His delivering power. We prayed and cast out the demons, and Natasha fell on the floor, totally quiet. She lay there for five to ten minutes, and when she stood up, she was a different girl—she was free. Then, Natasha and her grandmother prayed to receive Jesus.

The next day, we made arrangements with the hotel for accommodations for the ministry team we would be bringing later for our healing meetings. Six months later, we flew into Kiev with a group of over one hundred people. Natasha was at the airport to meet me. She knew one sentence of English, and she said, "I love Jesus."

I saw Natasha in Ukraine four or five times after that. She married and had children, and she remained totally free in Jesus. And, her mother, father, brother, and sister-in-law also became Christians.

This is how miracles create ripples of God's grace. Mary and I went to Kiev to arrange a meeting, met three ORU students, and prayed for a young girl's deliverance from demons, out of which salvation came to her and her family. We later returned and held our healing meetings, which Natasha attended, and more people were saved. Entire lives were changed. That's a miracle package, delivered via connections with a large ministry and its mission.

Miracle Packages Through a Process

A miracle may not come into your life in the exact manner you would like or that you had imagined. A particular need may pave the way for God to bring forth the miraculous, but the road may become treacherous as your miracle makes its way toward you.

You've probably heard the old saying, "Necessity is the mother of invention." It may also be said,

A specific need will arouse your desire for a miracle, but then you will need to persevere to receive it.

"Desperation gives birth to design." In other words, a specific need will arouse your desire for a miracle, but then you will need to persevere to receive it.

This is what happened to me some years ago when I became very ill. I could not eat, and my stomach burned all the time. I began to lose weight, and I couldn't sleep, to the point that I became so weak I could hardly walk across the floor. In all of this anguish, I became depressed. It was hard for me to even read my Bible. I couldn't speak the Scriptures I had memorized over the years and had spoken so often, because it was difficult for my mind to focus. Of course, I went to doctors and underwent all kinds of tests, but they could find nothing wrong with me. It was distressing. One of the doctors said I needed counseling, because he thought I had a mental problem. I thought, *It's not my mind that's burning; it's my stomach.*

I prayed continually, and my staff and church did, too. I lost twenty pounds, and it was easy to see I was going downhill quickly. I canceled my traveling schedule, and my life appeared very bleak.

Finally, I changed doctors, and the new doctor ordered more tests. Even though he didn't have conclusive proof, I felt a glimmer of hope when he told me, "I believe you have parasites."

He continued with a long series of tests for parasites. Although the tests never indicated a positive result for them, the doctor was convinced that this was what was causing havoc in my body. He gave me strong antibiotics to take for a short period of time.

One night, while I was experiencing deep depression, I went to bed and had an unusual dream. Receiving dreams from God is not a normal occurrence for me. Once in a while, I've had spiritual dreams, but not often.

In this dream, I was in a European city and the sun was rising. I was walking up a hill that was part of a very busy street in the city. In my dream, I thought, *I'm well; look at me. I have the energy to walk up this hill. I feel fine. I'm going to call my office and tell them to start booking me, because I am fine.*

I awakened and quickly realized it wasn't true—I was still just as sick, and my stomach burned. However, in my spirit, I knew that I *would* be fine. I was in the process of receiving a miracle.

From that time forward, I got better. I'll never forget the first morning I smelled coffee again. It was a wonderful aroma, and I was elated to partake of something so normal to life. In fact, I stopped and thanked God for a good five minutes because the coffee smelled so good! Gradually, my appetite came back, and food tasted pleasant. And, increasingly, my energy returned. As it did, I regained my clarity of thought. Once again, things became clear, and I had focus. The depression definitely left me.

When people would ask me, "Well, are you going to get better, or is there a problem?" I would say, "I will be fine." Within two months, I began to travel again.

Two years after I had the dream, Sarah and I held a meeting in Naples, Italy, and we saw God do some fabulous things in that city. We drove to the meeting in the early evening, so it was still light out. As we started up a busy street, I thought to myself, *Why is this street so familiar to me?*

Then, I remembered. It was the street in my dream! That dream had been a fantastic revelation of God's wonderful love to me in my time of crisis—a promise of renewed health and of continued ministry. Because He had healed me, I could resume holding healing meetings around the world to bless others.

> **The dream had been a fantastic revelation of God's wonderful love to me in my time of crisis.**

I share this story with you to encourage you that a miracle package is not always instantaneous; it can be a process. I wanted a miracle of instant deliverance. I wanted God to touch me, and I wanted to be totally well. My miracle did not come quickly, but it did come.

BUILDING BRIDGES FOR MIRACLE PACKAGES

Although human beings have been connected to one another since Adam and Eve, our differences—of geographic location, language, culture, ethnicity, and so forth—may prevent miracles packages from being "delivered" unless the Lord intervenes to bridge the separation. Let me tell you how the Lord sent me out to offer such a link, so that His power and presence could be demonstrated to those who came from an entirely different culture than I.

In 2010, our ministry took a team of approximately 120 Americans to Morocco. I've been to Morocco three times, and I love the country, its people, and the response I've had there. The man who owned the tour company we were using, and who was a committed Muslim, had become a good friend. He asked me, "Do you want to go out to dinner with a group of Sufi Muslims?"

I had not had much opportunity to meet with Sufi Muslims, so I said yes.

Another name for Sufi is Dervish, and these people represent a small percentage of the Islamic movement. They like to experience Allah and are somewhat of an offshoot of Islam, yet they are committed to Muhammad and the Koran.

I went to the dinner and found that the guests were mostly businessmen—there was just one other woman there. When we sat down to talk, they asked me, "What are you doing in Morocco?"

I said, "I'm here to build bridges, not burn them. I would like to have a healing meeting here, because in the Koran it says that Jesus heals. I would like to pray for sick Muslims in the name of Jesus and see them healed."

I think that rocked their boat. I told them how I had been to Muslim countries all over the world, held healing meetings, and seen people transformed by the name of Jesus and the power of His Word. They were open to me. One of them said, "I want to ask you a personal question."

I said, "Okay, if I can answer, I'll try."

He said, "What do you do when you feel dry in your heart? What do you do when you are in that kind of position?"

I was shocked to be asked such a frank question by a Muslim, much less a Sufi Muslim, because they desire to experience God's presence. I said, "Basically, I've been a born-again Christian since I was sixteen. I am now seventy-nine. I have dry times. When I do, I read the Bible more, I pray more. I try to be around Christians of strong faith, because it helps pull me up out of it. I believe people go through arid times in their walks, but if you press into God, He talks to you and reveals Himself to you."

That broke the ice, and we went around the table in a circle, asking questions. There was a nice rapport. They asked me, "Have you read through the Bible?" I said, "Yes, fifty-five times." "Oh," they said, "then you know that it prophesies in the Bible that Muhammad will come? Have you seen that?"

I said, "No, I haven't."

They said, "Well, maybe you will see it when you read though the Bible the fifty-sixth time. But our understanding is that it is there."

These were the kinds of questions and answers they had, but the presence of the Holy Spirit at that table was unbelievable. We continued talking about Jesus, our faith, and the Koran. I believe a lot of bridges were built. God can work miracle packages if we lay a bridge of commonality—based on our knowledge, needs, experiences, hopes, and desires—between our differences.

> **God can work miracle packages if we lay a bridge of commonality between our differences with others.**

The Holy Spirit spoke to me and said, *Now, share with them a prophetic Scripture.*

I told them how the Holy Spirit gives me prophetic Scriptures for people. I asked them if they would mind if I gave them a Scripture out of the Bible in the name of Jesus. They said, "No, we wouldn't mind at all."

I gave Scriptures to everyone at the table, and the presence of God again came down upon us. We wept, and it was a very special time. One of the men said, "I'm going to get a musician here in the restaurant because I want to sing a song for you in Arabic called 'The Love of God.'" I didn't understand the song, but we all understood the reality of the presence of God with us.

I asked them, "Do you think I can come back and have a healing meeting, just for Sufi Muslims?" They said, "We believe you can do that." I said, "Of course, I am going to teach the Bible and pray in the name of Jesus."

God knows how to package miracles, doesn't He? He does it in the power of the Holy Spirit and the Word of God. I believe I will go back to Morocco and have a miracle healing meeting, and I believe it will be with Sufis.

The Sufis also told me something curious about the Berbers, who are the indigenous people of Morocco. Sixty-four percent of Moroccans are Berbers, and they have gone to the government and said, "We want to return to our roots. Our roots are not Islam. In the seventh century, we became Islamic because we were forced to. Before that, we were Christians."

I asked them, "What will the government say?"

"Their response will be no."

"What will the Berbers do?

"They will worship Jesus anyway."

We have a big God, and He does big things. He does not see our differences with other peoples; He sees our common need for His Son and for the Holy Spirit. He knows that miracle packages that impact other peoples for Christ can come only when we set aside our differences and come together with them to partake of Him "*in spirit and truth*" (John 4:24).

Persevering for Your Miracle Package

It's a difficult challenge to hold fast through distressing circumstances and adversities while waiting for a miracle package. However, if you do hold on, in due time, your faith will reap the miraculous.

> **If you hold on, in due time, your faith will reap the miraculous.**

Some years ago, I met a woman named Ochibo who was a Japanese pastor, and she told me her testimony. A Christian woman from America had come to Japan with her husband, who was in the military. When this woman saw an article in the newspaper featuring Ochibo and describing her doctorate and professorship, the Lord said to her, *I want you to tell her about Me, and I want you to send her a Christian book once a month, for twelve months.*

She called Ochibo and explained what God had spoken to her, telling her that she would be sending her a Christian book once a month for twelve months and that she would like her to read the books.

Ochibo responded, "I don't want any Christian books. Don't send them to me. If I get it, I will throw it into the wastebasket. I will not read it. I am not interested in being a Christian. I am a Buddhist, and that's what I'm going to remain. That's what I and my family are, and that's what I'm going to continue to be."

But the Christian woman felt that God had spoken to her and that she was to do this. So, once a month, for twelve months, she sent Ochibo a book, and then she called her, asking, "Did you get the book I sent you?"

"Yes, I just threw it in the trash."

At the twelfth month, the woman called and said again, "Did you get the book?"

"Yes, I got the book," Ochibo replied. "I told you not to send me those books. I just threw that one in the trash, too."

The woman replied, "I won't send you any more books, because God only told me to do this for twelve months."

However, that night, Ochibo had a dream in which she had a visitation from Jesus Christ, and she had a far-reaching experience with Him. Afterward, Ochibo called the woman and told her how she had met Jesus through her dream. They had a wonderful time visiting on the phone; they were both thrilled and excited, and the American started to mentor her.

Ochibo thought her family would love what had happened to her, and she told her mother, sister, and brother. They were from a wealthy, well-known family, and they were not thrilled. In fact, her brother beat her. Ochibo said that it didn't make any difference; she maintained her faith in Jesus.

Then, her sister, who also was a professor at the campus where Ochibo taught, told her that she was an embarrassment to her. She also informed her that she used to think Ochibo was wonderful, but now that she was a "crazy Christian," she was no longer welcome in her home.

But Ochibo persevered and prayed, and, today, all her family members serve God. Ochibo pastors a church of more than 500 people. She also has a "prayer mountain," similar to the one Dr. Cho established in Korea to give people a private, quiet place to pray for an extended time.

If we're listening to God, and we persevere, as the American military wife and Ochibo did, He will bring about miracle packages. Nothing is impossible for God. Here are three basic but essential keys to receiving your miracle package:

1. Look to God

In the book of Genesis, we read about a time when Jacob had a terrible problem in front of him. He'd experienced other serious difficulties before, but this one was perhaps the worst he'd ever confronted because it could cost him his life. He had to face his brother, Esau, whom he hadn't seen in twenty years. Jacob had needed to flee his family and his home all those years ago because Esau wanted to kill him. Frankly, it was

Jacob's fault that there was animosity between them, because he had cheated Esau out of the blessing and had taken advantage of him to gain his birthright. Likewise, some of the problems you are dealing with may have been caused by you, and you may be thinking, *Then, God can't do the impossible, because it's my fault.* Yes, God can still do the impossible, even when you have done wrong. Let's look at what Jacob did, starting with the backdrop to his story.

> **God can still do the impossible, even when you have done wrong.**

Jacob was living in Padan Aram, or Mesopotamia, in the city of Nahor. He was wealthy, and he had two wives, two concubines, and eleven children. God told him, "*Return to the land of your fathers* [the Promised Land] *and to your family, and I will be with you*" (Genesis 31:3). So, he packed up his family and all his belongings and began the journey home, but, the whole time, he knew he would have to encounter Esau. When he sent messengers ahead to tell Esau he was coming, they reported that Esau was riding out with four hundred men to meet him.

Jacob could have said, "I'm not going to face Esau; I'm going to go back." But if he returned to Padan Aram, he'd have to face his father-in-law, Laban, who was a major reason he had left, because Laban had cheated him and had become increasingly jealous of him.

So, what did he do? He looked to God.

I find it interesting that when God told Noah to build the ark, He told him to put in one window, and that window faced up; it was on the roof. (See Genesis 6:16.) When you look around, you can get in trouble. And, sometimes, when you look within yourself, you can get into trouble. But if you look up to God, then He can take the "impossible" and make it possible through His power and grace.

So, Jacob looked up to God and had a prayer meeting, asking Him for deliverance. Then, the Bible says, a "*Man*" met him and wrestled with him all night, until He said to Jacob, "*Let*

Me go, for the day breaks" (Genesis 32:26). What was Jacob's response? *"I will not let You go unless You bless me!"* (verse 26).

That's being aggressive, and I have learned that God likes aggressiveness. I haven't found anybody about whom God has said, "Oh, he's too aggressive in his faith." God is always saying, "Come on up; get aggressive." (See, for example, Hebrews 4:16.)

Jacob had said, *"I will not let You go unless You bless me!"* and he was blessed. When he encountered Esau, he discovered that his brother had forgiven him, and he was welcomed with open arms. Later, God told Jacob,

> *Be fruitful and multiply; a nation and a company of nations shall proceed from you, and kings shall come from your body. The land which I gave Abraham and Isaac I give to you; and to your descendants after you I give this land.* (Genesis 35:11–12)

All of this happened because Jacob looked to God and wouldn't let go of Him. (See Genesis 31:1–3; 32–33.)

2. Don't Give Up

The second key is found in a parable Jesus told about a widow and a judge, through which He taught us how to pray and hold on until the impossible becomes possible. Even when we're pressed to the wall, we do not need to give up.

> [Jesus said,] *"There was in a certain city a judge who did not fear God nor regard man. Now there was a widow in that city; and she came to him, saying, 'Get justice for me from my adversary.' And he would not for a while; but afterward he said within himself, 'Though I do not fear God nor regard man, yet because this widow troubles me I will avenge her, lest by her continual coming she weary me.'"* Then the Lord said, *"Hear what the unjust judge said. And shall God not avenge His own elect who cry out day and night to Him, though He bears long with them? I tell you that He will avenge them speedily. Nevertheless, when*

the Son of Man comes, will He really find faith on the earth?" (Luke 18:2–8)

The judge was unfair. Some of you may be dealing with people like that, but you have to remember that God knows how to work on them.

The widow probably didn't have a lot of money, and she most likely didn't have family to help her, so she ended up going to the judge for help. But he turned her away, saying, in effect, "I don't want to be bothered with you. I don't like people, and I don't like widows, so just get out of here."

Did she give up? No. Could the impossible become possible? Let's find out. She went back again, and when the judge saw her, he probably said something like, "You, again? Don't bug me. You're a little, unknown woman, and I don't want you here, so get lost."

But she didn't "get lost." She went back again and again, until the judge said, *"Yet because this widow troubles me I will avenge her, lest by her continual coming she weary me"* (verse 5).

Jesus said we need to pray in the way the widow appealed to the judge—with persistence and perseverance. He was telling us that the game is not over until you win. We need to take to heart the purpose for which He told this parable: that we *"always ought to pray and not lose heart"* (verse 1).

> **Jesus said that we *"always ought to pray and not lose heart"* (Luke 18:1).**

If you give up, you're never going to win, but if you hold on in prayer, you will see the miracle packages God has for your life. He will take the seemingly impossible situation you're in and make it possible.

Our ministry took a team of about 150 people on a ship bound for Ruse, Bulgaria, on the Danube River. The majority of the team was to disembark there for our two nights of healing meetings. I was also to conduct a ministry training school there during the day, so one of the staff people and I got off the ship a little early to take an overnight train to Ruse, and we arrived the day before the ship was to come to port.

After we got there, the pastor in Ruse told me our team would never be allowed off the ship. A Youth With A Mission ship had come and docked there the previous year, but none of the staff members had been permitted ashore. This pastor told me, in so many words, "Your people will never get off; it'll never happen; you can hang it up and forget it." He went on telling me that the ship would dock, but they would not get off. He was sure that, rather than having 150 people at the meeting, the only ones present would be myself and the staff member who had ridden the train with me.

You know, some people are just full of good news.

I went to the hotel and prayed, *God, am I going to believe his words more than Your Word?* God's Word says that I always triumph in Christ. (See 2 Corinthians 2:14.) It doesn't say "a third of the time," and it doesn't say "half of the time." It says "*always*." So, again, the game is not over until we win.

The next day, I taught at the ministry training school. The ship was scheduled to dock at three o'clock in the afternoon, and I experienced some anxiety about what the pastor had said. But I prayed, "No, God, I'm not going to be anxious. I will always triumph in Christ; all things are possible to him who believes; You can take the impossible and make it possible," and so on.

I taught and preached at the school until almost three. In my heart, I prayed, *God, I believe You. I believe they're going to get off that ship.*

At three thirty, my son-in-law, Reece, walked into the auditorium. They were off the ship.

The icing on the cake was when my daughter, Sarah, preached, and a boy with a blind eye was healed. If we had doubted, that never would have happened.

Don't give up. The game is not over until you win!

3. Ask, Seek, Knock

The third point comes from another of Jesus' teachings recorded in the gospel of Luke.

> *And He said to them, "Which of you shall have a friend, and go to him at midnight and say to him, 'Friend, lend me three loaves; for a friend of mine has come to me on his journey, and I have nothing to set before him'; and he will answer from within and say, 'Do not trouble me; the door is now shut, and my children are with me in bed; I cannot rise and give to you'? I say to you, though he will not rise and give to him because he is his friend, yet because of his persistence he will rise and give him as many as he needs."* (Luke 11:5–8)

Now, think about this. At midnight, would you like someone to come knocking on your door, saying, "Hey, I'd like to borrow three loaves of bread"? You might call back to him, "Well, go buy some. There must be a convenience store nearby."

The situation described in this parable was more serious than we might think, according to our modern perspective of things. In those days, people's doors contained a fold-up bed, because they lived in small quarters. At night, they would lock the door and let the bed down. Then, the family members would all climb into the one bed. Therefore, at midnight, the husband would be in bed with his wife and all his children.

Can you picture someone knocking on the door and asking for bread in the middle of the night under those conditions? The husband would have to awaken his wife and children (if they weren't awake already from the knocking), get everyone out of bed, lift up the bed, unlock the door while the wife or another family member went to get the bread, give the person the bread, then lock the door again, lower the bed, and have everyone get back in. After that, they would have to hope they could all get back to sleep!

Jesus said that it wasn't because the person was a friend, but because he kept knocking, that the man got tired of being disturbed and said, "Okay, we'll get up and get you the bread!"

That's the way to pray. Never give up until you win. Jesus said so.

When we held healing meetings in Vera Cruz, Mexico, a woman gave the following testimony one night: When she was in her early fifties, she was in a car accident, and her shoulder was severely injured. She underwent surgery in which pins were inserted, but she was told she would never lift her arm again.

So, this woman prayed, "God, I'm going to believe You to restore my shoulder." She stood on the Word and stood on the Word, and nothing happened. However, she kept saying, "God, I'm believing You to restore my shoulder."

Five years later, while she was cooking, she reached for something in the cupboard using the arm with the bad shoulder. She had the total use of her hand, arm, and shoulder.

When a miracle happens to one person, it builds faith in others to receive, also.

After she gave this testimony, there were about a hundred miracle healings of shoulders in the meeting. Do you see that when a miracle happens to one person, it builds faith in others to receive, also? God is so economical that He gets extra mileage out of the one miracle. This is a great example of a miracle package.

In a similar way, because God did a miracle to enable our team to get off that ship in Ruse, Bulgaria, we were able to do more than minister to the pastors at the training school; we were also able to hold our healing meetings in the evenings. God wanted the boy who had been born with a blind eye to be healed. At that time, the people in Bulgaria had barely come out of Communism. God demonstrated that the Bible is true and that He can make the "impossible" possible.

At the conclusion of His parable, Jesus told us what to do to receive miracles by describing intense persistence—not giving up.

> So I say to you, ask, and it will be given to you; seek,
> and you will find; knock, and it will be opened to you.
> For everyone who asks receives, and he who seeks
> finds, and to him who knocks it will be opened.
> (Luke 11:9–10)

How did Jesus teach us to move from the impossible into the miraculous? First, He said, we are to ask. Now, any of us can ask. I can ask any nine things in one minute. Asking is not hard. And so, you may say, "Well, I asked God for a miracle, and nothing happened."

Did you keep believing, or did you give up? The second point Jesus made in the above statement is that we need to seek.

At one point, Sarah was going through a hard time with her faith. I was in Japan at the time speaking at a conference for Dr. Cho, and I had a horrible dream about her. I had asked God to deliver her, but, in the dream, her situation was even worse. I awoke, got out of bed, and began to pray in the Spirit. Then, I fasted. In other words, I began to seek, and God answered, bringing Sarah through this difficult period.

Seeking is like spiritual warfare. We don't say, "Oh well, He didn't answer me." If you have not yet received an answer to prayer, you may need to fast and get into intense prayer. You may need to pray for a longer period of time than you have prayed. Often, I use the times when I am driving in my car to pray in the Spirit. There are days when I can get in an hour of praying in tongues that way.

Still, you may say, "I've asked, and I've been seeking, but nothing's happened." Well, don't give up, because the next step is to knock.

Now, knocking gets "violent." The Bible says, *"From the days of John the Baptist until now the kingdom of heaven suffers violence, and the violent take it by force*" (Matthew 11:12). The *New International Version* puts it this way: "*...the kingdom of heaven has been forcefully advancing, and forceful men lay hold of it.*"

How aggressive are you willing to be to see God move, taking the impossible and making it possible?

There was a time when I began to gain a little extra weight, and I thought, *I need to exercise.* So, I had a trainer work with me. She taught me how to use an exercise band, and it strengthened me. Although it helped, I still wanted to lose more weight.

My trainer told me, "It's not about just losing some inches and weight, but it's about staying healthy." She took me from using the exercise band to lifting weights. I compare the exercise band to the "asking" part of prayer and the weights to the "seeking" part. These were little weights; they started at five pounds. But then I moved to ten-pound weights, and I saw that twelve-pound ones were next. The weights were a challenge, and I began to gripe about them, saying, "Oh, these weights are so hard."

My trainer said, "If you don't quit talking negatively about it, you'll end up not doing them at all."

I replied, "Oh, that's the end of that. I love weights. I love weights. Weights are wonderful."

However, I still didn't get all the results I wanted. My weight was better, I was losing inches, my energy was good, but I didn't have what I *desired.* To get it, I would need the "knocking" type of faith.

My trainer told me to do a workout with a weight ball. We went through the exercise, and I said, "That's impossible."

The first time I tried doing the exercise, I could not do it, but I kept trying. It was strenuous, and it called for all the strength and control I had. But, today, I can do the exercise twenty times in a row.

Every day, I had to bear down on that exercise and press in with a determination that would "move a mountain." That's "knocking" faith.

If we will do what Jesus tells us to do, "impossible" miracle packages will become possible ones. Believe Him for your miracle package. Believe that He can bring it to you, no matter what form it comes in, through your perseverance in faith—through asking, seeking, and knocking.

If we will do what Jesus tells us to do, "impossible" miracle packages will become possible ones.

Rest Stop
on Your Pathway to Miracles

1. What "miracle packages" have you seen—miracles that affect not only the person who receives them directly, but also others, as God's grace and power ripples out from them?

2. Memorize Hebrews 10:23 and 1 Corinthians 10:13.

3. Meditate on Luke 11:9–10.

4. The fruit of the Spirit is listed in Galatians 5:22–23, and one of the fruit is *"longsuffering,"* or *"patience"* (NIV). Memorize this passage and think about what the word *"longsuffering"* or *"patience"* means to you as you look to God for your miracle.

5. Intense persistence in asking, seeking, and knocking will be fortified by a knowledge of God's faithfulness and a commitment to be faithful to Him. Read and then speak aloud Scriptures such as the following: Deuteronomy 7:9; Psalm 31:23; Psalm 101:6; Psalm 119:90; Lamentations 3:22–23; Matthew 24:45–47; 1 Corinthians 1:9.

BIBLICAL EXAMPLES AND SCRIPTURES RELATING TO MIRACLE PACKAGES

- *Miracle of the smoking oven and burning torch*:
  Genesis 15:7–21

- *Miracle of Isaac's birth*:
  Genesis 17:15–19; 18:10–14; 21:1–8

- *Miracle of Hagar's well*:
  Genesis 21:9–21

- *Miracle of Jacob's deliverance from Esau*:
  Genesis 31:1–3; 32–33

- *Miracle of Solomon's wisdom*:
  1 Kings 3:4–14; 4:29–34

- *Miracles of Jesus*:
  Luke 4:16–21; John 21:25; Acts 10:38–39

- *Miracle of Peter's spiritual preservation*:
  Luke 22:31–34; John 21:15–17

- *Miracle of the outpouring of the Spirit at Pentecost*:
  Acts 2

- *Miracle of Paul's deliverance from conspiracy*:
  Acts 23

CHAPTER 13

MIRACLES OF OPPORTUNITY
Open Doors and Unexpected Blessings

Miracles of opportunity are open doors from God that enable us to fulfill His purposes in our lives. Some require special alertness on our part. They may be right at our fingertips, but we don't see them because we're not actively looking for them. The Bible teaches that we are to stay spiritually alert until Jesus returns, and one of the ways we can do this is by recognizing the opportunities for miraculous events He provides us. Rewards will come if we stay watchful. We need to take Jesus' reminder to heart: *"Watch, therefore, for you do not know when the master of the house is coming...lest, coming suddenly, he find you sleeping. And what I say to you, I say to all: Watch!"* (Mark 13:35–37). We need to take part in the opportunities He sends our way.

Opportunities may also come in the midst of situations we don't like or don't realize God has allowed for a purpose. He permits curious circumstances to come our way at times to give us open doors for the miraculous. Through the years, I have found that, many times, circumstances that seem unhelpful at first are opportunities in disguise.

I thank God for the miracle of opportunities. We never know what doors God may open, so we need to be discerning in regard to the people and circumstances He brings into our lives.

MIRACLE OPPORTUNITIES FOR WITNESSING

God is an "opportunist" and wants us to listen to the Holy Spirit and learn how we can use the openings He provides for us to tell others about Him. Just as a surfer will wait for the right break in the tide and the right wave to ride back to shore, we need to be watchful for the movement of the Spirit.

To Those You Meet as You Go About Your Life

Earlier, I mentioned how I often witness while traveling by plane. Let me tell you about another such instance that illustrates a miracle of opportunity. Once, when I was returning home from Indonesia, a Japanese businessman boarded the plane at our layover stop in Tokyo and sat down beside me. He spoke English perfectly, so I thought, *Perhaps this is an opportunity*. I prayed in the Spirit so that I would be sensitive and not turn him off. Then, I asked him about his work, and he told me he dealt with steel corporations and came to the United States a lot. He appeared to be successful and a very nice gentleman.

He asked me, "What do you do?"

My opportunity to witness opened. I told him that I taught the Bible, had a daily television program that reached two billion viewers every weekday, and had traveled to Buddhist, Communist, Hindu, and Muslim countries and found that I loved them all. I loved the Buddhists because they taught peace and had wonderful values for living. I so appreciated the Communist countries' rich heritage of religious teachings. I loved the Hindus because of their family values and because their principles of life were outstanding. I concluded by saying I'd read most of the Koran and gone to many Muslim countries and had fallen in love with the people. I then said, "Let me tell you what I am."

He responded, "You are a Christian, correct?"

"I would call myself a Jesus person," I said. "When I studied Buddhism, I saw that though they had wonderful values, they had no way for me to approach a perfect God; they offered nothing by which I could remove my sin. I also didn't find what I needed in Hinduism to get me to God. Their values were outstanding, but, again, there was no way for me to approach a perfect God. Though I loved the Muslims, I didn't find anything in the Koran that could address my sin issue, either;

I could only work and work and hope that God would take me to paradise.

"But when I heard about Jesus, I learned that He was God's Son, that He was perfect, that He never sinned, and that He shed His blood and gave His life for my sins. God raised Him from the dead. When I received Jesus, He took my sin, and now I have a way to approach God."

The man sat quietly as I spoke. I told him how I had invited Jesus into my life, and how He walks with me and talks with me. I said that He's the author of my Bible, the book that comes from His heart. "I don't call myself a Christian. I am a Jesus person," I repeated.

He said, "No one has ever told me this before."

I gave him a card with the sinner's prayer on it, and I felt that he would pray to receive Christ. We had a wonderful time during our flight, and I saw him later coming through customs. Perhaps I will never see him again, but I believe a "God opportunity" transpired the day I flew from Tokyo to San Francisco.

Watch for opportunities to share your faith, too, because they don't always take place where you might think. They can happen in a store, a taxicab, or anywhere else the Spirit of God decides to move.

> **Watch for opportunities to share your faith because they don't always take place where you might think.**

Rarely will people turn you down if you ask, "Can I pray for you?" Strangers of all ages and all walks of life will accept a prayer. Opportunity is always at your door. Be available, warm, and considerate. You don't have to be "religious," just loving.

To Muslim "Gentiles"

In the early church, the rejection of Christ by a number of the Jews at Antioch prompted a dramatic turning point in the apostles' ministry:

> *Then Paul and Barnabas grew bold and said, "It was necessary that the word of God should be spoken to you first; but since you reject it, and judge yourselves unworthy of everlasting life, behold, we turn to the Gentiles."*   (Acts 13:46)

Perhaps a quote from the prophet Isaiah flashed through Paul's mind at the time and gave him fresh direction and inspiration for his God-given mission:

> *And now the LORD says, who formed Me from the womb to be His Servant, to bring Jacob back to Him, so that Israel is gathered to Him (for I shall be glorious in the eyes of the LORD, and My God shall be My strength), indeed He says, "It is too small a thing that You should be My Servant to raise up the tribes of Jacob, and to restore the preserved ones of Israel; I will also give You as a light to the Gentiles, that You should be My salvation to the ends of the earth."*   (Isaiah 49:5–6)

The call to take the gospel to both Gentiles and Jews is for each and every one of us. We can have miracle opportunities to share Christ with those who do not know Him.

One of the greatest opportunities I have had to minister to Muslim Gentiles was in Detroit, Michigan. After having ministered in Muslim countries for many years, my heart began to go out to mosques in the United States. I didn't see a lot of mosques, but, every now and then, I would see one in a certain city, and I would think, *How can we reach people in that mosque? No Christian is allowed in a mosque—certainly not a woman, and definitely not a Christian woman.*

Yet, in His wonderful love and wisdom, God can turn a negative situation into a positive one. He can take what looks like a closed door and make it an open door of opportunity.

I love to go to Detroit, especially to Word of Faith Church, whose pastor is Bishop Keith Butler. Bishop Butler has traveled with me to Pakistan twice and has a great passion for the nations and for the lost. Word of Faith is a church character-ized by prayer and strong faith in God's Word.

I spoke at this church several years ago for a two-day seminar on the gospel of John, and my topic was "The Seven 'I Am's' of Jesus." In one of the morning sessions, I made this bold statement: "The largest num-bers of Muslims in the United States are in Dearborn, Michigan. I believe God could open a door for me to have a healing meeting in a mosque. If He can open big doors overseas in Islamic countries, why can't He open the door to the Muslims in our nation?"

> **"If God can open big doors overseas in Islamic countries, why can't He open the door to the Muslims in our nation?"**

I did not speak this as a prophetic word. I said it casually to the crowd.

That morning, among those in attendance was a woman who worked in the political sphere. She heard my statement, and it challenged her. Afterward, she called me and said, "I work in the government. I know an imam, a leader of a mosque, who per-haps would be open to having a healing meeting in his mosque."

God bless her. She began to call and try the doors for such an opportunity, and she gained an interview for me with one of the major Islamic leaders in the Dearborn area.

Our global director, Stephen Kiser, went with me, and we sat down with a Shiite imam who had been in the States for more than fourteen years and was the leader of The House of Wisdom mosque in Dearborn. He brought a board member to hear what we had to say.

I shared with him how much I love the Muslim people and how much I like to pray for the sick, especially in Muslim coun-tries. I told him how I had been in Pakistan, Sudan, and other Islamic countries and had held large healing meetings, and I told him I had videotapes of the meetings. He was surprised.

He did not question or argue with me, but he told me very bluntly that he was not interested. He said it would not work in his mosque; it just wouldn't happen. He also shared with me that he had been a chaplain to the navy in Iran and that, periodically, he would go back there. In no way did he offer me an opportunity to do what I wanted to do in his mosque.

When I tell you everything I wanted to do, you will understand his hesitation. Not only did I want to have a healing meeting and invite the Muslims of the Dearborn area to come and be healed, but I also wanted to broadcast a recording of the meeting on our television program. I wanted to share it with our worldwide audience and show them what God can do in the Islamic world.

As I said, he was quite negative toward my proposal, and so was his board member. However, I didn't give up. I didn't think that because someone told me, "You can't do it," God couldn't do it.

At the end of our meeting, as I was preparing to leave, he said to me, "The next time you're in Detroit, I would like you to come to my home, pray for my wife, and have dinner with us. Would you be willing to do this?"

I thought, *Of course, I would be willing.* It was an unusual open door, and I agreed.

Six months later, I was in the Detroit area, and Stephen called the imam and set up a time for us to have dinner at his home. He was so gracious to us. His wife, a very lovely American who had converted to Islam, hosted a beautiful dinner. We took our time and listened to what he shared about Iran, his life, and the wisdom he felt in the Islamic community. After perhaps an hour, he said to me, "Marilyn, what is it that you want to do in the mosque?"

I told him again, "I would like to have a healing meeting. I would like to advertise it and invite Muslims to come, and then pray for the sick. Also, I would like to record the meeting on DVD, as well as interview you, and then present it on my telecast to an audience of over two billion people."

He said, "Marilyn, I believe we can do this." He went to get the Koran and looked up what was written about Jesus. As I mentioned previously, the Koran says Jesus heals the sick.

Six months later, we went to The House of Wisdom in Detroit and held two nights of healing meetings. The women had their heads covered, and I also dressed appropriately. The first night, the meeting was in the mosque itself, where they have their general meetings. There was not a big crowd (perhaps one hundred people attended), but I knew this was an awesome opportunity. In the past 1,400 years, there had not been an open Christian healing meeting in a mosque, much less a Christian woman speaker.

> **In the past 1,400 years, there had not been an open Christian healing meeting in a mosque, much less a Christian woman speaker.**

The iman and I had rehearsed exactly what would happen during the service. He would introduce me, give a small Islamic sermon, and then introduce two of his young leaders, who would participate in the program by reading from the Koran. One was a teenage boy and the other was a young girl. After that, I would speak and then pray for people's healing.

After the young people read from the Koran, the imam introduced me again by explaining that the Koran says Jesus heals. He told how we were friends and how I had come to preach about Jesus from the Bible and to pray for the sick.

I tell you openly and honestly that I taught in that mosque as I would teach in a Christian church. I had chosen one miracle of Jesus from John 5:1–9, which we will look at shortly, and I told the people how Jesus had healed the crippled man at the pool of Bethesda. I preached about how Jesus is the same yesterday, today, and forever, and how He wanted to heal the sick that night. I was allowed thirty minutes to speak, and we were able to record the entire service on DVD.

Then, I asked God to give me words of knowledge for the different sicknesses of those in the audience, and, when He did, I had the people stand. I prayed for their needs in the name of Jesus. I asked people to extend their hands toward those in need, and they joined me in praying in the name of Jesus. I shared Psalm 107:20, *"He sent His word and healed them, and delivered them from their destructions."* I sent the Word into their bodies and asked God for total healing. I then asked them to share their testimonies. The teenage boy who had earlier read from the Koran had a great miracle of healing in his eye and came forward to testify. Several others testified of healings in their backs. It was a short meeting but a good one.

Afterward, we shared refreshments. I sat down at a table, and a Muslim man approached me and asked me to pray for his wife's healing. It was another unusual opportunity, and I found him to be warm and courteous.

The second night, we were invited to a dinner hosted by the imam. There were eleven other imams there, plus various leaders from the Islamic community. Also in attendance were a Spirit-filled Catholic priest and a rabbi. I was encouraged because the imam was quite open to building bridges of communication. That night, I again taught from the Bible. I talked about Jesus and prayed for the sick. And, once more, people came to my table and wanted me to pray for them. It was a wonderful evening.

I presented the imam and his wife with my own personal Bible and encouraged him to read the four Gospels. He replied by saying, "I've read the Bible once. I will read it again."

We had negative responses from two of the imams, who became very angry and left the dinner. However, the rest were warm and open to us. They presented me with a lovely clock, which I keep in my office as a reminder of what God did in those services.

You might be thinking, *This was just a small meeting.* But what God did was to shatter history. Remember, this had never been done in over 1,400 years.

I've asked the imam if he thought it would be possible for me to hold a healing meeting in Tehran, Iran. All I can say is that he has not been negative.

I spent a brief time in his office as we recorded an interview with him, and we have shown this interview on our television program. What God will do with all of this, I do not know. But I believe Muslims will come to know Jesus Christ as their personal Savior and invite Him to be Lord of their lives.

Since those meetings, the imam's wife has had a baby. Recently, they invited me to come and spend the night in their home. I have not taken advantage of that opportunity yet, but I would like to when I return to Detroit.

In addition, I have been offered another opportunity to speak in a mosque in Indonesia. We cannot think that God will not open opportunities for the miraculous! We need to watch for those doors and not give up, because we have a miracle-working God. He wants to work miracles in your life, if you will let Him.

> **God wants to work miracles in your life, if you will let Him.**

Some people may question why I want to pray with Muslims, since they are at odds with Israel. I believe that as people from all walks of life—Muslims, Buddhists, Hindus—experience the love of God and His healing power, the Spirit of God will change them from within. When I came to know the Lord, I experienced love for my fellow man, and as love becomes the dominating factor, there will be less hatred, and we will all be blessed, including Israel. My prayer is that Israel will also experience our wonderful God.

MIRACLE OPPORTUNITIES FOR HEALING THROUGH WORDS OF KNOWLEDGE

Some miracle opportunities come through words of knowledge concerning people's sicknesses. The Scriptures say, *"For the LORD gives wisdom; from His mouth come knowledge and understanding"* (Proverbs 2:6), and *"To one is given the word of wisdom through the Spirit, to another the word of knowledge through the same Spirit"* (1 Corinthians 12:8).

Several times, I have mentioned instances when I have received words of knowledge from God during healing meetings about people's illnesses and asked them to stand and be healed, such as I did in the mosque in Michigan. We see various examples of words of knowledge that led to healing in the Bible. For example, we previously noted how Naaman the Syrian was healed through Elisha the prophet. Elisha had received a word from God that Naaman should dip seven times in the Jordan River, and then he would receive his healing. (See 2 Kings 5:1–14.)

In the New Testament, Jesus had a word of knowledge for healing when He went to Jerusalem for the Passover feast.

> *Now there is in Jerusalem by the Sheep Gate a pool, which is called in Hebrew, Bethesda, having five porches. In these lay a great multitude of sick people, blind, lame, paralyzed, waiting for the moving of the water. For an angel went down at a certain time into the pool and stirred up the water; then whoever stepped in first, after the stirring of the water, was made well of whatever disease he had. Now a certain man was there who had an infirmity thirty-eight years.*
> (John 5:2–5)

Jesus caught sight of this man, and He must have inquired about him, because the Bible indicates He learned that he had been in this condition for some time. Jesus asked him, *"Do you want to be made well?"* (verse 6). He gave the man his opportunity for a miracle.

The sick man answered Him, *"Sir, I have no man to put me into the pool when the water is stirred up; but while I am coming, another steps down before me"* (verse 7).

God the Father had revealed to Jesus the manner in which the man would be healed, and Jesus said, *"Rise, take up your bed and walk"* (John 5:8). The man was instantly cured, and he took up his bed and walked, as Jesus had told him to. (See verse 9.) Later, we see that Jesus received an additional word of knowledge about him when He told him, *"See, you have been made well. Sin no more, lest a worse thing come upon you"* (verse 14).

Another biblical instance of a word of knowledge is when Jesus spoke with the Samaritan woman at the well and told her that she'd had five husbands and was living with a sixth man. The accuracy of Jesus' knowledge of her life, when this was the first time He had ever met her, was a means by which the woman came to faith in Jesus as Messiah and experienced spiritual rebirth. This is also an example of a "package miracle," since her encounter with Jesus led to the salvation of many in her town. (See John 4:3–42.)

Recently, I had a meeting in Richmond, Virginia, where I was privileged to preach and participate in another miracle of God involving a word of knowledge that I gave during the service. A woman was healed, and this is an excerpt of the testimony I received from her:

> I had the pleasure of sitting under the anointed message that you preached on this past Sunday, April 3, 2011. I attended both services, but my healing took place at the 11:30 service. This is what happened. You asked for everyone that had a tumor, wart, or cyst to stand up. For a minute, it didn't register, because I had been carrying that cyst in my breast so long I forgot to stand up. Over the years, as I would have my yearly checkup, my doctor would tell me that if they removed the cyst, it would leave a large hole in my breast because the mass was so large. Thank God, every year they checked, it was never cancerous. The Holy Spirit jolted me and prompted me to stand up. You began to pray, and afterward you said, "Now, check yourself." I looked around and told my fiancé, "I don't think I should check myself here." After service, I got caught up with the brothers

and sisters and left church later than usual. We went out to grab a bite and went home. We sat around, watched a movie, talked, and my fiancé went home. I went to my room to prepare for bed, and I was reminded to check myself. When I checked, to my surprise, that large mass was gone. I kept checking because it had been there so long I thought it moved to another position. I couldn't find it anywhere. As large as it was, it was impossible for it to be hiding. Needless to say, I began to leap and shout and praise the Lord. IT IS GONE! BY JESUS' STRIPES I WAS AND AM HEALED!!! PRAISE BE TO GOD! Thank you, Dr. Hickey, for your obedience to God. May He continue to use you mightily for His glory.

MIRACLE OPPORTUNITIES FOR GAINING WEALTH

God can provide in the midst of any financial lack we have.

God can also provide miracle opportunities for us to receive the finances we need and to gain wealth during times of economic hardship. Often, when we are faced with a lack of finances, we feel that our problems must be the worst in the history of mankind. But, to illustrate what God can do, I want us to look at a horrible circumstance in 2 Kings 6:24–29 in which God intervened in a desperate situation to bring about a miracle of provision and material wealth. If He can intervene in such a situation, He can also provide in the midst of any financial lack we have.

Hold on to your stomachs, because this is strong stuff. In the days of Elisha, there was a famine in the city of Samaria, the capital of the northern kingdom of Israel. The famine was so terrible that the people were literally starving to death. This situation was not due to a lack of rain but because the city was surrounded on every side by the army of the Syrian king, Ben-Hadad. Remember him? He was the king who previously had wanted to capture Israel but could never do it because God always told Elisha what he was about to do. (See 2 Kings 6:8–23.) Now, Ben-Hadad had taken his entire army and besieged Samaria so that no one could enter or leave the city, and no food or other supplies could be delivered.

> *And it happened after this that Ben-Hadad king of Syria gathered all his army, and went up and besieged Samaria. And there was a great famine in Samaria; and indeed they besieged it until a donkey's head was sold for eighty shekels of silver, and one-fourth of a kab of dove droppings for five shekels of silver. Then, as the king of Israel was passing by on the wall, a woman cried out to him, saying, "Help, my lord, O king!" And he said, "If the LORD does not help you, where can I find help for you? From the threshing floor or from the winepress?" Then the king said to her, "What is troubling you?" And she answered, "This woman said to me, 'Give your son, that we may eat him today, and we will eat my son tomorrow.' So we boiled my son, and ate him. And I said to her on the next day, 'Give your son, that we may eat him'; but she has hidden her son."* (verses 24–29)

Because the people were desperate for food, they were actually boiling their own children and eating them. Now, I know you're thinking, *Marilyn, this is disgusting.* I know it is. However, stay with me because I want you to learn the truths that unfold through this story.

Cursed Situations

This siege and the resulting famine was a cursed situation for the Israelites. Curses are birthed from sin and disobedience, and they bring death. Sickness, disease, and poverty are all results of curses that come upon human beings because of sin. There are curses that result from sexual sin, idolatry, and rebellion, just to name a few. Curses may even be passed down from parents, grandparents, or great-grandparents; these are often called "generational curses."

The Bible has something interesting to say about the nature of curses: *"An undeserved curse does not come to rest"* (Proverbs 26:2 NIV). In other words, a curse can't come upon a nation or a person without a reason. If you are engaging in sexual sin, then a curse is upon your life. If you are cheating your company by embezzling money, then you are in disobedience and sin, and a curse will come.

Some Christians think they can get away with disobedience and not pay any consequences for it. For example, they may say, "It doesn't really matter if I don't tithe, because that's an Old Testament teaching, and we're in New Testament days. Besides, I need this money more than the church does. Have you seen the way the pastor dresses? Have you noticed all the shoes his wife owns? What about that fancy car they drive? Why, they don't need my money!"

Curses don't come without a reason, my friends. God wants our obedience.

The first part of the curse that affected Israel was the attack by the army of Syria. Ben-Hadad had said, in effect, "We're going to take over Israel once and for all and make it ours." Why had this terrible curse come upon Israel? I believe it was because the king, Jehoram, kept the nation in idolatry. Jehoram was the same king who had wanted to kill the Syrians Elisha had spared, and the same king who'd gotten into trouble when he'd gone to war against the Moabites. His father was Ahab, and his mother was Jezebel, who'd introduced Baal worship to Israel. Actually, the whole family was nothing but a bunch of thugs. An *"undeserved curse"* cannot come, but if you choose to practice idolatry, then, here comes the curse.

Now, the Syrian king, Ben-Hadad, wasn't too swift, either. Previously, we saw that he had already witnessed the results of miracle after miracle of God's provision (see, for example, 2 Kings 5:1–18; 6:11–23), but he still refused to repent and serve Him. He was put in situations where he could be delivered from the curses on his life by turning to the one true God. But, apparently, the old king just loved to sin, and he was determined to conquer Israel anyway.

I know some Christians who must be related to Ben-Hadad. They see miracle after miracle, but their hearts don't change. They complain, "I know that so-and-so was healed of cancer, but it won't happen for me. Healing isn't for everyone, you know." What is the result? *Pop goes the miracle!* Instead of getting a wonderful deliverance, some people stay in rebellion and live out their curses.

You have to step out in faith and believe God for your miracle. If you recognize that you are in a cursed situation, then you have to ask for His help. If you don't know how a curse came to your family, ask God, and He will tell you. He doesn't get angry if He has to answer questions, because He loves to teach us to win. If you are living in sin, the Holy Spirit will reveal your sin and help you to clean up your act. Curses bring death, but miracles bring life. The Bible instructs us to *"choose life"* (Deuteronomy 30:19).

> **If you don't know how a curse came to your family, ask God, and He will tell you.**

Blame versus Trust

What did King Jehoram do about the dire situation Israel was facing? When he heard that people were eating their children because the famine was so severe, he got very angry, but for the wrong reason.

> *Now it happened, when the king heard the words of the woman, that he tore his clothes; and as he passed by on the wall, the people looked, and there underneath he had sackcloth on his body. Then he said, "God do so to me and more also, if the head of Elisha the son of Shaphat remains on him today!"*
> (2 Kings 6:30–31)

It is easy to blame others for our sins and troubles. We may hear the Word of truth that can change our lives, but we fail to put it into practice. Instead, we grumble, "I know I should tithe, but everything in my house is falling apart, the bill collectors are knocking at my door, and my car won't run. I can't afford to tithe." As the situation gets worse and worse, so do our attitudes. "If so-and-so hadn't said I could be prosperous, then I wouldn't have these troubles in the first place!"

Israel was in such a desperate state that some people were boiling their children and eating them, but God was going to bring an opportunity for deliverance. Our circumstances can get better, in spite of ourselves. Elisha knew what was going on in the city, but he wasn't nervous. He wasn't sitting at home, biting his nails, having a pity party, and fretting that there wasn't any food. He had seen enough miracles in his life to know that God was faithful to His Word and that deliverance was just around the corner. Elisha wasn't trusting in King Jehoram or Ben-Hadad. He knew the living God was his source.

Our Power Source

When "famines" occur in our finances, the first thing we like to do is talk about the situation. We tell our neighbors and friends all about our terrible money problems. We move away from faith and into foolishness, and then we really have difficulties. We may start to blame God and other people, such our spouses, our children, and our pastors. But, as we have seen, talking about our problems makes things worse. It brings darkness and can be spiritually deadly. (See, for example, Proverbs 15:4; 18:21; James 3:5–11.) Living in darkness keeps us from the truth. But Jesus is the light of the whole world. If we keep our eyes focused on Him during our financial famines, He will penetrate the darkness with the truth of God's Word. (See John 8:12.)

Let me give you an analogy. Having the power of electricity is an amazing advantage that we often take for granted. For example, when you want light in your bedroom, you turn on the switch and have it instantly. Because the power of electricity was channeled through the electrical wires to that switch, when you flipped it on, light appeared through the elements of the lightbulb. The point is that electricity can be channeled to the right place at the right time.

In a similar way, if there is a financial famine in your house, Jesus is ready to "pour on the power." You can simply say, "Jesus, I have a great need here in my life. I need a miracle to get on my feet again." Jesus loves this kind of prayer. He is the power source of your miracle. He can send His power to "turn on the switch" and bring you wisdom and provision in relation to your problem. You may think your problem is unique in the world, and it may be. However, Jesus can channel His power directly to your specific need and bring you into the light of the "Promised Land."

> **Jesus can send His power to "turn on the switch" and bring you wisdom and provision in relation to your problem.**

I'm not going to sit in the darkness and talk about the problems that want to block my pathway. I see them as opportunities in disguise. Jesus is my power source, and I want Him to be such a great light in my life that people will see that light in the midst of their own darkness. Hurting people will know that my God is a God of miracles and begin to believe for their miracles, too.

Elisha knew this truth, and he proclaimed what God could do in the midst of that terrible famine in Israel. He told King Jehoram,

> *Hear the word of the LORD. Thus says the LORD: "Tomorrow about this time a seah [about twelve pounds] of fine flour shall be sold for a shekel, and two seahs of barley for a shekel, at the gate of Samaria."*
>
> (2 Kings 7:1)

This word from God was tremendous news. If you were starving, wouldn't this be good news to you? Yet, wouldn't you know, in the midst of such wonderful news, there was an officer of the king who didn't believe Elisha. *"An officer on whose hand the king leaned answered the man of God and said, 'Look, if the LORD would make windows in heaven, could this thing be?'"* (2 Kings 7:2).

The attitude of the king's officer is like the attitude of some Christians. They hear the Word of God, but they reject it because they don't believe He is a God of miracles. The Lord was about to do a miracle for Israel—and even for the king's officer—but this man was operating in doubt and unbelief. Elisha knew God was going to open the windows of heaven and bring this miracle. Yet what did he say to the unbelieving officer? *"You shall see it with your eyes, but you shall not eat of it"* (verse 2).

A Mighty Deliverance

Get ready, because Israel was about to receive a mighty miracle by a peculiar circumstance. Sometimes, your pathway to miracles may take some unexpected turns.

> *Now there were four leprous men at the entrance of the gate; and they said to one another, "Why are we sitting here until we die? If we say, 'We will enter the city,' the famine is in the city, and we shall die there. And if we sit here, we die also. Now therefore, come, let us surrender to the army of the Syrians. If they keep us alive, we shall live; and if they kill us, we shall only die."* (2 Kings 7:3–4)

These men became bold, and, at dusk, they got their walking sticks and headed for the Syrian camp. They were very hungry and tired, yet they had a hope that kept them going.

The closer they got to the site, the more they noticed how quiet it seemed. No one was even watching the entrance. They walked into the camp, and guess who they saw? Nobody. That's right, nobody. They found abandoned tents, horses, donkeys, clothing, and *food.*

They ran over and began to eat and eat. They were so hungry, they didn't even count their calories. This was simply wonderful—all kinds of food around, and no one to bother them. (See 2 Kings 7:5, 8.)

Where do you suppose the Syrians were that day? This is what the Word says:

> *For the* LORD *had caused the army of the Syrians to hear the noise of chariots and the noise of horses; the noise of a great army; so they said to one another, "Look, the king of Israel has hired against us the kings of the Hittites and the kings of the Egyptians to attack us!" Therefore they arose and fled at twilight, and left the camp intact; their tents, their horses, and their donkeys; and they fled for their lives.* (verses 6–7)

Here we see the miracle God performed. He caused the Syrians to hear a great noise that sounded like thousands of men and horses rushing toward the city. The first thing the Syrians thought was that Jehoram had gotten the Hittites and the Egyptians, who had the two largest armies in the area, to come and attack them. They became so terrified that they fled for their lives and left all their material possessions behind.

The lepers had found an abundance of food and material wealth sitting there for the taking. After they ate, they tried on clothes. On and on they went, eating and admiring the wealth of the Syrians. Finally, though, one of them said, in effect, "Hey, don't you think we should go back and tell the people of Israel that we found food? Let's share our blessings with everyone else at home."

So, the lepers went back to the city. I imagine them in this way: their bellies were fat, they were burping, and they were wearing beautiful clothes. They cried out to the gatekeepers of the city, in effect, "The Syrian army is gone! Come and see all the food that they left, and all the clothes and jewelry and money. Hurry! Go to the camp and eat." (See verses 9–11.)

You can imagine what the city people must have thought as they listened to and looked at the four lepers. Note what happened after the king's messengers confirmed their story:

Then the people went out and plundered the tents of the Syrians. So a seah of fine flour was sold for a shekel, and two seahs of barley for a shekel, according to the word of the LORD. Now the king had appointed the officer on whose hand he leaned to have charge of the gate. But the people trampled him in the gate, and he died, just as the man of God had said, who spoke when the king came down to him. (2 Kings 7:16–17)

As you can see, the people of Israel raced to the Syrian camp. They were all trying to get there at once because they were starved. And what happened to the officer who didn't believe Elisha's prophecy? Elisha told him that he would see the wealth and the food, but he wouldn't partake of it. Well, the king told this officer to help the crowd get through the gate in an orderly manner. But these people were wild with hunger, so when the he opened the gate, hundreds of people came rushing toward him. He couldn't get out of the way in time, and—crunch—the hungry mob trampled him, and that was the end of him.

When you choose to believe God, the gate of blessing will swing open as you obey Him.

God had a plan for the people of Israel, a blessing of opportunity for provision and wealth. He spoke through His prophet Elisha and told him there would be food. You can either believe God for miracles, or you can be like the king's officer. When you choose to believe Him, the gate of blessing will swing open as you obey Him. There will be abundance, not lack. We are the chosen people of God. We are supposed to take the spoils and be filled to our hearts' content.

I encourage you to say these confessions:

I will overcome my financial famine. I will believe God to meet my needs. I will give to God and expect the windows of heaven to open for me. I will walk in the light and not in darkness. I will proclaim what God can and will do in my life. I will open the gates of

God's kingdom and life in prosperity. I will take the spoils from the devil and claim my miracle.

I pray that the Lord will work miracles of opportunity in your life that exceed what you expect and what you can imagine (see Ephesians 3:20), as you make yourself available to the leading of the Holy Spirit. It's only by God's Spirit that our eyes can be opened, so that we can discern the exciting opportunities He has planned for us.

REST STOP
ON YOUR PATHWAY TO MIRACLES

1. Think of a negative situation that has occurred in your life and write it down. Then, write down the outcome of this situation. Was it favorable? Did it present an opportunity? If it was unfavorable, how might you have responded to it as an opportunity?

2. Read and memorize Matthew 28:18–20.

3. In the above Scripture, whom did Jesus direct to *"Go"*?

4. Ask God what He would like you to do to reach the unsaved, including recognizing the opportunities He has opened for you. Write down the guidance you receive.

5. What financial miracle of opportunity do you need? Write it down and pray about it, trusting God to open doors for you with a blessing of provision.

BIBLICAL EXAMPLES AND SCRIPTURES RELATING TO MIRACLES OF OPPORTUNITY

- *Miracle of Joseph interpreting Pharaoh's dream*:
  Genesis 40:1–41:45; 45; 50:15–21

- *Miracles under Gideon*:
  Judges 6:1–8:32

- *Miracles under Samson*:
  Judges 14–16

- *Miracle of Samuel's calling as a prophet*:
  1 Samuel 3

- *Miracles under David*:
  2 Samuel 22

- *Miracle of provision and wealth for the Israelites in Samaria*:
  2 Kings 6:24–7:20

- *Miracle of salvation for the Samaritan woman and her town*:
  John 4:3–42

- *Miracle healing of crippled man*:
  John 5:2–9

- *Miracle of Gentile conversions*:
  Acts 13:44–48

- *Miracle of Lydia's conversion*:
  Acts 16:11–15

CHAPTER 14

MIDNIGHT MIRACLES

Your Darkest Hour May Bring Your Greatest Miracle

Most of us don't think of midnight as a time for miracles. "Midnight" often seems to symbolize the darkest times in our lives, or when time seems to have run out for hope or rescue. Yet the "midnight hour" may bring our greatest miracles.

God's midnight miracles eclipse adverse situations and demonstrate His power through such things as judgments, rescues, calls on people's lives, and healings. At the "midnight hour," I've seen cancer disappear, blind eyes and deaf ears open, and tumors vanish.

In this chapter, we will be looking at eight "midnight miracles" in the Bible—four from the Old Testament and four from the New Testament. I think it so interesting that God chooses to move in the dark of the night. But, when you think about it, midnight is actually the point at which we break into a new day....

1. THE MIDNIGHT MIRACLE OF THE PASSOVER

Our first midnight miracle is the Passover deliverance of the Israelites. God's people had been enslaved and persecuted by the Egyptians for 400 years. Eighty years before their exodus, the pharaoh had ordered the death of their male babies, because he feared the Israelites were growing too numerous and strong. However, a deliverer was born—a baby who had been slated for death by Pharaoh but was hidden by his family and then rescued by none other than Pharaoh's own daughter. The baby's name was Moses.

It was one of the darkest times in the history of Egypt, but it was one of the most miraculous times for Israel.

Moses left Egypt at the age of forty after trying to save the Israelites in his own way, and he became a shepherd. Forty years later, God called him to deliver His people out of their slavery. When the reigning pharaoh refused to release the Israelites, God sent plagues on the Egyptians. Because of these plagues, it was one of the darkest times in the history of Egypt, but it was one of the most miraculous times for Israel. (See Exodus 2–4.)

Following God's instructions, Moses and his brother Aaron went to the pharaoh nine times, announcing various plagues on Egypt if he would not free the Israelites, but Pharaoh's heart was hardened, and he refused. (See, for example, Exodus 7:1–13.) I'm sure it wasn't God's desire to punish the Egyptians in this way, but their leader stubbornly refused to heed the God of Israel, even after the miraculous demonstrations of the plagues. In addition, the Egyptians in that day served about 2,000 gods and goddesses but did not acknowledge the one true God.

The fact that Pharaoh refused to let Israel go was no surprise to God. The Lord had said to Moses at the time when He'd first called him to be Israel's deliverer,

> *I am sure that the king of Egypt will not let you go, no, not even by a mighty hand. So I will stretch out My hand and strike Egypt with all My wonders which I will do in its midst; and after that he will let you go.*
> (Exodus 3:19–20)

The Lord had also told Moses that the Israelites would have favor with the Egyptians and receive "*articles of silver, articles of gold, and clothing*" (verse 22) from them when they left.

I won't describe the previous nine plagues because I want you to see what God did at this special hour of midnight when the tenth plague struck Egypt.

And the LORD said to Moses, "I will bring yet one more plague on Pharaoh and on Egypt. Afterward he will let you go from here. When he lets you go, he will surely drive you out of here altogether."　　(Exodus 11:1)

So, Moses went to see Pharaoh one last time:

Then Moses said, "Thus says the LORD: 'About midnight I will go out into the midst of Egypt; and all the firstborn in the land of Egypt shall die, from the firstborn of Pharaoh who sits on his throne, even to the firstborn of the female servant who is behind the handmill, and all the firstborn of the animals. Then there shall be a great cry throughout all the land of Egypt, such as was not like it before, nor shall be like it again. But against none of the children of Israel shall a dog move its tongue, against man or beast, that you may know that the LORD does make a difference between the Egyptians and Israel.' And all these your servants shall come down to me and bow down to me, saying, 'Get out, and all the people who follow you!' After that I will go out." Then he went out from Pharaoh in great anger.　　(verses 4–8)

The Israelites were spared from this tenth plague of death through the first Passover. God also instituted a continuous observance of the Passover feast for His people. As we saw in chapter 2 of this book, the Passover observance is a revelation of the sacrificial Lamb of God (Jesus).

Now the LORD spoke to Moses and Aaron in the land of Egypt, saying, "This month shall be your beginning of months; it shall be the first month of the year to you. Speak to all the congregation of Israel, saying: 'On the tenth of this month every man shall take for himself a lamb, according to the house of his father, a lamb for a household.'"　　(Exodus 12:1–3)

The first month of the year signifies a new start. We, too, experience a new beginning as we "take the Lamb for ourselves," receiving Christ's Spirit, Christ's mind, and Christ's words into our lives. (See, for example, Matthew 26:26; Romans 8:11; 1 Corinthians 2:16; John 15:7.)

God told Moses, "*Now you shall keep* [the lamb] *until the fourteenth day of the same month. Then the whole assembly of the congregation of Israel shall kill it at twilight*" (Exodus 12:6). Note that the lamb was to be slaughtered at dusk, or twilight. The Hebrew word for "*twilight*" in this verse means "between the evenings." This meaning thrills me so much, because I have often taught about the morning and evening sacrifices. The Jews had two evenings—one at three o'clock, which was the time the evening sacrifice was killed, and the other at six o'clock. Jesus hung on the cross and died at the ninth hour, meaning nine hours after sunrise, or three o'clock in the afternoon—the time of the evening sacrifice. (See, for example, Mark 15:20–38.) Exciting, isn't it? God had every detail lined up in this precursor to Jesus' sacrifice.

"*And they shall take some of the blood and put it on the two doorposts and on the lintel of the houses where they eat it*" (Exodus 12:7). Each Israelite family applied the blood by dipping a cluster of hyssop into it and hitting it against the two sides of the door and its upper post. Under the old covenant, there was no forgiveness, holiness, or relationship with God without the blood covenant. And Jesus told His disciples at the Last Supper, "*This is My blood of the new covenant, which is shed for many for the remission of sins*" (Matthew 26:28). The new covenant is based on the "Passover" that resulted from Jesus' sacrifice, for there would be no forgiveness, redemption from sin, holiness, relationship with God, indwelling of the Holy Spirit, or eternal life without Jesus' blood covenant.

The final plague—the death of the firstborn—came to Egypt at midnight. But the Israelites were not affected. Not only did they have the blood of the sacrificed lambs over their doorways, but they also had eaten the meat of these lambs. In this way, they had the lamb "inside" and "outside" of them. The Passover in Egypt was the greatest deliverance miracle the Israelites experienced, because it saved their firstborn from the judgment of death. "*By faith* [Moses] *kept the Passover and the sprinkling of blood, lest he who destroyed the firstborn should touch them"* (Hebrews 11:28). This was, again, one of the greatest prophetic revelations of Jesus Christ, the Lamb of God, who came to save us from eternal death. *"And* [Christ] *is the head of the body, the church, who is the beginning, the firstborn from the dead, that in all things He may have the preeminence"* (Colossians 1:18). We can have the Lamb inside us—Jesus is our *"hope of glory"* (verse 27)—as well as His blood on the "outside" of us to protect us from the onslaught of our enemy, the devil. *"They overcame* [Satan] *by the blood of the Lamb..."* (Revelation 12:11).

This midnight miracle also set God's people free from Egyptian slavery. The Egyptians were so anxious to have them leave that they gave them their wealth, just as God had said they would. Psalm 105 affirms, *"[God] brought them forth also with silver and gold: and there was not one feeble person among their tribes"* (verse 37 KJV). The Israelites were free, they were healthy, and they had a future—the Promised Land. And it happened at midnight.

> We can be spiritually free, be physically healthy, and anticipate a future with God in eternity through the blood of the Lamb.

We can be spiritually free, be physically healthy, and anticipate a future with God in eternity through the blood of the Lamb of God. Jesus has made those provisions for us, if we will receive them.

2. THE MIDNIGHT MIRACLE
OF ESCAPE FROM ENEMIES

The second "midnight" occasion has to do with Samson, one of the last ruling judges of Israel. His birth came about after the Angel of the Lord appeared to his parents, Manoah and his wife, and told them they would have a son who would begin to deliver the Israelites from their enemies, the Philistines. (See Judges 13.) After a number of escapades in his life, in which he demonstrated remarkable strength, Samson went to Gaza, a Philistine city. The Gazites surrounded him in the night and waited for him at the gate of the city, with a plot to kill him in the morning. Somehow, Samson heard of the scheme. It could be that the Lord awoke him and told him to get out of there.

Anointed by God and possessing supernatural strength, Samson arose at midnight, pulled down the gates of the city, put them on his shoulders, and eluded his would-be captors, carrying the gates to the top of a hill. (See Judges 16:1–3.) That hill stood about a mile away from the city of Gaza.

The barriers of the city could not stop him, and neither could the plot of his enemies. Can you imagine the Philistines awakening and saying, "Where are the gates of the city? Those were for our protection!" When they looked, they spotted them at the top of the hill. It was obvious that only the man whom they sought to kill could have put them there.

> **You may feel hemmed in by enemies, but God will give you strength for your deliverance.**

This feat of strength and escape happened at midnight, at one of Samson's darkest hours, when forces lay in wait to ambush him. You may feel hemmed in by enemies, but God will give you strength for your deliverance. He brings midnight miracles, and He will do so for you, if you will keep your eyes on Him and not give up.

3. THE MIDNIGHT MIRACLE OF A KINSMAN-REDEEMER

The third midnight miracle centers on a romance, the story of Ruth and Boaz.

Ruth was a young Moabite widow who left her own family and country to follow her widowed and destitute mother-in-law, Naomi, back to her hometown of Bethlehem in Israel. Ruth had given her heart to the living God, openly confessing to Naomi, "Your God will be my God." (See Ruth 1:16.)

However, this was a dark time for Ruth. She was carrying the grief of losing her husband. She probably missed her relatives, her people, and many of the things she had been accustomed to in Moab. Then, after arriving in Bethlehem, she had to go out to glean leftover grain in the fields, like a beggar, in order to provide food for Naomi and herself. The Israelites had a policy that crops were not to be picked clean so that the poor could gather food for themselves. (See, for example, Leviticus 19:10.)

As Ruth worked in the fields of Boaz, who was an important man in the city of Bethlehem, she received his favor. He understood that she was a Moabite, and he was attracted by her devotion to Naomi, her hard work, and her personal character. So, he asked his men to take care of her as she gleaned in his fields, requested that she join his workers for meals, and secretly commanded that extra grain be left behind on purpose for her. At the end of the first day, Ruth arrived at home with over a bushel of barley—a great amount for a day's work. Her mother-in-law questioned her and discovered that this abundance had come from Boaz, who was one of her deceased husband's relatives. Naomi knew the customs of her people, which provided for the "redemption" (including marriage) of a widow by a close family member. She told Ruth it would be a good thing for her to stay in Boaz's field until the end of the harvest, because there she would be protected from potentially unsavory men on other estates.

When the harvest was over, one could almost see the gleam in Naomi's eyes as she told Ruth the plan she had in mind.

> *My daughter, shall I not seek security for you, that it may be well with you? Now Boaz, whose young women you were with, is he not our relative? In fact, he is winnowing barley tonight at the threshing floor. Therefore wash yourself and anoint yourself, put on your best garment and go down to the threshing floor; but do not make yourself known to the man until he has finished eating and drinking. Then it shall be, when he lies down, that you shall notice the place where he lies; and you shall go in, uncover his feet, and lie down; and he will tell you what you should do.*
>
> (Ruth 3:1–4)

Ruth followed her mother-in-law's advice, and the Bible says, *"Now it happened at midnight that the man was startled, and turned himself; and there, a woman was lying at his feet"* (Ruth 3:8). Wait, when did this happen? At midnight.

Boaz asked, "Who *are* you?"

She answered, *"I am Ruth, your maidservant. Take your maidservant under your wing, for you are a close relative ["kinsman-redeemer" NIV]"* (verse 9).

Boaz then told her,

> *Blessed are you of the LORD, my daughter! For you have shown more kindness at the end than at the beginning, in that you did not go after young men, whether poor or rich. And now, my daughter, do not fear. I will do for you all that you request, for all the people of my town know that you are a virtuous woman. Now it is true that I am a close relative; however, there is a relative closer than I. Stay this night, and in the morning it shall be that if he will perform the duty of a close relative for you; good; let him do it. But if he does not want to perform the duty for you, then I will perform the duty for you, as the LORD lives! Lie down until morning.*
>
> (verses 10–13)

Ruth lay at his feet until morning. When she got up to leave, he sent her home with six measures of barley—an abundance—most likely to let Naomi know that he had agreed to the arrangement.

In order for Boaz to become Ruth's husband, he had to be able to fulfill the following: (1) he had to be a close relative of her dead husband, (2) he had to have the money to buy her husband's land (the land her husband would have inherited from his father, if he had lived), and (3) he had to "redeem" her by marrying her. Not every man would have chosen such a circumstance for his marriage, because his firstborn son from the union usually bore the name of the deceased husband, thereby preserving the husband's memory and lineage. But he accepted the terms, and they were married after the closer relative declined these terms.

Ruth and Boaz had a son named Obed, who became the father of Jesse, who became the father of David, king of Israel. Even more remarkable, they became an integral part of the genealogy of Jesus Christ, who was descended from David. When did all this begin? It started at midnight.

You may be unmarried and lonely; you may feel there's no one for you. It could be a dark time in your life, but it could also be the time when God brings you an outstanding mate. Keep your faith in God while trusting Him to be your ultimate Redeemer and Provider.

> **Keep your faith in God while trusting Him to be your ultimate Redeemer and Provider.**

4. THE MIDNIGHT MIRACLE OF DELIVERANCE THROUGH PRAISE

If it's a dark time for you, get up and praise the Lord! The author of Psalm 119 went through various difficulties (see verses 49–61), but he still declared, *"At midnight I will rise to give thanks to You, because of Your righteous judgments"* (verse 62).

Let me tell you about a midnight miracle of praise that Paul and Silas experienced. These men were God's missionaries, and they met with pressing circumstances as they spread the gospel. When they were in Philippi, they encountered a slave girl who had a *"spirit of divination"* (Acts 16:16). She was being used by her masters to make money telling people's fortunes. The Greek word translated *"divination"* in the above verse is *puthon* (python). Python was, according to mythology, a huge serpent, slain by Apollo, who was a Greek "god" with prophetic powers.

This slave girl followed Paul and Silas around for days, shouting, *"These men are the servants of the Most High God, who proclaim to us the way of salvation"* (verse 17). Although she was correct, the spirit behind her ranting was demonic, and it grieved Paul, so he cast the evil spirit out of her.

The men who had made their living by the slave girl's powers were furious when Paul commanded the spirit to come out of her, causing her to lose her ability to see into the future. (I think she became a believer, although the Bible doesn't say this.) Her masters brought Paul and Silas to the city magistrates and told them, in essence, "These men, being Jews, have made a lot of trouble for our city." The people of the city came against them, as well. The magistrates ordered them to be beaten and imprisoned, and the keeper of the prison, or jailer, put them in an inner prison and fastened their feet in stocks.

Clearly, this was a dark time for Paul and Silas, but it was also a time of opportunity for God, made possible by their spirit of praise. Instead of looking at the stocks or complaining about the pain they were in, the two men looked up to Him and had a praise service. And, wouldn't you know, God showed up at midnight!

> *But at midnight Paul and Silas were praying and singing hymns to God, and the prisoners were listening to them. Suddenly there was a great earthquake, so that the foundations of the prison were shaken; and immediately all the doors were opened and everyone's chains were loosed. And the keeper of the prison, awaking from sleep and seeing the prison doors open, supposing the prisoners had fled, drew his sword and was about to kill himself.* (Acts 16:25–27)

The keeper of the prison was frightened because, if the prisoners escaped, he would be put to death, so he was about to end his own life. Paul called to him, *"Do yourself no harm, for we are all here"* (verse 28). A guard brought a light, and the jailer asked Paul and Silas, *"Sirs, what must I do to be saved?"* (verse 30). The two men he had just imprisoned were about to become an eternal blessing to him.

Paul and Silas took the best opportunity we can ever have. They led the man and his household to Christ. Now, the jailer tended to their wounds and fed them, and he and his family were baptized. It was truly a midnight miracle. The next day, Paul and Silas were released. (See Acts 16:16–40.)

You may find yourself in a dark situation, such as addiction, divorce, sickness, disappointment, defeat—the "beatings" we go through in life. But you can turn to God. At your midnight hour, you can praise Him, and He will shine His light on you, transform you, and give you a new beginning. Midnight—God's perfect time for a miracle!

> **At your midnight hour, you can praise God, and He will transform you and give you a new beginning.**

5. THE MIDNIGHT MIRACLE OF A RESURRECTION

Sometime after the incident at Philippi, Paul and Luke were in the city of Troas, and *"on the first day of the week, when the disciples came together to break bread, Paul, ready to depart the next day, spoke to them and continued his message until midnight. There were many lamps in the upper room where they were gathered together"* (Acts 20:7–8).

Many of the believers in Troas had gathered in this upper room to hear Paul's teaching. Paul lectured into the night because he was preparing to leave the next day, and he wanted to be sure they had a strong foundation for their faith in Christ. Then, a tragedy occurred:

> And in a window sat a certain young man named Eutychus, who was sinking into a deep sleep. He was overcome by sleep; and as Paul continued speaking, he fell down from the third story and was taken up dead. But Paul went down, fell on him, and embracing him said, "Do not trouble yourselves, for his life is in him."...And they brought the young man in alive, and they were not a little comforted.   (verses 9–10, 12)

Eutychus had died, but now he was alive! Paul's action reminds me of how the prophets Elijah and Elisha, at separate times, stretched themselves over the dead body of a widow's son and restored him to life through the power of God.

After Eutychus was resurrected, the believers returned to the upper room of the house. They had something to eat, and then Paul continued talking until daylight. When they left the gathering, the believers were not only encouraged by the teaching Paul had brought them, but they were greatly comforted by this midnight miracle of resurrection. (See Acts 20:7–12.)

God continues to miraculously resurrect people today, physically raising them from the dead. And the ultimate resurrection for all believers will be the resurrection of our bodies in the likeness of Jesus for eternity: *"The body is sown in corruption, it is raised in incorruption....In a moment, in the twinkling of an eye, at the last trumpet...the dead will be raised incorruptible, and we shall be changed"* (1 Corinthians 15:42, 52).

6. THE MIDNIGHT MIRACLE OF PRESERVATION

Paul later experienced still another midnight miracle. After being arrested and imprisoned, he appealed his case to Caesar. So, he was taken, along with several other prisoners, on a long voyage by ship to Rome under the custody of a Roman centurion named Julius. After the group had made several stops along the way and changed ships, Paul received a word from the Lord that they should not proceed with their planned voyage from Fair Havens, where the ship was currently in port, because it would end in loss of life, as well as the destruction of the ship and cargo. Yet Julius trusted the advice of the ship's helmsman and owner, who wanted to move on, more than he did Paul's warning.

Soon after they set sail, a storm as bad as you can imagine hit them. They were beaten by waves and a typhonic wind *"called Euroclydon"* (Acts 27:14). This name denoted typhoon whirlwinds that blew in all directions. They were in a precarious situation.

Those on board began to fast. They may not all have been Christians, but they fasted and prayed.

Then, Paul stood and told them that an angel from God had appeared to him, telling him that they would all be saved because God wanted him to speak to Caesar. He reassured them that God had also granted the life of everyone on board ship.

On the fourteenth day of the storm, it looked to the rest of the travelers as if all hope was gone, even though Paul had spoken those words of encouragement. Then, *"about midnight"* (Acts 27:27)—the darkest time in an already dark situation—the sailors discovered that the ship was near land.

Paul told them to break their fast and eat so that they would have strength to survive the coming shipwreck, and so they all partook of a meal. Then, as they attempted to reach land, the ship was broken up and destroyed, but all 276 people who had been on board survived—just as God had said.

When did the sailors first recognize they had finally found land? At the midnight hour. (See Acts 27.)

Even though we are following God, we may still enter into a tempest, but He will deliver us, perhaps at a time that seems least likely to us. When I find myself in such circumstances, I pray, *"Open my eyes, that I may see wondrous things from Your law"* (Psalm 119:18). Wondrous things from God's law enlighten me in my dark times, assuring me that His promises work. He is the God who gives us a new day to live and serve Him.

> **Wondrous things from God's law enlighten me in my dark times, assuring me that His promises work.**

7. THE MIDNIGHT MIRACLE OF TRANSFORMATION

At the beginning of creation, *"the earth was without form, and void; and darkness was on the face of the deep. And the Spirit of God was hovering over the face of the waters"* (Genesis 1:2). Time had not yet been instituted on earth when God's Spirit moved upon the face of the waters in divine creativity. I think that the world's original darkness may have been one of its midnight hours, but God transformed the earth's *"void...and darkness*" into a wonderful, vibrant, life-giving environment. He will do the same in our lives.

I experienced such a transformation in my life several years ago. We all have trials, but, as I mentioned in chapter 12, I once became seriously ill, apparently due to parasites. That was truly a "midnight hour" in my life. I had no idea I could be so sick. I didn't have the energy to walk across the room, and even thinking was hard.

This infection occurred before my daughter, Sarah, and her husband, Reece, became the senior pastors of Orchard Road Christian Center, the church Wally and I founded. Reece wanted me to make a statement about my illness to the members of the church because he said people might think it was something worse. He also wanted me to ask for prayer. I did ask. I requested prayer that my appetite would return and that I could sleep and renew my energy.

Every day, one of the women in our church would bring over our evening meal. It was such a blessing. I couldn't eat much, but Wally could. This woman would always say to me, "This is temporary." But the devil would whisper in my ear, *You will never travel again.*

My midnight experience lasted only seven months, and the Lord miraculously healed me. The devil had said I would never travel again, but just the opposite occurred. God has brought to pass more trips to other countries than I ever expected, and I've also had greater miracles in my life since then.

God's midnight miracles demonstrate His love for us and humble us. My midnight experience gave me more compassion for the sick, and it increased my faith. And, during the period when I couldn't travel but had to stay at home, I learned many things from the Lord. Yes, midnight-dark moments can usher in miracle times.

The darkness we face can be spiritual, financial, physical, mental, or emotional. Perhaps you're in the worst storm of your life, and it looks as if you'll never make it. If you feel this way, you are in the same club as many others. Keep your faith in Jesus, and you'll make it. Allow Him to transform the darkness with His light, and you will arrive securely at the shores of His love and grace.

8. THE MIDNIGHT MIRACLE OF THE BRIDEGROOM'S RETURN

I want to share one more midnight miracle: *"And at midnight a cry was heard: 'Behold, the bridegroom is coming; go out to meet him!'"* (Matthew 25:6). Jesus told us, *"Now when these things [signs of His second coming] begin to happen, look up and lift up your heads, because your redemption draws near"* (Luke 21:28.) As the bride of Christ, we need to be ready in the darkest time for the full revelation of Jesus Christ to the world. Don't look down, but lift up your head. *"Let us be glad and rejoice and give Him glory, for the marriage of the Lamb has come, and His wife has made herself ready"* (Revelation 19:7).

Are you ready for His return? The preparation for this ultimate event begins at the same place as the preparation for entering your pathway to miracles. Through the principles in this book, you can (and I hope you have already begun to) attain many types of miracles. Yet the greatest of miracles, and the place where they all begin, is to receive Jesus Christ as your Lord and Savior.

> **The greatest of miracles, and the place where they all begin, is to receive Jesus Christ as your Lord and Savior.**

I mentioned previously that I always carry with me cards that have the sinner's prayer printed on them, which people can use to pray for salvation and become reconciled with their heavenly Father. Don't get upset if I talk about being a "sinner." We all are, but God didn't leave us there. He provided a means to wipe away our offenses so we can be in relationship with Him. Would you like to know what those cards say? It's quite simple:

Dear heavenly Father, I know that You have a plan for my life, because You created me and You love me. You created heaven to be my eternal home with You.

Forgive me of all my sins, my failures, and my past. I believe the blood of Your Son, Jesus, cleanses me from all my sin. I repent of my sins and invite You, Jesus, to come into my heart and be my personal Savior. Thank You for saving me, according to what the Bible tells me in Romans 10:13—whoever calls on the Lord shall be saved. Amen.

If you prayed this prayer with sincerity, you are born again. I welcome you to the family of God! This is the greatest miracle of your life. I want you to hook up with a faith-filled, Bible-believing Christian church. Ask God to lead you to one, and then become involved in it. Pray and read your Bible daily so that you can learn more about your faith and grow in your relationship with God.

THE POWER BEHIND MIRACLES

The baptism of the Holy Spirit refers to an anointing that gives us supernatural power to live for God and serve His purposes in the world.

As you begin your new life in Christ, I want you to know that the power behind all the miracles I've described in this book is God—God the Father, God the Son (Jesus), and God the Holy Spirit. I don't know what path my life would have taken if it hadn't been for the Holy Spirit's continual presence with me. Through my husband, Wally, God led me to receive the wonderful gift of being "baptized" in God's Holy Spirit, and my prayer is that you would receive this gift, as well. Although every believer has God's Spirit living inside him, the baptism of the Holy Spirit refers to an anointing that gives us supernatural power to live for God and serve His purposes in the world. (See, for example, Acts 2; 10:44–46; 19:1–6; Mark 16:17.)

In Wally's book, *Life Lessons*, he shared,

Early in my Christian walk, I had been in a gray area in my religious life (some would've called me backslidden). Then God connected me with some on-fire Pentecostals. They were encouraging me to become baptized in the Holy Spirit with the evidence of speaking in tongues. This was new to me, so I prayed something like this: "Lord, this new thing I'm learning about—the baptism of the Holy Spirit—if it is of You, show me in Scriptures that no one else has used with me."

After praying that prayer, I was reading along in 1 Corinthians 2:9: "...*Eye has not seen, nor ear heard, nor have entered into the heart of man the things which God has prepared for those who love Him.*" Then, in 1 Corinthians 2:13, I found: "*These things we also speak, not in words which MAN'S WISDOM teaches, but which the HOLY SPIRIT TEACHES....*"

The Lord seemed to illuminate those verses and say in my heart: "The French-speaking child learns to speak French from the wisdom of his or her French-speaking mother. The English-speaking child learns to speak English from the wisdom of his or her English-speaking mother. There's only one language not taught through 'man's wisdom,' and that is the heavenly language that the 'Holy Spirit teaches.'" I took this as the answer to my prayer, and received my heavenly language, one taught to me by the Holy Spirit, in just a matter of days.

Ask God to baptize you in His Holy Spirit. He will do it. Begin to praise Him and receive the outpouring of His Spirit in your life. Jesus said, "*If you then, being evil, now how to give good gift to your children, how much more will your heavenly Father give the Holy Spirit to those who ask Him!*" (Luke 11:13). The Holy Spirit will teach you the truth of God's Word, give you power for ministry, and enable you to fulfill the plans God has for you. (See, for example, John 16:13–15; Acts 1:8; Romans 15:18–19; Ephesians 5:9.)

Traveling the Pathway to Miracles

I never would have traveled my pathway to miracles if I had not been encouraged to receive the baptism of the Holy Spirit. My life, as I now know it, would not exist. Thankfully, God pricked my spiritual ears and revealed to me then, in a way that I finally understood, that He had something so wonderful ahead for me. Personally ministering to thousands, broadcasting to billions through television, and visiting over 125 countries was way beyond my expectation. My life has been a pathway of miracles, but my life is not over. I believe more miracles are coming.

By the time this book is printed, I will have been in Karachi, Pakistan, speaking to an audience of 200,000-plus people. It will have been the largest meeting I have ever held, surpassing a previous meeting in Pakistan with 120,000 people. I will also have been to Hong Kong for healing meetings, and in Beijing, China, for teaching sessions with 3,000 cell leaders. I anticipate upcoming healing meetings in Turkey, with Iranian refugees, as well as the Turkish people. In addition, I am believing God for unusual opportunities to preach the gospel not only in Israel, but also in the Gaza Strip.

"And [Jesus] *said to them* [and us!], *'Go into all the world and preach the gospel to every creature'"* (Mark 16:15).

We have eternity to look forward to, but before we cross over, we have other portions of the pathway to travel on this side of God's "pearly gates." Remember, miracles are for *you,* and, in all things, I pray you'll have a blessed journey on *Your Pathway to Miracles!*

REST STOP
ON YOUR PATHWAY TO MIRACLES

1. Are you in an "Egypt" situation, needing freedom, health, and a future? Pray the Scripture *"Let My people go"* (Exodus 5:1) over your problems.

2. Is there a particular "enemy" that has dogged you, as the Philistines dogged Samson? What "gates" do you have to pull down in the name of Jesus to overcome that enemy?

3. What dark situation(s) do you need to praise God in? Write them down, as well as corresponding Scriptures of praise.

4. Are you prepared for Jesus' second coming? If you have not yet prayed the "sinner's prayer" and received Jesus as your Savior and Lord, do so today by praying the prayer at the end of this chapter.

5. If you have already prayed to receive Christ, are you currently living for Him? If you are not, re-dedicate your life to Him and begin serving Him. *"If we confess our sins, He is faithful and just to forgive us our sins and to cleanse us from all unrighteousness"* (1 John 1:9).

6. What miracles have occurred in your life since you first started reading this book? Write them down.

7. For what miracles are you currently praying and speaking the Word with expectation?

BIBLICAL EXAMPLES AND SCRIPTURES RELATING TO MIDNIGHT MIRACLES

- *Miracle of Israel's midnight Passover and exodus*:
  Exodus 11:1–12:42

- *Miracle of Samson's midnight escape*:
  Judges 16:1–3

- *Miracle of Ruth's midnight betrothal to her kinsman-redeemer*:
  Ruth 3

- *Miracle of Paul and Silas's deliverance from prison through praise*:
  Acts 16:16–40

- *Miracle of Paul's preservation from shipwreck*:
  Acts 27

- *Miracle of Eutychus' resurrection*:
  Acts 20:7–12

- *Miracle of Jesus, the Bridegroom, coming for His bride, the church*:
  Matthew 24:29–25:13; John 14:1–3; 1 Thessalonians 4:14–17; Revelation 19:7–9; 21:1–5

ABOUT THE AUTHOR

As founder and president of Marilyn Hickey Ministries, Marilyn is being used by God to help cover the earth with the Word. Her Bible teaching ministry is an international outreach via television, satellite, books, CDs, DVDs, and healing meetings. She has established an international program of Bible and food distribution, and she is committed to overseas ministry, often bringing the gospel to people who have never heard it before.

Marilyn, along with her late husband, Wallace Hickey, founded the Orchard Road Christian Center in Greenwood Village, Colorado. She has two grown children, five grandchildren, and four great-grandchildren.

A Special Invitation

Please contact me by mail or e-mail and let me know that you have prayed to receive Christ and the baptism of the Holy Spirit and have found a Bible-believing church. I also look forward to hearing about your miraculous experiences of God's power as He works in the circumstances of your life.

If you're in the Denver area, you are very welcome to visit Orchard Road Christian Center. And, of course, wherever you may be in the world, you can always send me your experiences and testimonies via the Internet through Marilyn Hickey Ministries or Orchard Road Christian Center.

God bless you!
Marilyn Hickey

Marilyn Hickey Ministries
Web Site: http://www.marilynandsarah.org/

Orchard Road Christian Center
8081 East Orchard Road, Greenwood Village, CO 80111
Web Site: http://orcconline.org/